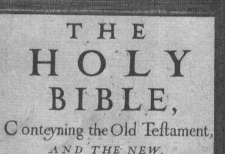

יהוה

# THE HOLY BIBLE,

Conteyning the Old Testament,

AND THE NEW.

*Newly Translated out of the Originall
tongues: & with the former Translations
diligently compared and reuised, by his
Maiesties speciall Commandement.*

*Appointed to be read in Churches.*

*Imprinted at London by Robert
Barker, Printer to the Kings
most Excellent Maiestie.*

ANNO DOM. 1611.

C. Boel fecit             in Richmont

# In The Beginning

# In The Beginning

## THE STORY OF THE
## KING JAMES BIBLE
### *and how it changed*
### *a* NATION, *a* LANGUAGE
### *and a* CULTURE

## Alister McGrath

Hodder & Stoughton
LONDON SYDNEY AUCKLAND

First published in Great Britain in 2001
by permission of Doubleday,
a division of Random House, Inc., New York.

10 9 8 7 6 5 4 3 2

British Library Cataloguing in Publication Data
A record for this book is available from the British Library

ISBN 0340 78560 8

Printed and bound in Great Britain

Hodder & Stoughton
A Division of Hodder Headline Ltd
338 Euston Road
London NW1 3BH

# CONTENTS

# LIST OF ILLUSTRATIONS

# PREFACE

I was born in 1953, the year of the coronation of Elizabeth II. Like every child born in Britain that year, I was given a copy of the Bible, by command of the queen. As a child, I often pored over the book, puzzled by its old-fashioned language, yet intrigued by the stories it told. It was a copy of the translation published in 1611, often referred to as the "Authorized Version," but more widely known as the King James Bible, after the king of England who ordered it to be produced.

As I grew older, I often wondered how the whole thing came about. How was the translation process started? Who were the people who had created it? What issues did they face? How did they go about producing the translation? How was it received? And why had Elizabeth II asked for this specific version of the Bible to be given to all born in the year of her coronation? What was so special about it?

As the years passed, the Bible I had been given as a child gradually fell to pieces. Its pages dropped out, one by one, and eventually it had to be thrown away. But the questions that puzzled me remained with me. Finally, nearly half a century after being given that book, I came to a decision. I would investigate the origins of the King James Bible, and tell the story of what I now knew to be a literary and religious classic. This book tells that tale, set against the backdrop of the tumultuous century of events which brought it into being. I hope you enjoy reading it as much as I have enjoyed telling it.

—ALISTER MCGRATH
OXFORD, JUNE 2000

# In The Beginning

# INTRODUCTION

The two greatest influences on the shaping of the English language are the works of William Shakespeare and the English translation of the Bible that appeared in 1611. The King James Bible—named after the king of England who ordered the production of a fresh translation in 1604—is both a religious and literary classic. Literary scholars have heaped praise upon it. Nineteenth-century writers and literary critics acclaimed it as the "noblest monument of English prose." In a series of lectures at Cambridge University during the First World War, Sir Arthur Quiller-Couch declared that the King James Bible was "the very greatest" literary achievement in the English language. The only possible challenger for this title came from the complete works of Shakespeare. His audience had no quarrel with this judgment. It was the accepted wisdom of the age.

The King James Bible was a landmark in the history of the English language, and an inspiration to poets, dramatists, artists, and politicians. The influence of this work has been incalculable. For many years, it was the only English translation of the Bible available. Many families could afford only one book—a Bible, in whose pages parents recorded the births of their children, and found solace at their deaths. Countless youngsters learned to read by mouthing the words they found in the only book their family possessed—the King James Bible. Many learned biblical passages by heart, and found that their written and spoken English was shaped by the language and imagery of this Bible. Without the King James Bible, there would have been no *Paradise Lost*, no *Pilgrim's Progress*, no Handel's *Messiah*, no Negro spirituals, and no Gettysburg Address. These, and innumerable other works, were inspired by the language of this Bible. Without this Bible, the culture of the English-speaking world would have been immeasurably impoverished. The King James Bible played no small part in shaping English literary nationalism, by asserting the supremacy of the English language as a means of conveying religious truths.

Yet the Bible is far more than a work of literature. For Christians—the world's largest religious grouping—the Bible tells the story of the creation of the world by God, and its redemption through Jesus Christ. The Bible speaks words of hope in the face of suffering and death. It tells of a New Jerusalem, in which pain, sorrow, and death are things of the past. Until the Bible was translated, many English-speaking Christians had to rely on their clergy to tell them about such things. The King James Bible enabled people to read these words for themselves, and shaped the contours of English-speaking Christianity in a period of unprecedented expansion and growth, as the great missionary undertakings of the late eighteenth and nineteenth centuries got under way. The ideas, language, and images of the churches of Africa and Australasia were deeply shaped by an English translation of the Bible that had been prepared centuries earlier.

The importance of the Bible went far beyond personal religious devotion and faith. It was central to the life of Western European society in a way that we cannot begin to imagine today. The story is often told of the great economic historian Jack Fisher, who was being pestered by a student for a reading list on sixteenth- and seventeenth-century economic history. Exasperated, Fisher finally gave his definitive answer: "If you really want to understand this period, go away and read the Bible." Throughout the sixteenth and seventeenth centuries, the Bible was seen as a social, economic, and political text. Those seeking to overthrow the English monarchy and those wanting to retain it both sought support from the same Bible. The Bible came to be seen as the foundation of every aspect of English culture, linking monarch and church, time and eternity.

The lives of countless men and women since then have been changed and moulded by the King James Bible. Refugees from England, fleeing religious persecution in the seventeenth century, took copies with them. It would be their encouragement on the long and dangerous voyage to the Americas, and their guide as they settled in the New World. Prisoners in English jails found solace in reciting biblical verses they had learned by heart, in the words chosen by the translators assembled by King James. The King James Bible became part of the everyday world of generations of English-speaking peoples, spread across the world. It can be argued that, until the end of the First World War, the King James Bible was seen not simply as the most important English translation of the Bible but as one of the finest literary works in the English language. It did not follow literary trends; it established them.

So how did this remarkable translation come to be written? What led to the production of this monument in the development of the English language? The full answer to this question is as fascinating as it is complex, and involves the Byzantine politics of Tudor and Jacobean England, the hopes and fears of English monarchs and would-be archbishops, and the surge of confidence and pride in England and its national language under "Good Queen Bess." To answer this question is to throw open the doors of a lost world—a world that was being transformed by the new technology of printing, in much the way that today's world has been changed by the Internet. As we prepare to tell the story of the greatest English Bible ever produced, we must close our eyes to our own world—a world in which books are plentiful, relatively inexpensive, and readily available, and in which English Bibles can be bought at any local bookshop and read, and enter another, very different universe.

Our story opens with a new invention that changed the face of Europe forever . . .

# 1

# UNKNOWN TO
# THE ANCIENTS:
# THE NEW TECHNOLOGY

New technology promises new riches to its pioneers. The development and commercial exploitation of television and computer technology in the twentieth century made fortunes for many, just as the railway and oil industries created a new wealthy social class in nineteenth-century Britain. In the fifteenth century, a new invention promised to revolutionize communications and generate untold riches for those fortunate enough to be in it from the beginning.

In 1620, the influential English philosopher Francis Bacon observed how three inventions had reshaped the world as he knew it.

> *It is well to observe the force and virtue and consequence of inventions, and these are nowhere to be seen nowhere more conspicuously than in those three which were unknown to the ancients, and of which the origins, though recent, are obscure and inglorious; namely, printing, gunpowder, and the magnet. For these three have changed the whole face and state of things throughout the world.*

Bacon here identified the three inventions that changed the face of the known world. Gunpowder altered the course of warfare irreversibly. The magnet, when used to construct a mariner's compass, allowed navigation to proceed even when the sun and stars could not be seen. These two inventions lay behind England's rise to greatness under Queen Elizabeth I in the late sixteenth century, as Bacon well knew.

Most important of all for the story of the King James Bible, the invention of printing made it possible for ideas to sweep across Europe and the oceans of the world, ignoring the barriers erected by anxious monarchs and bishops to safeguard the familiar and comfortable old ways. To understand the importance of this invention, we need to consider the social revolution that had engulfed Europe during the later Middle Ages. A new middle class emerged, convinced of the possibility of changing the world.

## THE SOCIAL REVOLUTION: THE NEW MIDDLE CLASS

THE MIDDLE AGES was witness to a massive social upheaval across much of Western Europe. The feudal system gradually crumbled, with wealth and power beginning to shift to a new merchant class. Under the feudal system, power and wealth were concentrated in the hands of a relatively small number of families. Especially during the fifteenth century, the influence of the traditional families began eroding. Control of some of the great cities of Europe slipped away from the aristocracy, and shifted to the growing number of merchants. These had made their fortunes through trading and dealing, and had little time for the old-fashioned attitudes of the traditional families. Throughout Europe, cities began to be governed by city councils dominated by the new merchant class. Traditional social structures were undermined by greater social mobility, increased wealth and spending power within the middle classes, and a surge in literacy and levels of educational achievement within the population as a whole.

This development was of immense significance in the shaping of a new Europe. The control of sections of society was slowly but surely shifting from the old patrician families to the entrepreneurs. The emerging breed of venture capitalists was looking for business opportunities. The great trade fairs of late medieval Europe—held at international crossroads, such as Geneva—became important catalysts for economic growth, encouraging trade across Europe. Investment opportunities were eagerly sought. Our story concerns one such opportunity—the invention of printing. The financial backing of the new technology of printing was quickly identified as one of the surest ways to make money. Investment in printing technology became increasingly attractive on account of a major social change—the rise in literacy. People began to read; someone had to produce the books they came to demand.

In the early Middle Ages, literacy was rare, and often limited to the clergy. It was common for the courts of Europe to employ clergy to handle their correspondence and archives. This was not because the clergy might bring some special spiritual quality or blessing to these matters, but simply because the clergy were just about the only people at the time who could read and write. But the new culture of the Italian Renaissance, which swept through much of Western Europe in the fourteenth century, saw literacy as being a social accomplishment, rather than just a useful administrative tool. Being able to read was now seen as the key to personal fulfilment; to own books was a statement of social status, sending out powerful signals concerning both the financial and intellectual standing of the household.

The Renaissance was a complex and highly dynamic movement, which had its origins in fourteenth-century Italy. At one level, it can be seen as a movement working for the renewal of culture, which based itself on the classical language, literature, and arts of Ancient Rome. Ancient Rome was seen as a fountainhead, a spring of fresh and flowing water, that could refresh and renew European culture, and liberate it from the barren and arid ideas of the Middle Ages. The Renaissance set out to promote written and spoken eloquence, and placed considerable emphasis on cultivating both reading and writing. To be literate was now more than a technical accomplishment, useful for keeping records and correspondence up to date. It was a sophisticated cultural achievement that opened the way to self-improvement and personal fulfilment—not to mention the hope of social advancement. The possession of books was now seen as a social virtue, raising the status of their owner within an increasingly literate culture.

The demand for books soared. The rise in literacy created a virtually insatiable appetite for reading material. Yet this new demand simply could not be met by existing book production techniques. These were painfully slow, and the price of books correspondingly high. Text and illustrations had to be painstakingly copied out by hand by specially trained scribes. Demand far outstripped the supply. The surge of interest in books caused many to wonder whether it was possible to develop a new way of producing them that would cut out the hugely expensive copying process. There was money waiting to be made for someone who could cut production costs, just as there was venture capital waiting to be invested in any new technology that could open the way to mass book production.

So how could books be produced cheaply? A short-term answer was found in the early part of the fifteenth century. Text and illustrations were engraved on wooden blocks, using a knife and gouge. A water-based brown ink, made from the bark of trees, was then applied to the block using an inking cushion. The block was then used to print copies of the image on single sheets of paper, which were bound together to produce a book. But it was only an interim solution. The blocks were costly to produce, and once cut to order, could not be used for any other purpose. It was ideal for short books—but for long works, such as the Bible, it was unrealistically cumbersome. A better solution had to be found. The man who found it was Johannes Gutenberg.

## JOHANNES GUTENBERG AND THE ORIGINS OF PRINTING

AS WE HAVE seen, the burgeoning demand for reading material throughout Western Europe created a huge market for books. Entrepreneurs began to realize the potentially lucrative business opportunity this offered. Suppose it were possible to invent a new way of producing books quickly and cheaply. If the process could be kept secret in its early stages, it could make its inventor and his backers immensely rich. This was the new philosopher's stone, which could turn all to gold. By 1450, five individuals were desperately seeking the answer, each with their own financial backers. Jean Brito of Bruges, Panfilo Casteli of Feltre, Johannes Gutenberg of Mainz, Laurens Koster of Haarlem, and Prokop Waldvogel of Avignon were urgently pursuing this new holy grail, which promised to make them rich beyond their dreams.

The solution was eventually found by Johannes Gutenberg, who made the breakthrough that finally established printing as the communication technology of the future. Similar ideas may have been under development around the same time in Prague and Haarlem. But in business, the key question is not about who else is in the race, it's about who gets there first. Johannes Gutenberg was the first to make the new technology work, ensuring his place in any history of the human race.

Gutenberg was born to the wealthy Gensfleisch family in the city of Mainz. Following a long-standing custom, he took his mother's name. He trained in metalworking, and became a member of Mainz' Guild of Goldsmiths. In 1430, he moved to Strasbourg, where he established a business making high-quality metal mirrors. These were much sought after by pilgrims to local cathedrals, who believed that they could reflect the healing power of sacred relics on their owners. It was pure superstition, of course—but even superstition could be exploited for profit.

Gutenberg's experience in working metals to create mirrors would come in useful as he laboured, in secret, to develop a new way of transferring ink to paper through the first printing press. Gutenberg's first experiments in new approaches to printing were carried out clandestinely in Strasbourg. They were hugely expensive, and Gutenberg had to borrow extensively to finance them. But Gutenberg regarded the costs as the inevitable result of any major business venture, and had every expectation of recouping all his costs once the technology was perfected. And secrecy was essential if he was to stay ahead of the opposition.

What Gutenberg developed was a printing system. It is important to appreciate that the printing press being developed by Gutenberg brought together a number of existing technologies, as well as one major innovation—movable metal type. The invention of movable metal type on its own would not have been enough to enable this breakthrough. Gutenberg's genius lay in creating a system that incorporated both new and old ideas, allowing a task to be performed with unprecedented efficiency.

Gutenberg's experimental printing process involved the kind of wooden screw press traditionally used to crush grapes for wine or olives for oil, or to compress bales of cloth. A similar press was already used in paper production, to squeeze water out of newly made paper. Gutenberg appears to have realized that the process that removed water from paper might also be used to print ink on to that same medium.

An initial difficulty that Gutenberg encountered was that the screw used to press the platen—that is, the flat plate that spreads the pressure from the screw across a wide area of paper—caused ink smudges. Turning the screw to increase the pressure on the paper also caused the platen to rotate slightly, and thus blurred the printed impression. Gutenberg got around this difficulty by inserting a vertical wooden box between the screw and platen. This box—which came to be known as a "hose"—allowed the smudge-free printing so characteristic of Gutenberg's early productions.

But what kind of ink should be used? One of Gutenberg's key

PORTRAIT OF JOHANNES GUTENBERG
BY AN UNKNOWN ARTIST

contributions to the development of printing was the invention of a new type of ink made from lampblack—the soot deposited by candle flames on cold surfaces—and varnish, which was suitable for this new approach to printing. The older printing technology used a water-soluble brown ink, which faded over time; the new process used a dark black ink, which was permanent. A range of water-soluble inks were available to medieval scribes. The liquid produced by cuttlefish and squid was employed to produce a sepia-colored ink, while a brown ink could be made by extracting the tannic acids found in gallnuts or tree bark. Egg white and gum acted as a media support for these inks.

Oil-based ink had been developed earlier in the Middle Ages. The new inks, based on "lampblack," had not been used extensively. The main reason for this was that most medieval books took the form of manuscripts made of vellum or parchment (calf- or lambskin), which did not readily absorb the oil. As a result, the ink did not always dry completely, and smudged easily.

Gutenberg developed printing techniques that allowed paper to come into its own as a medium for the new technology. The origins of rag- and fibre-based papers can be traced back to second-century China. The Arab invasions of western China in the eighth century led to the Arabs acquiring this new technology; in turn, they passed it on to Europe, and the first European paper mill was established in eastern Spain in 1074. But the technology spread slowly across Europe, and the first German paper mill was not founded until 1390, at Nuremberg. The reason for this slow advance is not difficult to establish. Paper was widely regarded as inferior to vellum. It cost less to produce than vellum, but it did not last as long. In addition, it had a tendency to absorb the water-based inks used in manuscript book production. Vellum was widely regarded as being superior on all counts.

Yet paper proved to be eminently suitable for the new process of mechanical printing, using metal type and oil-based inks. Although Gutenberg produced a small number of printed Bibles using vellum (or parchment; the two terms are more or less interchangeable), his technology effectively marked the end of vellum as a publishing medium. An additional factor here was that vellum did not absorb any kind of ink, whether water- or oil-based. As a result, the pigments were deposited on the surface of the material, rather than absorbed within it. The pigments could thus easily be rubbed off the surface of vellum through constant use. The imprint on paper, in contrast, remained permanent.

Gutenberg's real breakthrough was the invention of movable type—that is, letters that could be reused after printing one book. Block-print technology—which had been known in Europe since the return of Marco Polo from Asia at the end of the thirteenth century—suffered a serious limitation. Each block had to be created specially for each page of a book; once it had been used, it could not be recycled or employed for any purpose other than reprinting exactly the same page. The process of carving the individual blocks was time-consuming. Errors could not easily be corrected. Gutenberg's solution allowed the reuse of type, and the ready correction of each page from "proofs."

Gutenberg's type had to be designed and produced in large quantities. The cost was huge. After Gutenberg had returned to Mainz in 1448, he was able to interest Johann Fust, a local goldsmith, in his invention. Fust backed Gutenberg to the tune of eight hundred gulden in 1450, and the same amount again in 1452—well over one million pounds by today's standards. The type was designed by Peter Schoeffer, and was probably cast in "speculum" metal—the same metal used by Gutenberg for the mirrors that gullible pilgrims believed reflected the spiritual powers of sacred relics in their direction. This metal consisted of an alloy of lead, tin, and antimony—the last being added to harden the metal, to ensure that it resisted wear. The method of casting type devised by Gutenberg would continue to be used until 1838, when David Bruce pioneered the first typecasting machine in New York.

There is evidence that Gutenberg initially printed about six short works—including a Latin grammar and an astronomical calendar—apparently partly to persuade Fust that his new invention really worked, partly to gain the experience of producing books, and partly to recoup his not inconsiderable operating costs.

Needing new investment urgently, Gutenberg wanted to persuade his patron that he was capable of the much greater project he had in mind. Fust allowed himself to be persuaded to make him a further loan, on condition that he become Gutenberg's partner in this great project. By 1452 all was ready to begin the work that Gutenberg regarded as his life's goal—the production of the first printed Bible.

## THE FIRST PRINTED BIBLES

WHY THE BIBLE? Two reasons may be given. First, it posed a challenge, which aroused Gutenberg's professional interest. The Bible is a large book, and to print it in its totality represented pressing the technology then available to its uttermost limits. The 1468 version of the Bible produced by Gutenberg—known as the "Thirty-Six-Line Bible," due to the number of lines of type in each column of print—runs to 1,768 pages. By the standards of the time, this was a phenomenal challenge. Few can resist the desire to rise to a challenge like that, and show that they have what it takes to meet it. Gutenberg's massive achievement instantly secured his place in history.

Second, the Bible was an immensely popular and influential work. Today, it remains the world's best-selling book. If any one book may be said to have shaped Western civilization, it is the Bible. The fifteenth century was a period of considerable growth in religious activity throughout Western Europe, which saw new interest develop in reading and owning copies of the Bible. Virtually every measurable parameter—such as the number of churches being built, donations to religious charities, or the numbers of those going on pilgrimages—points to a surge in interest in religion at this time. The rise of movements such as the "Modern Devotion" led to a growing interest in reading religious books—supreme among which was, of course, the Bible itself.

The ability to read had once been the exclusive preserve of the clergy. By the beginning of the fifteenth century, this literary monopoly was in the process of being decisively overthrown. During the Renaissance—the cultural movement that began in Italy and swept northward—the ability to read and write was regarded as of immense importance. The development of printing meant that works available earlier only to a charmed clerical circle were now available to a much wider readership. The demand for religious books spiraled. And the book in greatest demand? The Bible.

The sheer length of the Bible—which consists of sixty-six books, thirty-nine of which are located in the Old Testament and twenty-seven in the New—made it a major publishing undertaking. The cost of copying it by hand was prohibitive. Yet many households saw the possession of a Bible as essential for the private matter of personal devotion, not to mention the rather more sordid and public matter of drawing attention to their social status. Studies of the household inventories of patrician families in early fifteenth-century Florence show that virtually every noble household possessed a copy of the New Testament, painstakingly copied out in manuscript. The demand for the Bible was immense; Gutenberg's invention suddenly made possible a new means of meeting this demand.

As far as can be established, Gutenberg began cutting the type for this project in 1449 or 1450. Composition began in 1452, and the printing was completed by 1456. During the final stages of the process, six compositors were employed, working simultaneously. The work had been divided up between them, with each compositor knowing exactly what section of the work he was responsible for. Each page had two columns of text, consisting of forty-two lines of type. It is not clear how many copies were printed. The most reliable estimate suggests that the print run for the work was tiny by modern standards—possibly as few as 185 copies were produced, of which about 40 still exist today. While most of these were printed on paper, a small number were printed on the more expensive vellum. The cost of this would have been considerable. Each printed Bible consisted of 340 folio sheets. As each calf hide yielded 2 folio sheets, 170 animal hides were required for each of the two-volumed Bibles. The investment required to produce a single Bible was thus considerable. The asking price for each Bible was thirty florins, estimated to be three years' wages for a learned clerk.

Gutenberg was a businessman, and knew that the production of a best-seller was a sure-fire way of making money. The investment he was forced to make in this new technology was huge—but so were the rewards that he could hope to reap. Nobody else had access to the technology that was essential for the task, and he thus had a virtual monopoly on the production of Bibles. He added another line of business; he began to print indulgences—pieces of paper, issued on behalf of the Pope or a local bishop, offering written promises of dispensations from time in purgatory (a matter to which I shall return in

SAMPLE PAGES FROM
THE GUTENBERG BIBLE, C. 1455

chapter 3). These slips of paper—which served the Church by raising funds for projects (such as funding Crusades or building cathedrals)—were initially handwritten. With the innovation of the printing press, however, indulgences could be printed by the thousands.

The importance of this point was realized by William Caxton (1422–91), England's first printer. Caxton learned the skills of printing in mainland Europe, and printed his first book in the city of Bruges. In 1476, Caxton returned to England, and set up his printing shop at Westminster. The first work Caxton published took the form of an indulgence, issued by John, Abbot of Abingdon, to a couple called Henry and Katherine Langley. The indulgence—the price of which, incidentally, is unknown, but likely to have been very high—assured the couple that their sins had been fully forgiven. The indulgence delicately hints that the couple were no strangers to the delights

STAINED GLASS PORTRAIT OF WILLIAM CAXTON
FROM STATIONERS' HALL IN LONDON, C. 1880

of the world, and consequently had rather a lot of sins to be absolved. In addition, they would receive the benefits normally associated with pilgrimages, without suffering the inconvenience of actually having to make them. It is likely that Caxton received a commission for every indulgence sold, and profited considerably as a result. It was hardly surprising that Gutenberg chose to muscle in on the trade. One reliable report suggests that he may have printed as many as two hundred thousand. His future seemed as rosy as it was secure.

In the event, however, Gutenberg did not end his life as a wealthy man. He lacked business sense, and ended up losing a serious legal battle with his partner, Johann Fust, over the repayment of loans. Fust promptly formed an immensely successful new partnership with Gutenberg's former employee Peter Schoeffer. The secrets of typesetting could not be kept for long, and the advantage Gutenberg enjoyed over his competitors was soon eroded. Printing houses sprang up throughout the 1460s to meet the new demand for printed books. Others grew rich through Gutenberg's invention, while he went on to die in poverty in 1468. By the end of the century, the production of printed Bibles was so firmly established that it had become virtually routine. Printed Bibles were of major importance for the private devotions of individual Christian families; their novelty value was, however, at an end. Prices had fallen dramatically. The cost of a Gutenberg Bible was equivalent to a large town house in a German city; by 1520, Bibles had become an affordable luxury.

Yet many were aware that another religious best-seller lay just over the horizon. The Bible printed by Gutenberg was in the Latin language—the language of diplomacy, of the Church, and of scholarship—but not of ordinary people. Yet the Bible was not originally written in Latin, but in the languages of the ancient world—in the case of the Old Testament, Hebrew, with a smattering of Aramaic, the great diplomatic language of the ancient Near East; in the case of the New Testament, Greek. For Western Christianity, the Bible has always been known as a translated book. This can be contrasted with the sacred text of Islam, the Koran, which is still read by Muslims in its original Arabic. The translation and publication of the Bible in the living languages of Western Europe was thus widely recognized as the next publishing landmark. Gutenberg's innovations put Germany ahead of the opposition. The first German Bible was printed by Mentelin of Strasbourg in 1466; by 1483, there were nine different vernacular German Bibles in print.

But there was not the slightest hint of an English version of the Bible being about to appear in print in the late fifteenth century—despite the best efforts of John Wycliffe and his followers to bring about such a development.

## A VERNACULAR BIBLE: THE WYCLIFFITE VERSIONS

ONE OF THOSE who pressed most vigorously for an English version of the Bible in the fourteenth century was John Wycliffe (c. 1330–84), often seen as a forerunner of the Reformation of the sixteenth century. Wycliffe argued extensively—in both English and Latin—for the translation of the Bible into his native English. The English people had a right to read the Bible in their own language, rather than be forced to listen to what their clergy wished them to hear. As Wycliffe pointed out, the ecclesiastical establishment had a considerable vested interest in not allowing the laity access to the Bible. They might even discover that there was a massive discrepancy between the lifestyles of bishops and clergy and those commended—and practised—by Christ and the apostles.

Consequently, Wycliffe threatened to destroy the whole edifice of clerical domination in matters of theology and church life. The translation of the Bible into English would be a social leveller on a hitherto unknown scale. All would be able to read Christendom's sacred text, and judge both the lifestyle and teachings of the medieval church on its basis. The very idea sent shock waves throughout the complacent church establishment of the day. Henry Knighton—an English chronicler interested in maintaining his rather comfortable

PORTRAIT OF JOHN WYCLIFFE

status quo—had no doubts of the dangers posed by what Wycliffe proposed. Christ put the clergy in charge of the church; what right had lay people to get involved in its affairs?

> *John Wycliffe translated the gospel, which Christ had entrusted to clerics and doctors of the church, so that they might administer it conveniently to the laity, and to lesser people according to the needs of the time and the requirements of their audience, in terms of their hunger of mind. Wycliffe translated it from Latin into the English—not the angelic!—language. As a result, what was previously known only by learned clerics and those of good understanding has become common, and available to the laity—in fact, even to women who can read. As a result, the pearls of the gospel have been scattered and spread before swine.*

Knighton here makes a somewhat laboured pun on the Latin terms *lingua anglica* (English language) and *lingua angelica* (angelic language). His lousy sense of humour apart, the concern he had was real, and was shared by many within the religious establishment of the era. Translating the Bible into English would break the clerical monopoly on this text, and allow it to be placed into the hands of the laity—or, even worse in Knighton's view, *women*. What Knighton feared was, of course, precisely what Wycliffe hoped for.

Wycliffe's follower Nicholas Hereford preached a series of sermons in English at Oxford in May and June 1382. They attracted considerable popular interest, not least because lay people could understand what Hereford was demanding—including his severe criticisms of the wealth of the Church and individual clergy, and the obsession with money and litigation that seemed to have become endemic within the Church. If neither the Church nor the king were prepared to sort things out, Hereford suggested that the laity might like to take things into their own hands. England had been thrown into chaos by the Peasants' Revolt of June–July 1381. The cause of the revolt was a punitive new tax of one shilling, imposed on all men and women over the age of sixteen. For a while, it seemed as if the social fabric of England was being torn into shreds. King Richard II lived in fear of a new outbreak of rebellion. Coming a year after this revolt, which had caused chaos in England, these were rightly seen as highly contentious and incendiary ideas. What excited the English laity caused serious anxiety in the cloisters of power. It is little surprise that the Archbishop of Canterbury summoned Hereford and others to London to explain themselves—in Latin, of course, for fear that any inquisitive lay people present might understand and approve of their proposals.

The evidence that Wycliffe himself undertook biblical translation from Latin into English is far from certain, and it is likely that history's final judgment on this matter will be that Wycliffe probably encouraged others to do what he personally lacked the time to undertake. Yet it is clear that Wycliffe's programme had the potential to revolutionize England—if it was allowed to happen. Wycliffe himself contrasted the divine authority of the Bible with the human authority of both king and Church. What would happen if the population of England were given access to the text of the Bible in a language they could understand? Might not the institutions of the day—fragile enough at the best of times—be liable to be overthrown in a frenzy of revolutionary activity?

One of Nicholas Hereford's sermons ended with the following words, which clearly implied that it was God's will—as revealed in the Bible—that the Christian population should rise up and seize the wealth of the clergy.

> *As there are no officers [of the state] specifically appointed for this purpose, it is necessary for you, O faithful Christian people, to take this matter into your hands and ensure this obligation is achieved. And I firmly hope that this will succeed, as I know with the greatest certainty that God almighty wishes it to be done.*

Divine authority was being cited for social upheaval. God was being invoked as the basis of radical change. It is little wonder that the state and church authorities panicked. As a result, the mere possession of a vernacular Bible was presumptive evidence of heresy in fifteenth-century England. Powerful vested interests were thus stacked up against the production of an English Bible. English kings and bishops feared that this might cause the English people to rise in revolt, and overthrow them.

Yet it was one thing to block the production of such a Bible in England. What would happen if an English translation of the Bible were to be produced abroad, and smuggled into England? The very idea of such a Bible was deeply unsettling to the English elite at this time. The development of the technology of printing in Europe meant that there was a very real threat of someone producing such a Bible as a business venture, aiming to make money out of it. What could be done to stop this? As events proved, this much-feared development would not take place until the 1520s. As expected, it proved formidably difficult to detect and prevent such importation.

But this is to run ahead of our story. One of the most remarkable facts of English history during the Middle Ages is that its ruling elite chose not to use their native language of English, except when dealing with social inferiors. The publication of the King James Bible in 1611 can be seen as the crowning literary and religious glory of a nation that had finally come of age, and took pride in its own language. Yet it took the English some generations to love, respect, and use their own language. So important is this matter to our story that I must tell something of the remarkable tale of how English emerged from obscurity to begin its remarkable advance to become the world's favourite language.

# 2

# THE RISE OF
# ENGLISH AS A
# NATIONAL LANGUAGE

The struggle for an English Bible was long and complex, reflecting the entrenched and vested interests of the medieval Church, and the caution and conservatism of politicians. Yet it also rested on a hesitancy on the part of many concerning the merits of the English language. It is not generally realized that the languages of the elite in English society in the early fourteenth century were French and Latin. English was seen as the language of peasants, incapable of expressing anything other than the crudest and most basic of matters. English was just fine when dealing with spreading dung on fields. But how could such a barbaric language do justice to such sophisticated matters as philosophy or religion? To translate the Bible from its noble and ancient languages into English was seen as a pointless act of debasement.

The story of the King James Bible cannot be told without an understanding of the remarkable rise of confidence in the English language in the late sixteenth century. What was once scorned as the barbarous language of ploughmen became esteemed as the language of patriots and poets—a language fit for heroes on the one hand, and for the riches of the Bible on the other. Gone were any hesitations about the merits of the English language. Queen Elizabeth I's navy and armies had established England's military credentials; her poets, playwrights, and translators had propelled English into the front rank of living European languages. The King James Bible consolidated the enormous advances in the English language over the centuries, and can be seen as the symbol of a nation and language that believed that their moment had finally arrived.

The growing tide of nationalism that broke out in the late fifteenth century, and which helped shape the massive political and religious upheavals that lay ahead in the sixteenth, gave a new significance to regional languages. National identity was both moulded and sustained by its cultural achievements. The growth of a literature in living European languages was widely seen as essential to the formation of national identities in France, Spain, and England. This development was viewed with dismay by those who wanted Latin to be the language of a new cosmopolitan European culture, such as Erasmus of Rotterdam and Sir Thomas More. Yet it proved to be irresistible.

What can be termed a "rhetorical nationalism" came to develop across Europe, including England. In his 1589 *Art of English Poesy*, written at the height of the Elizabethan Age, George Puttenham declared that English was just as sophisticated as Greek or Latin, and perfectly capable of expressing the full range of human emotions and thoughts.

> *And if the art of Poesy be still appertaining to utterance, why may not the same be with us as well as them, our language being no less copious pithy and significative as theirs, our conceits the same, and our wits no less to devise and imitate than theirs were?*

To write in English—or translate into English—was a political act, affirming the intrinsic dignity of the language of a newly confident people and nation. And why should that nation not have its own Bible in its own language?

If any nation managed successfully to suppress demands for a Bible in its own language during the fifteenth century, it was England. A German Bible was published at Strasbourg in 1466. An explosion of translations (always based on the Latin Vulgate text) followed, so that by 1483 nine printed translations were accessible. Martin Luther's German translation of the New Testament (1522) was built on a solid tradition of translation stretching back for two generations. French Bibles were available by 1500. But the translation of the Bible into English, in whole or in part, remained illegal under a decree of 1408 known as the "Constitutions of Oxford."

Some essentially fictional works of devotion, which some people—unfamiliar with the original texts of the gospels—might assume to be translations of part of the gospels, were indeed in circulation in English at this time. These were carefully vetted to ensure that they were acceptable to the church authorities of the day. Direct knowledge of the biblical text was still regarded as far too dangerous a thing to be permitted to the laity. In any case, some argued, English was too crude and unsophisticated a language to cope with the great themes of the Christian religion.

## THE TRIUMPH OF FRENCH AND THE MEDIEVAL NEGLECT OF ENGLISH

THE ENGLISH LANGUAGE went through a period of severe neglect in the Middle Ages. The conquest of England by the Normans in 1066 had led to the suppression of English in public life. French—or, more accurately, the form of Anglo-French that arose after the Norman conquest—dominated public discourse, particularly government departments and the courts. The English upper classes spoke Anglo-French as a matter of principle, to distinguish themselves from the lower classes, who spoke Middle English, in much the same way as the

Russian nobility in the nineteenth century preferred French to their native Russian.

It must be noted that this development was not restricted to England. Throughout Western Europe, the French culture and language were basking in their ascendancy. The French court was seen as embodying the noble ideals of chivalry in their most refined and advanced forms, and was widely imitated throughout Europe. The University of Paris came to be regarded as the embodiment of the ideals of scholarly excellence and educational achievement, and further increased the prestige of France as a cultured nation. The great thirteenth-century Italian writer Brunetto Latini, who numbered Dante Alighieri among his students, wrote one of his most influential works in French. On being asked to justify this decision, he commented:

> *If anyone should ask why this book is written in Romance, according to the French language, when I myself am Italian, I should say that this is for two reasons. First, because I happen to be writing in France. And second, because that language is the most delectable and common to all people.*

This widespread perception that French had established itself as the lingua franca of the cultural elite of Europe inevitably led to English being dismissed as a crude language, incapable of conveying the subtle undertones necessary for diplomacy, the fine distinctions of philosophy, and the complexities of legal and financial negotiations. English would do very well for the common labourer; French was the language of choice for the elite.

But the form of French that was spoken in thirteenth-century England was the dialect associated with Normandy. While this enjoyed a certain prestige at that time, the political and cultural ascendancy of Normandy was already becoming seriously eroded. Shifting alliances during the thirteenth century meant that political power came to be firmly linked with the city of Paris. The French of the Paris region was now the language of choice. By the fourteenth century, the form of French spoken in England had become the subject of ridicule in cultured French society. Aware of this, those English gentry who could afford it arranged for their children to be educated in Paris, to avoid the indignity of being thought crude and unrefined by the arbiters of cultural sophistication.

## A Turning Point:
## The Fifteenth Century

THE FIFTEENTH CENTURY saw the dawn of the English nationalism that would prove to be so vigorous under Elizabeth I. A sense of national solidarity—a shared identity as a people—began to emerge in the first half of the fifteenth century, and was directly linked to a growing regard for (and use of) the national language. Slowly but surely, English began to displace French in discourse of the public arena. Grammar schools gradually stopped teaching French, and concentrated on offering education in the English language. A surge of literary and religious works began to appear in English around this period—such as Geoffrey Chaucer's *Canterbury Tales*, and *Sir Gawain and the Green Knight*. No longer did the English feel they had to be apologetic when using their own language.

Signs of anxiety within the establishment concerning the future of the French language in England were evident early in the fourteenth century. In 1332, Parliament laid down that "all lords, barons, knights and honest men of good towns must exercise care and diligence to teach their children the French language." The university authorities at Oxford, alarmed at the tendency of both dons and students to speak English, attempted to impose Latin and French on an increasingly unwilling academic institution.

The potential importance of the growing use of English for the religious life of the nation can be seen in many ways. The liturgy of the Church was in Latin, as was the Bible, which was read as part of that liturgy. While the popular view of the late medieval English church is that it was dominated by the Latin language, it needs to be realized that French was also extensively used. Many senior English clergy spoke neither English nor Latin, but only French. An eyewitness account of the consecration of the bishop of Durham in 1318 discloses the remarkable fact that the new bishop could not even read the Latin words he was required to repeat during the service. After several attempts to pronounce the Latin word *metropoliticae*, he announced—in French—his intention to leave that word out, and get on with the remainder of the service. This valiant attempt came to grief over the Latin word *enigmate*, at which point the bishop—again, in French—complained that nobody could possibly read aloud a word like that. It is little wonder that Christianity seemed to many fourteenth-century English people to be a religion whose business was conducted entirely in one of two foreign languages. Reaction against this developed outside the church hierarchy.

The reign of Henry V (1413–22) is often seen as marking a turning point in securing new respectability for the English language. The military defeat of the French armies at Agincourt mirrored a corresponding cultural defeat of the French language in England. That military victory would prove to be short-lived; the linguistic victory proved to be permanent. The same Henry V who vanquished the French at Agincourt began the trend of using the English language in his letters. The influence of the king's example can be seen in a resolution of the Brewers' Guild of London, probably dating from 1422, in which they formally declared that their guild would now conduct its business in English, not French, following the example of both king and Parliament.

The Hundred Years War (1337–1453) served to consolidate the growing popular impression that French was the language of England's enemy. It was no accident that Shakespeare placed the following words in the mouth of Jack Cade in *Henry VI, Part II*:

*He can speak French; and therefore he is a traitor.*

PORTRAIT OF WILLIAM SHAKESPEARE
BY AN UNKNOWN ARTIST

The French defeat of a larger English army at Formigny in April 1450 marked the end of any serious possibility that England might retain its French possessions. For the first time, English longbowmen were defeated in an open battle, having been forced to dislodge from their traditional defensive positions by the use of artillery, and then were overrun by a French heavy cavalry charge. At Castillon (1453) the French destroyed the last English army with cannon, handguns, and heavy cavalry. This battle led to France's recovery of Guienne and was the final major engagement of this long and increasingly pointless war.

The war with France at an end, English became the language of choice of the upper classes and government departments. No longer was English dismissed as the language of the lower classes; it was now the language of choice of a nation with an increasing sense of national identity and shared purpose, strengthened by England's growing maritime enterprise. While this would reach its zenith during the Elizabethan era, it was clearly foreshadowed in the closing years of the fifteenth century.

## RELIGION AND THE VERNACULAR: THE YORK MYSTERY PLAYS

THE GROWING IMPORTANCE of English in relation to matters of religion can be illustrated in many ways. Perhaps one of the most interesting developments was the establishment of mystery plays in great northern English cathedral cities, such as Chester and York. The York mystery plays are widely regarded as being the finest example of this genre, and deserve our attention.

By 1350, the ravages of the Black Death upon the northern English city of York had ended. The city entered into a new phase of prosperity, and was second only to London in terms of its financial and social importance. The city celebrated its new wealth and status by staging a series of plays on and around the feast of Corpus Christi. Like Easter, Corpus Christi was a movable feast, and could fall on any date between 23 May and 24 June. This ensured reasonably good weather for the cycle of plays. The plays in question depicted the creation, fall, and redemption of humanity, drawing extensively on biblical narratives.

The long sequence of events between creation and the last judgment was broken down into manageable segments, each of which was entrusted to one of the city's guilds. Trouble was taken to ensure that the guild had some natural relationship with the biblical scene being acted out. Thus the Marriage at Cana in Galilee (at which water was changed into wine) was entrusted to the Guild of Vintners, the Last Supper to the Guild of Bakers, and the Death of Christ to the Guild of Butchers.

The impact of these mystery plays was immense, and they came to play a major role in York's popular religious culture. The intermingling of images, actions, and words offered a powerful and attractive account of the central themes of the Christian faith, and offered both stimulation to the imagination and education for the mind. Most important of all, *the plays were performed in English*—or, more accurately, the Yorkshire dialect of the late fourteenth and early fifteenth centuries. Where the Church offered a liturgy, Bible readings, and sermons only in Latin—which few outside the intellectual elite understood—the play cycle offered religious teaching in the vernacular. Its appeal was considerable. So the question naturally arose: why was the Bible not also available in this way?

The demand for a printed Bible in the English language became an issue of increasing importance in the late Middle Ages. There was clearly a growing market for such a work. It also had the potential to become a classic of English literature, allowing a definitive form of the English language to establish itself through the widespread usage, public and private, that such a work was guaranteed to enjoy. If any printed work could shape the contours of a living Western European language, that work was a vernacular Bible.

## ENGLISH:
## A LANGUAGE OF CULTURE AND LEARNING?

IT WILL BE OBVIOUS that there were powerful vested interests within the Church that opposed the "Englishing" of the language of religion. Indeed, one of the most significant developments of the fourteenth century is the association that came into being between the deliberate decision to use English and opposition to the religious status quo. Opposition to translating the Bible into English rested on real fears that the English peasantry might be encouraged to rise against their masters. After all, had not the peasants of the south of England, angered by the imposition of additional taxes in 1381, captured London and beheaded the Archbishop of Canterbury? The religious establishment spoke Latin and French; English was the language of its potential opponents.

Alongside such fears on the part of the religious establishment, however, was a more complex anxiety within English academia concerning the very nature of the English language itself. To its Latin- and French-speaking critics, English was a barbarous language, lacking any real grammatical structure, incapable of expressing the deep and nuanced truths of the Bible in particular, and the Christian faith in general. This complaint, which had been implicit in much fourteenth-century dismissal of English as a serious language of faith, became explicit in an important debate at Oxford in 1401. Richard Ullerston defended English against its critics valiantly, but ultimately in vain. The debate concluded that English was not an appropriate language for the translation of the Bible. It was but a small step from this literary judgment to the essentially political decision to ban the English language altogether from every aspect of English church life. This decision, taken in 1407 by Thomas Arundel, Archbishop of Canterbury, had special relevance for the issue of biblical translation:

> *We therefore legislate and ordain that nobody shall from this day forth translate any text of Holy Scripture on his own authority into the English, or any other, language, whether in the form of a book, pamphlet or tract; and that any such book, pamphlet or tract, whether composed recently or in the time of John Wycliffe, or in the future, shall not be read in part or in whole, in public or in private.*

English thus became the language of the religious underground. To write in English was tantamount to holding heretical views. Even as late as 1513, John Colet—then Dean of St. Paul's Cathedral, London—was suspended from his position for translating the Lord's Prayer into English.

Even within official church circles, the serious problems caused by the 1407 decision were acknowledged, even if only in private. Two years later, Arundel himself authorized the English translation of a small book of meditations on the gospels entitled *A Mirror of the Life of Christ*. The book was not, strictly speaking, a gospel translation, but a rather pious and mawkish work of fiction, which places predictably sentimental—but most emphatically not biblical!—words into the mouths of gospel characters. The New Testament records few words of Mary, the mother of Jesus. The *Mirror* makes up for this deficiency by providing a rich feast of Marian sayings. It is possible that, precisely because the work was so obviously *not* a biblical translation but essentially a free work of fiction and speculation, Arundel felt he could authorize it without contradicting himself.

Yet the growth of English as the national language could not be inhibited. Political and cultural factors made its ultimate triumph inevitable. Those who fought the rise of the national language began to find that they were powerless in the face of a major cultural trend. It proved impossible to stop the relentless advance of the tide of English nationalism, increasingly linked with the adoption of the English language. Those who were once apologetic and defensive about the vernacular now used it with pride. Speaking English was an affirmation of national identity. In 1527, John Rastell, one of Henry VIII's advisers, noted that "the universal people of this realm had great pleasure and gave themselves greatly to the reading of the vulgar English tongue."

A widening gulf began to emerge between the increasingly confident native language of government, law, and business, and the archaic Latin of the Church. Even the clergy were affected by this development, and found themselves increasingly living in two different worlds—the sphere of everyday life, in which English was the language of choice, and the more rarefied world of the Church, in which Latin alone was used. Increasingly, the clergy found mastering Latin to be both tedious and pointless. Linguistically, the Church seemed to be cut off from the life of the English nation. It was an untenable position; the question was not *whether* but *when* the Church would abandon its resistance to the relentless Englishing of England.

As the confidence of the laity grew, so did the intensity and depth of their criticisms of the clergy. To add insult to injury, these criticisms went far beyond the traditional litanies of discontent—that clergy were overpaid, underemployed, and greedy—to include allegations of incompetence in the Latin language. As more and more laity mastered Latin, they became painfully aware of the shortcomings of the clergy's grasp of this learned language. The clerical refusal to allow the English people to read the Bible in their own language was now increasingly interpreted as a sign of fear on the part of an embattled Church.

Yet it would be wrong to suggest that the Church was the last bastion of Latin in an increasingly Anglophone culture. England's two universities—Oxford and Cambridge—remained wedded to Latin as the lingua franca of academic life. The university sector of Paris was widely known as the "Latin Quarter" precisely because Latin was the preferred—indeed, at times the only—language of scholarship and academic debate. An examination of the contents of the main Oxford library at the beginning of the seventeenth century suggests that, even at this late stage, only about one book in every hundred was in English, the remainder being virtually exclusively in classical languages. While English, as we have seen, had made massive inroads as the language of preference in national politics, legal matters, and economics, the academic world remained committed to the use of Latin.

In part, this rested on pure arrogance, and a desire to maintain a *cordon sanitaire* between the riches of classical literature and the masses. Perhaps more understandably, Latin was seen as the language of a pan-European academic culture, which allowed scholars from one country to discourse with their colleagues from abroad. Erasmus, who spoke no English, was able to spend time at both Oxford and Cambridge, using Latin as the medium of his conversations and lectures. The academic world was thus the last bastion of Latin in England as even the Church of England had ceased to use this language to any significant extent by the 1540s.

This chapter has chronicled the relentless advance of English as a national language. In the sixteenth century, a further factor contributed to the growing prestige of the English language. The movement we now know as "the Reformation" surged into prominence on the Continent of Europe. One of its leading themes was that the Bible ought to be translated into the everyday languages of Europe, including English.

The scene was therefore set for a powerful amalgamation of religion and nationalism, which made the production of an English Bible inevitable. Where once an English Bible was derided as crude and potentially heretical, it would now be seen as a symbol of national pride and international status.

# 3

# THE GREAT TUMULT:
# THE REFORMATION

History gives names to its great movements in which new ways of thinking and acting are swept into power. Often, those names are chosen by scholars many generations after the events that they describe. The theme of this chapter is the movement known as "the Reformation." The Reformation was unquestionably a religious movement—but it was also a movement that embraced and encouraged massive social, political, and economic change. Like both the French and Russian Revolutions, the origins and causes of this development are complex, and are still not completely understood. There is no doubt, however, that one factor is of major importance to our story—the rise of individualism in the Renaissance.

## THE RISE OF INDIVIDUALISM

AS WE HAVE seen, the Renaissance can be thought of as the immensely creative and dynamic period in European culture that had its origins in fourteenth-century Italy. Certain historians, most notably

Jakob Burckhardt (1818–97), argued that the Renaissance gave birth to the modern era, in that it was in this era that human beings first began to think of themselves as *individuals*. In the early Middle Ages, people had been happy to see themselves simply as parts of a greater whole—for example, as members of a great family, trade guild, nation, or Church. This communal consciousness of the Middle Ages gradually gave way to the individual consciousness of the Renaissance. Florence became the new Athens, the intellectual capital of a brave new world of individuals, each in control of his destiny. Burckhardt's definition of the Renaissance in purely individualistic terms can be challenged at several points. But in one sense, Burckhardt is unquestionably correct: something novel and exciting developed in Renaissance Italy that proved capable of exercising a fascination over generations of thinkers.

The new social mobility of the late Middle Ages meant that these new ideas were not going to be limited to Italy. Scholars and merchants, travelling to Italy on business in the early fifteenth century, brought the new ideas of the Renaissance home with them. Italy rapidly became a cultural icon of sophistication—many of Shakespeare's plays are set in Italian cities for precisely this reason. The new emphasis on the individual affected just about every aspect of European culture.

The new merchant class was impatient with what it saw as the conservatism of the old order. Old-fashioned attitudes were getting in the way of economic development. Power was still largely held by the old aristocratic families, who had managed their estates in the same ways for centuries. The medieval Church was also seen to be part of this traditional social order, with a vested interest in maintaining the status quo. All of this was called into question by the new social mobility and "can-do" attitude of the rising merchant class. Individuals should be free to change things. Power should rest on achievement, not family connections. Wealth should be actively created through trade, not passed down passively from one generation to another.

For the purposes of this story, the most important change was religious. Christians became dissatisfied with approaches to their faith that stressed its external aspects—such as just attending church. They demanded a form of Christianity that was relevant to their personal experience and private worlds. They didn't want just to be told what the Bible said—they wanted to own and read it for themselves. Religion was about personally appropriating the Christian faith, and making it a living reality in the experience of the individual lay person. A new confidence surged within the ranks of the laity. Why should the clergy have such power and influence, when the laity were now just as well educated as the former?

A hunger for reform that saturated the air of Europe in the first decade of the sixteenth century is well illustrated by one book—the *Handbook of the Christian Soldier*, published in 1503 by Erasmus of Rotterdam. The work was a demand for reform—but it was more than that. It set out a compelling vision of the church of the future, in which the laity would play their full role, wresting power and influence from the discredited clergy. Even the most humble ploughman would read his New Testament as he worked the fields. It was a vision that combined the Romanticism of the English pastoral literature of the late sixteenth century, and the hard-nosed realism of Europe's most powerful advocate of personal and institutional reform. Erasmus did not want to eliminate the clergy, who, he insisted, had a continuing role to play as the educators of the laity. But the prestige, power, and wealth that many of them had once enjoyed would be a thing of the past. The laity had come of age; the future belonged to them. And knowledge of the Bible was the key to this vision for the future.

Erasmus's work became a best-seller. If anyone needs confirmation of either the growing power of the printing press at this stage in European history, or the appeal of the ideas that Erasmus developed, they need only look at the printing history of this book. By 1515, it had achieved cult status. Originally published in Latin, it was soon translated into the most influential living European languages. The

PORTRAIT OF ERASMUS OF ROTTERDAM
BY QUENTIN METSYS (C. 1465/6-1530)
OF THE ANTWERP SCHOOL

work both reflected and intensified the hunger for change. It was only a matter of time before radical change took place.

In the first two decades of the sixteenth century, Western Europe was like a dry tinderbox. It was merely awaiting a spark before it burst into flame. But what sort of spark might ignite this explosion? In later years, European revolutions would generally be triggered by political events—such as the assassination of the Austrian Archduke Francis Ferdinand in 1914, which was the immediate cause of the First World War. If the great tumult of the sixteenth century was set off by one person or event, it is widely agreed that the event in question was Martin Luther's famous posting of the Ninety-Five Theses against indulgences of October 31, 1517.

## MARTIN LUTHER:
## PIONEER OF REFORM

MARTIN LUTHER (1483–1546) is widely regarded as one of the most significant of the reformers. Luther was born on November 10, 1483, in the German town of Eisleben, and named after Martin of Tours, whose festival fell on November 11, the day of Luther's baptism. Hans Luder (as his father's name was spelled at this stage) moved the following year to the neighbouring town of Mansfeld, where he established a small copper mining business. Luther's university education began at Erfurt in 1501. His father clearly intended him to become a lawyer, not unaware of the financial benefits this would bring the family. In 1505, Luther completed the general arts course at Erfurt, and was in a position to move on to study law.

As events turned out, his study of law never got very far. At some point in June 1505, Luther was returning to Erfurt from a visit to Mansfeld. As he neared the village of Storterheim, a severe thunderstorm gathered around him. Suddenly, a bolt of lightning struck the ground next to him, throwing him off his horse. Terrified, Luther cried out, "St. Anne, help me! I will become a monk!" He kept his word. On July 17, 1505, Luther entered the most rigorous of the seven major monasteries at Erfurt—the Augustinian priory. Luther's father was outraged at the decision, and remained alienated from his son for some considerable time.

Why should Luther have screamed these words? We shall never know for sure. The reference to St. Anne is perhaps the easiest part to understand; she was the patron saint of miners, and would have featured prominently in his father's prayers. Yet lying behind Luther's cry lies a medieval worldview that is difficult for the modern reader to fully appreciate. The past is indeed a strange country, in which things were done differently. Luther's mental world included a number of fixed landmarks that have crumbled over the centuries, and are not always easy to recognize today. One was a fear of death and what lay beyond.

PORTRAIT OF MARTIN LUTHER
BY LUCAS CRANACH THE ELDER (D. 1586)

The Middle Ages had developed an immensely sophisticated view of the afterlife, resting in part on some biblical texts, and perhaps in greater part on the human love for speculation and imagination. Dante's great fourteenth-century work *The Divine Comedy* sets out the geography of hell and purgatory in great detail. This cartography of hell echoed the popular beliefs of the time, to which Luther was heir. His views on this matter were those of his age, even if he held them with greater intensity than many.

Luther feared the wrath of God, whom he knew at this stage only as a vengeful and righteous figure, dispensing salvation to the few and eternal punishment to the damned. He knew hell to be a place in which the damned writhed in agony in a sulphur-laden atmosphere, tormented by fire. It was a terrifying thought, which preyed heavily on the young Luther's imagination, perhaps coupled with more popular beliefs of fiends and devils lurking in woods and dark places, awaiting their opportunity to snatch unwary souls and take them straight to hell. The incident of 1505 seems to have crystallized all the fears and anxieties that had been building up within his troubled mind, unresolved. The bolt of lightning brought to the surface Luther's dark broodings, and released the emotional pressure that had been accumulating.

Whatever the explanation may be for this action, Luther chose to enter the Augustinian priory at Erfurt. It was an austere place—yet it guaranteed Luther his place in heaven. Was not becoming a monk the surest way to avoid hell? Were there not stories about monks who had abandoned their monastic habit, and been turned away from the gates of paradise because they were not properly dressed for the occasion? Luther wanted to know—and know for certain—that he would escape hell and arrive safely in paradise. What other option did he have?

These ideas were widespread at the time, and Luther was in many ways faithfully reflecting the settled beliefs of the Western European Christian community—a community that embraced Church and state, and gave every indication of intellectual and cultural permanence. Were these beliefs not grounded in the Bible, and guaranteed by the Church, as the authorized guardian and interpreter of that sacred text? We are all limited and shaped by the apparent assumptions of our culture, held to be self-evidently true, which become absorbed as essential pieces of furniture of the mental worlds we inhabit. These seemingly unshakable assumptions were to prove vulnerable, not least through the growing demand—pioneered by people such as Luther himself—that individual Christians should have the right to read and interpret the Bible for themselves, rather than meekly receive and accept the official views of the Church.

Luther took up his position as professor of biblical studies at the University of Wittenberg in 1512. This was perhaps not the greatest academic accolade of the period. Wittenberg would have been near the top of a league table of insignificant European universities. It had been founded by a local prince about ten years earlier, in the vain hope of establishing a university that would outperform the neighbouring university of Leipzig. By the time Luther arrived, the fledgling university was having trouble enrolling students, not least on account of the lack of a high public profile. By the time Luther had finished with it, of course, Wittenberg would have a gratifyingly high profile—but not for reasons of which its founder would have approved.

Luther's position involved extensive lecturing on the text of biblical works. We know that he lectured on the Psalms between 1513 and 1515, and that he went on to lecture on Paul's letter to the Romans in 1515–16. By then, Luther was having serious misgivings about many of the teachings of his Church, not least those concerning how salvation was achieved, and whether the individual believer could be assured of that final salvation.

Much scholarly ink has been spilled over exactly when Luther changed his mind about how salvation is achieved and secured. There is perhaps most support for the view that Luther began to develop a new understanding of how salvation comes about as he wrestled with the Psalter, and then the letter to the Romans, in 1515. In a later recollection of his youthful anxieties, dating from the year before his death, Luther noted how he found a passage in Paul's letter to the Romans to be a stumbling block to him. Paul speaks of the "righteousness of God" being revealed in the gospel (Romans 1:17). But how could this be good news? All that this meant was that God, being righteous, would reward those who deserved it with eternal salvation, and would damn those who were sinners.

There can be no doubt that Luther saw himself as a man who was deeply sinful. He observed the rules of his order with the utmost scrupulosity. As he later recalled: "I was a good monk, and kept the rule of my order so strictly that I can say that, if ever a monk got to heaven by his monastic discipline, that was me." But Luther was plagued with self-doubt and morbid thoughts. He was utterly convinced that he was a sinner—and that sinners could expect only condemnation at the hands of a righteous God. It was a terrifying thought.

Then—possibly in 1515—Luther had a new insight. We shall never be sure exactly how and when Luther arrived at his new way of thinking. We do, however, have his own account of what happened. He meditated daily on the words of Paul, which he found so problematic, hoping against hope to have the answer to his questions. Finally, he arrived at his conclusion. The "righteousness of God" of which Paul spoke so highly was not the righteousness by which God was righteous, but a righteousness given to us by God. The gospel was indeed good news, in that God provided the righteousness needed for salvation. Individual humans were not being asked to be righteous and hence be saved—they were being offered precisely the righteousness that was demanded as a condition of entry into paradise. Luther exulted at his discovery, which changed everything.

*This immediately made me feel as though I had been born again, and as though I had entered through open gates into paradise itself. From that moment, the whole face of Scripture appeared to me in a different light.*

There is also some debate over exactly where Luther's insight took place. A somewhat cryptic remark in one of Luther's personal recollections has been the subject of much interest. Luther wrote of being granted his theological insight in a room identified by the Latin abbreviation *cl*. What could this mean? One obvious interpretation would be that the abbreviation is to be understood as *cloaca*—a semipolite Latin term for "latrine" or "privy." This possibility has evoked considerable discussion. For example, John Osborne's 1961 play *Luther* represents Luther as achieving theological insight at the same moment as he experienced relief from a long-standing bout of constipation.

This might initially seem somewhat improbable. Nevertheless, Luther himself saw a link between Satanic temptation and latrines, even if that connection might well be puzzling to most modern readers. In a recollection dating from Christmas 1531, Luther quotes a popular poem concerning the monk who is caught by the devil reading his prayers on a latrine:

> Devil:  *Monk on the latrine!*
> *You shouldn't be reading matins here!*
> Monk:  *I am purging my bowels*
> *While worshiping almighty God.*
> *You can have what goes down*
> *While God gets what goes up.*

Interesting though this possibility might be, there is another (and rather more plausible) explanation of the mysterious Latin abbreviation *cl*. The term could be an abbreviation for the heated room in the Wittenberg monastery, which was a favourite haunt of monks feeling the cold in winter.

This debate aside, the relevance of Luther's insight cannot be ignored. What Luther was proposing, based on his reading of key sections of the Bible, was that the righteousness required for salvation was not acquired through scrupulous monastic observance, or through individual moral achievement—it was the free gift of God. As Luther wrestled with this issue over the period 1514–17, it seemed to him that the entire Church of his day had lapsed into a complete misunderstanding of what Christianity was all about. The Church seemed to Luther to stress achieving, meriting, or even downright purchasing forgiveness and eternal life, when in fact this was offered by God as a gift. What humans could never achieve, or hope to acquire, was given them as a gift by a gracious God. It was clear to Luther that this was the central theme of the Bible, and that the Church had lost sight of it. And if it had lost sight of so central a theme, how could it be called a "Christian" Church?

These worrying questions, which dogged Luther's thoughts throughout this period, were brought to a focus when Johann Tetzel arrived in Wittenberg in October 1517 to sell indulgences. For many scholars, the incident that resulted triggered the massive upheaval we know as "the Reformation."

## THE INDULGENCE CONTROVERSY

POPULAR RELIGION IN the late Middle Ages involved a fear of purgatory—a place of purification, through which the medieval Church taught that souls must pass before they could enter into heaven. The belief was sanctioned by the Church, and was widely endorsed by medieval theologians. While there was some disagreement on the fine detail, the basic idea was simple. Before dead souls could enter into the presence of God, their sins needed to be "purged." This process of purification took some time. The argument over how long rivalled in detail and pointlessness the legendary scholastic debate over the number of angels that could dance on a pinhead. But the bottom line was clear: the more you sinned, the longer you spent in purgatory. And it was not a nice place to stay.

No wonder, then, that much theological effort went into finding ways of getting around purgatory altogether, or at least minimizing the amount of time to be spent there. An encrustation of popular beliefs had become attached to the idea of purgatory, throwing it wide open to abuse and exploitation. One such belief was that the living had the option of shortening the time their loved ones spent in purgatory—including the purchase of "indulgences." An indulgence can be thought of as a piece of paper, issued with the authority of the Church, that promised reduction of the time spent in purgatory. The invention of printing revolutionized the trade in indulgences. They could be printed and sold in the thousands. It was no wonder that printers such as Johannes Gutenberg and William Caxton chose to cash in on these items. The Church, of course, took its cut of the proceeds, and used them for what it regarded as good causes—such as the building of new churches.

In April 1506, Pope Julius II laid the foundation stone of what would eventually become the greatest church building in Christendom—St. Peter's, Rome. The original church, built on the site of St. Peter's tomb in the fourth century, had fallen into disrepair. Julius dreamed of building a spectacular new building, which would be one of the architectural wonders of the age. A host of artists—including Raphael and Michaelangelo—were signed up to work on the building, which was not completed until 1614. It was clear from the outset that it would be formidably expensive to construct. Massive funding was needed. But how was this money to be raised?

One fund-raising strategy that was vigorously pursued was a new indulgence sale. The marketing of these indulgences was subcontracted to professional "pardoners," who had no hesitation in talking up the benefits offered by their products. In 1517, perhaps the most famous indulgence peddler of all arrived in Wittenberg. The scene was set for a showdown. Johann Tetzel's message was fairly straightforward: sin—no problem. Just buy an indulgence, carefully tailored to your needs and your ability to pay, and forget all about it. In fact, why limit this to yourself? How about your dead relatives, now languishing in purgatory? Get them out! Was there ever a better investment? In an age when people knew how to enjoy sin, there was no shortage of clients. Tetzel even wrote a nice little jingle advertising his services:

*As soon as the coin in the coffer rings,*
*The soul from purgatory springs!*

Some Germans objected to this practice. They were irritated that German money was being used to build an Italian church. Luther's objections were much more fundamental. The sale of indulgences was offensive and unnecessary. Forgiveness did not need to be purchased, and in any case was not for sale. It was freely offered to all on account of Christ's death on the cross—and that was the end of the matter.

Furious with Tetzel and the Church, which sanctioned his high-pressure sales technique, Luther did what comes natural to academics—he penned a series of scholarly objections to the practice. These

Ninety-Five Theses against indulgences were then nailed to the door of the castle church at Wittenberg on the eve of October 31, 1517. It was a natural spot for Luther to place his objections. The castle door served as a general university noticeboard. As Luther's objections to indulgences were written in Latin, he may well have hoped to interest some passing academics in his concerns. If this was the case, we have no record whatsoever of any such interest.

But there was another reason for choosing to display his objections on this door on this date. The castle church at Wittenberg contained a vast collection of relics, which were due to be displayed the following day, on November 1—All Saints' Day. These were rumoured to offer dispensation from purgatory of several million years for those fortunate enough to see them. They were thus viewed with considerable interest. Luther's hope was that the thoroughly venial motives of the visitors to the church might lead to them reading his theses, and revising their views. If Luther was right, who needed indulgences or relics? Yet these theses were written in Latin, and seem to have had limited impact. Few of those who passed by them would have understood them.

Luther also sent a copy of the theses to Archbishop Albert of Mainz, asking him to intervene to prevent the sale of indulgences. The archbishop regarded the theses as a direct challenge to his authority, and forwarded them with a letter of complaint to Rome. However, this had less impact than might have been expected. Luther's protest came at a time when the papacy needed the support of Frederick the Wise—Frederick was one of a small group of German princes who had the right to elect the next Holy Roman Emperor—to secure the election of its favored candidate to succeed Maximilian in this position. Summoning Luther to Rome might be taken as a provocative assertion of Roman authority in Germany, which would embarrass Frederick. To provoke Frederick in this way might be to lose his support for the candidate whom the papacy wanted to succeed Maximilian. As a result, Luther was not summoned to Rome to answer the charges laid against him, but was examined locally in 1518 by the papal legate Cajetan. Luther refused to withdraw his criticisms of the practice of selling indulgences.

Yet Luther was not prepared to let the matter drop. Reform was needed. Initially, his reform programme was limited to introducing radical changes to the theological curriculum at the University of Wittenberg. There would be more lecture material on the Bible, and much less on Aristotle and the scholastic theologians. Yet even Luther's most ardent admirers would concede that these changes were not exactly going to set the Continent of Europe on fire. Hardly anyone had heard of the University of Wittenberg. What Luther was proposing amounted to little more than tinkering with theological textbooks at a university that attracted few enough students anyway. The impact of Luther's proposals on popular culture and the Church at large would be severely limited if he continued to campaign in this manner.

Realizing this, Luther made a momentous decision: he would raise his sights. No longer would he limit his campaign to the academic world; he would take it to the people, using a language the people could understand and addressing issues that concerned them.

## TRANSLATION AND POWER: THE REFORMATION AND THE VERNACULAR

IN 1520, LUTHER took the decisive steps that would lead to the fledgling Reformation breaking free from the limited confines of academia, and becoming a popular movement. He began writing works in German, rather than the more scholarly Latin. Luther would continue to use Latin when it suited him; after all, he wanted his ideas to travel throughout Europe, and Latin was the cosmopolitan language of his day. Yet Latin was a language of exclusion, which ensured that common people could not share in the political and religious discussions of the elite. Luther chose the most accessible and inclusive language of the region to reinforce his message of reform. The arcane language of the Church would be set aside in order to allow Luther to speak directly to his fellow Germans in their native language.

Luther, however, recognized that language was not the only factor in reaching a wider audience. He needed to adapt his writing style as well. He, therefore, published three popular pamphlets in 1520, arguing the case for reform with wit and vigour. The first of these—*The Appeal to the German Nobility*, published in August 1520—was perhaps the most important. In it, Luther set out—in German—the need for reform, and castigated the Church and its clergy for their unwillingness to deal with the matter. So if the Church would not reform itself, what could be done? Luther's answer was as simple as it was radical: the German laity should press for the reform that the Church sought to evade.

Luther now added a more fundamental demand. The laity should have the right to read and interpret the Bible for themselves. Why should they depend on the Pope to interpret the Bible for them? Were there not vested interests here? What was special about the Pope, anyway? And why did the Bible have to be locked away from the people, imprisoned in the fetters of a dead language that only a charmed circle could read? Why could the educated laity not be allowed to read the Bible in their own languages for themselves, and form judgments on whether what the Church taught and practised was in line with the biblical material?

Erasmus produced a new Latin translation of the New Testament in 1516, based on the original Greek texts. That was useful, in Luther's view. But most laity could not read this learned language. What *they* needed was the New Testament to be translated accurately into the language they used in their everyday lives. Giving the laity access to the Bible in their own language would let them see how they had been duped by the clergy. Having realized the need for such a translation, Luther decided the task was too important to leave to anyone else. He would do it himself, and translate the New Testament into German.

Making the Bible available in the German language thus became a priority. Luther argued that the medieval church had built walls around the Bible, in an attempt to exclude ordinary Christians from reading and interpreting it. The Bible was treated as a fortified city, with walls designed to keep the ordinary people out. Luther saw himself as a latter-day Joshua. He would cause the walls of this new Jericho to come tumbling down. The medieval Church, he argued, tried to exclude the laity from reading the Bible, by preventing it from being read in a language they could understand. He, Luther, would change all that. The Bible would be available in German! And so the massive task began, in which Luther would painstakingly translate the Bible from its original languages into the everyday language of his people.

If the Bible was available in the vernacular, all could read it and judge the teachings of the Church for themselves. As a result, power could pass from the hierarchy of the Church to its ordinary people. The Reformation was a movement of popular empowerment, in which the laity would be given the right to judge the Church, and demand its reform and renewal. Not surprisingly, this was seen as profoundly threatening by the church establishment, which promptly made every attempt it could to suppress Luther's ideas. On June 15, 1520, the papal bull *Exsurge Domine* was issued, condemning Luther's teachings, and giving him sixty days to retract his opinions or face being denounced as a heretic. This was accompanied by the public burning of Luther's books in the Piazza Navona in Rome, and demands for his books to be destroyed.

These repressive measures met with severely limited success. Germany at this time consisted of a myriad of territories, governed by princes, each of whom treasured his independence. In the case of Saxony, in which Luther was active, the local prince was Frederick the Wise. Although he was a traditional Catholic who had no wish to quarrel with his Church, Frederick saw no reason to take action against Luther, despite urgings from Rome to suppress the upstart priest who was causing such difficulty for papal authority in the region. Luther had succeeded in mobilizing popular opinion behind his stand. The papal bull was pelted with filth and torn down by mobs in many German cities and universities. Erasmus dismissed the bull with contempt. Luther's crime, he argued, consisted in two matters. "He has attacked the Pope's crown and the monks' bellies." The real threat of Luther's revolt, as Erasmus so clearly realized, was to the power and wealth of the Church.

This is precisely what many in the Church feared. Lay access to the Bible was about power as much as it was about encouraging personal spirituality. Pressure for the Bible to be placed in the hands of the ordinary person was an implicit demand for the emancipation of the laity from clerical domination. One incident in the history of this period illustrates this point—the Great Disputation at Zurich, which took place in January 1523.

The Reformation in the Swiss city of Zurich began in January 1519, after Huldrych Zwingli (1484–1531) was installed as the "people's priest" in the closing months of 1518 at the Great Minster, which still dominates the old city. Zwingli's demands for reform— especially his insistence that the Bible should be the norm of all church teachings and practices—gradually met with acceptance within the city. At some point in 1520, the Zurich city council required all its priests to preach according to Scripture, avoiding "human innovations and explanations."

A minor crisis arose in Lent 1522, when some of Zwingli's followers broke the fast traditionally observed at this time of year. During a period in which it was traditional to eat only vegetables or fish, it seems that some of Zwingli's supporters succumbed to the sensuous and forbidden pleasures of a kind of sausage. (Sadly, the precise details of the matter have been lost to us.) The city council reaffirmed their commitment to the observance of the Lenten fast a few weeks later on April 9, and fined Herr Froschauer—a prominent Zurich printer—a trivial amount for allowing it to be broken in his house.

There the matter might have rested, as the city council clearly hoped it would.

Zwingli was having none of this, however, and saw it as a convenient moment to force an issue. Seven days later, he published—on Froschauer's presses, as it happened—a treatise arguing that he was aware of no place in Scripture that required that believers should abstain from eating meat during Lent. A similar debate also developed during the same year concerning clerical marriage. Aware of growing tensions over the progress of reform in Zurich, the city council decided to hold a public debate, and invited Zwingli to present the case for the Reformation, and the Bishop of Constance to send representatives to oppose the Reformation and argue for the retention of traditional Catholic beliefs and practices.

The debate was held on January 29, 1523, at the Zurich town hall. All of Zurich's citizens were invited to hear the debate, and judge the issues for themselves. The outcome was a personal triumph for Zwingli. The Bishop of Constance's representatives insisted on speaking in Latin, a language understood by relatively few of the worthy citizens of Zurich. Zwingli spoke in Swiss German, the native language of his people. The impressions created were as memorable as they were permanent. Catholicism was perceived as alien to Zurich. The use of the vernacular was decisive in winning the debate for the Reformation. It offered power and choice to the people, bypassing the vested interests of social and ecclesiastical elites.

As events at Zurich made clear, the citizens of Europe could offer a compelling challenge to the power and authority of the Church. It was all part of the great pattern of the age—the shift of influence from traditional authorities to the rising mercantile classes. The key to the theological empowerment of the laity was to allow them to read the Bible for themselves, and act on what they found. The pressure for the translation of the Bible, and publication of the resulting translations, became irresistible.

## The Pressure for
## Translation of the Bible

By 1525, Luther was widely seen as the leading light of the growing movement for reform within the Western European church. His
ideas were being debated and discussed across Europe. Two ideas can
be seen as underlying both his critique of the Church and his proposals for reform.

1. The church had lost sight of the basic New Testament idea that
   salvation is given by God as a gift, not earned as a reward;
2. The key to the reform and renewal of the Church was to put the
   Bible in the hands of lay people.

Luther developed this second idea with special force in his 1520 writing *The Appeal to the German Nobility*. The reform of the Church and
the correction of its errors depended on increasing the biblical literacy of the laity. That vision was shared by Erasmus, and set out in his
*Handbook of the Christian Soldier*. While Erasmus preferred to use
Latin, he knew the limitations of many of his readers. If the most
humble layperson did not understand Latin, then he must be able to
read the Bible in his own language—French, German, Flemish, or
English. Erasmus himself was well aware of the power and lure of this
vision:

> *I totally disagree with those who are unwilling that the Holy
> Scriptures should be translated into everyday languages and read
> by unlearned people. Christ wishes his mysteries to be made
> known as widely as possible. I would wish even all women to read
> the gospels, and the letters of St. Paul. I wish that they were trans-
> lated into all the languages of all Christian people—that they
> might be read and known not just by the Scots and Irish, but even
> by the Turks and Saracens. I wish that the farm laborer might sing
> parts of them at his plough, that the weaver might hum them at*

*his shuttle, and that the traveller might ease his weariness by recit-ing them.*

The Old Testament was written in Hebrew (apart from a few sections in Aramaic), and the New Testament in Greek. The most widely available text of the Bible was a Latin translation known as the "Vulgate." The origins of the Vulgate lie in the translation work of some early Christian writers such as Jerome in the late fourth and early fifth centuries. For Jerome, it was important that the Bible should be available in the official language of the Roman Empire. The fall of the Roman Empire in the fifth century did not, however, lead to the end of Latin as an international language. If anything, Latin became increasingly important as time progressed, and was well placed to become the language of scholarship and diplomacy when the so-called "Dark Ages" finally lifted over Europe around the year 1000.

Jerome's Latin translation now became increasingly important as a business proposition, as demand for the Bible in Latin increased. A twelfth-century syndicate of stationers in Paris reckoned they could make a quick profit by publishing—in manuscript form, of course—a Latin version of the Bible. It is this Paris version of the Vulgate that would go on to become widely used and accepted within medieval Christianity. When a medieval Christian writer talks about "the Bible," it is quite likely that it is this specific Latin translation of the Bible that is being referred to.

Not everyone could read Latin, though; in any case, as Erasmus would make clear, there were some big problems with the accuracy of the Vulgate translation. In 1516, Erasmus declared that this tradition-al Latin translation of the Bible was awash with translation mistakes. Once Erasmus began his scholarly work in earnest, it did not take him long to expose problems with this widely used Latin translation. Convinced of the importance of studying the New Testament in its original Greek, Erasmus travelled to various libraries to take notes on the best Greek manuscripts of the original text. The outcome was devastating. The Latin text was shown to include seriously misleading errors in translation. Erasmus's solution was simple: he would point out these errors, and offer a new Latin translation of the New Testament, which would correct them. In 1516, he combined in a single volume the first printed Greek New Testament and a new Latin translation, based directly on the original Greek, which avoided the errors that had crept into the Vulgate.

Erasmus, who had always been noted for his waspish wit, seems to have rather enjoyed pointing out these errors, perhaps anticipating the pandemonium they would cause. Two of these translation mistakes are particularly interesting, as they illustrate how easily some contentious theological ideas came to be based on rather shaky biblical foundations.

The opening of the third chapter of Matthew's Gospel tells of how John the Baptist appeared in the wilderness of Judea, and proclaimed the need for repentance on the part of his audiences. The Vulgate offers the following account of the ministry of John (Matthew 3:1–2):

*In those days, John the Baptist came, preaching in the wilderness of Judaea, and saying: "Do penance, for the kingdom of the heavens is close to hand."*

Few of the late medieval readers of this text could miss the implications of what was being said, given the highly developed theory and practice of penance of the era. John seemed to be demanding that they "do penance"—that is to say, to find a priest, confess their sins, and carry out any acts of penance this priest might require of them. The Vulgate version of the passage suggested that John's words were firmly connected to the penitential system of the Church, so that this network of penitence was sanctioned by Holy Writ.

Erasmus would have none of this. The Greek original could not possibly mean "do penance." The most natural translation was "repent"—a demand for an inward change of mind and heart. What might, therefore, be taken as an endorsement of the Church's complex and somewhat cumbersome mechanics of penance was thus converted, at a stroke, into a simple demand for a personal change of heart. It was subjective change that was required of converts. The involvement of the institution of the Church was no longer necessitated—or even implied—by the passage. Repentance was now a private matter of the individual before God.

The first two chapters of Luke's Gospel narrate the events linked with the birth of Jesus Christ. One of those events is what Christians often refer to as the "annunciation"—that is, the message of the angel Gabriel, delivered to Mary, that she was to bear a child who would be the savior of the world. The Vulgate translation of the opening section of this account reads like this (Luke 1:28):

> And the angel went in, and said to her: "Hail, O one that is full
> of grace! The Lord is with you! Blessed are you among women!"

Erasmus was scathing about this translation. The words of the angel could not possibly be translated as "Hail, O one that is full of grace!" Perhaps it could be rendered as "Hail, O one that has found grace!" or "Hail, O favoured one!" The implication of the passage was that Mary had found God's favour—not that she could bestow that favour on others.

The angelic words we have just noted (in Latin: *ave gratia plena!*) were often interpreted in the Middle Ages as meaning that Mary was like a reservoir, full of God's grace. She could, therefore, be a source of God's grace to those who needed it, and who could access this grace through prayer to her. Whatever Erasmus may have thought of this belief—which lay behind much Marian theology of the Middle Ages and beyond—he had no time for the translation that ultimately lay behind it. It seemed to him to be a clear example of a theological opinion that was firmly grounded in an untenable Latin translation.

The importance of these points for existing English versions of the Bible must be noted. The famous Wycliffite versions of the Gospels, for example, were not translations from the original Greek, but from the Latin of the Vulgate. The Wycliffite versions thus reproduced the translation mistakes of the Vulgate, more or less faithfully, in English. While the resulting text had the undoubted advantage of being an English translation, it nevertheless had the severe disadvantage of being an *inaccurate* English translation.

So what other treasured theological opinions of the Middle Ages might be shown to rest on untenable biblical translations? Erasmus's work was seen as opening a Pandora's box, scattering doubt and uncertainty within the Church. What other beliefs might need to be revised? And an additional point emerged from the two examples we have noted. Both can be argued to privilege certain parts of the Christian community. The Matthew text suggests that the clergy have superiority over the laity; after all, penance was provided by clergy to laity. The Luke text implies the superiority of Mary over other Christians, in that she is replete with the grace that others are so desperately seeking.

Might there not be other errors, which would lead to a radical revision of the existing order of things? Might not the process of more accurate translation show that the clergy had kept the laity in submission to them without good reason? This was certainly an idea that Martin Luther explored in *The Babylonian Captivity of the Church* (1520), which argued that the institution of the Church, and especially its clergy, had oppressed the laity. It was time, Luther declared, for the tables to be turned. There was one certain remedy by which this captivity of the laity could be ended—biblical translation.

These developments may have taken place on the Continent of Europe, far away from the shores of England, but they were essential to the long process that led to the production of the King James Bible. The pressures that led Luther to translate the Bible into German were being felt throughout Europe. It would only be a matter of time before the tidal waves of the Reformation crashed against the shores of England. The seeds of the King James Bible were sown in the 1520s, as the pressure for a Bible in the English language gradually became irresistible.

PORTRAIT OF HENRY VIII BY HANS HOLBEIN
THE YOUNGER (1497/8-1543)

# Henry VIII
## and the English Reformation

IF ANY EVENT may be said to have prepared the ground for the translation of the Bible into English, it was the Reformation in England, which began under Henry VIII. Henry came to the English throne in 1509, and set himself the agenda of making the realm of England a significant European power. The origins of the English Reformation are probably best understood in terms of Henry VIII's concern to ensure a smooth transition of power after his death through producing a son as heir to the English throne. His marriage to the Spanish Catherine of Aragon had produced a daughter, the future queen, Mary Tudor. The marriage had not only failed to produce the requisite son and heir, it had also reflected the political realities of an earlier generation, which saw an alliance between England and Spain as essential to a sound foreign policy. The weakness of this assumption had become clear by 1525, when Charles V declined to marry Henry's daughter by Catherine. Henry, therefore, began the process by which he could divorce Catherine.

Under normal circumstances, this procedure would not have been expected to encounter any formidable obstacles. An appeal to the Pope to annul the marriage would usually have secured the desired result without difficulty. Popes were generally open to granting favours to kings; after all, they might need a return favour in due course. However, the situation regarding Henry VIII was not normal. At this time, the city of Rome was under virtual siege by the army of the emperor Charles V, and the Pope (Clement VII) was feeling somewhat threatened as a result. Catherine of Aragon was the aunt of Charles V. Clement would hardly wish to offend Charles V at such a sensitive moment by allowing Henry to divorce one of Charles's relatives. As a result, the request for a divorce failed. As if to add insult to injury, Clement VII informed Henry that he would be excommunicated if he married again.

Henry VIII was less than happy about this decision. He wanted a male heir badly, and felt that the Pope's intransigence was indefensible. Henry's response was to begin a programme of persuasion, at both national and international levels, designed to assert both the independence of England as a separate province of the Church, and the autonomy of the English king. Henry wanted to break free from the power of the Pope by being able to take control of the affairs of the English Church. On November 3, 1529, Henry convened a Parliament with the intention of reducing the power of both Church and clergy. At this stage, it may be noted, Parliament lacked the independence that would become such a significant feature of English politics in the early seventeenth century under James I.

The English clergy initially refused to concede these points, fearing an erosion of their influence and status. This prompted Henry to bring in more severe measures to help the English clergy realize the errors of their ways. The most important of these took place over the period 1530–31, during which Henry argued that the English clergy, by virtue of their support for Rome, were guilty of praemunire (a technical offence that can be thought of as a form of treason, in that it involves allegiance to a foreign power—namely, the papacy). Faced with this threat—which, incidentally, could incur the death penalty— the clergy reluctantly agreed to at least some of Henry's demands for recognition of his ecclesiastical authority. Henry knew perfectly well that the threat of a traitor's death would help his clergy cope with their theological difficulties over his demands.

Henry was presented with an opportunity for the further advancement of his aims in August 1532, when the Archbishop of Canterbury, William Warham, conveniently died. Henry replaced Warham with Thomas Cranmer, who had earlier indicated his strong support for Henry's divorce proceedings. Cranmer was finally consecrated archbishop (possibly against his will) on March 30, 1533. Meanwhile, Henry had begun an affair with Anne Boleyn, and Anne became pregnant in December 1532. The pregnancy raised all kinds of legal niceties. Henry's marriage to Catherine of Aragon was annulled by an English court in May 1533, allowing Anne to be crowned queen on 1 June. Her daughter, Elizabeth Tudor—the future Queen Elizabeth I—was born on September 7.

Henry's divorce of Catherine immediately led to the threat of excommunication. Henry now determined to follow through the course of action on which he had embarked, by which his supreme political and religious authority within England would be recognized. A series of acts were imposed in 1534. Among them, the Succession Act declared that the crown would pass to Henry's children. The Supremacy Act declared that Henry was to be recognized as the "supreme head" of the English church. The Treasons Act made denial of Henry's supremacy an act of treason, punishable by death. This final act led to the execution of two prominent Catholic churchmen, Thomas More and John Fisher, both of whom refused to recognize Henry as supreme head of the English church—a title they believed belonged only to the Pope.

Henry now found himself under threat of invasion from neighbouring Catholic states. The mandate of restoring papal authority would have been a more than adequate pretext for either France or Spain to launch a crusade against England. Henry was thus obliged to undertake a series of defensive measures to ensure the nation's safety. These measures reached their climax in 1536, when Henry ordered many English monasteries to be closed, and their assets to be seized by the crown. To some extent, this was designed to eliminate potential centres of resistance to his reform measures; the main motivation for this move, however, seems to have been financial. Henry benefited considerably from the income resulting from the sale of monastic lands and buildings.

The dissolution of the monasteries provided Henry with funds for his military preparations. Negotiations with German Lutherans were begun with the object of entering into military alliances. At this point, Lutheran ideas began to be adopted in some official English formularies of faith, such as the "Ten Articles" of 1536. This short statement of faith, which never had much influence in England or elsewhere, was an ingenious way of suggesting that Henry was sympathetic to Lutheran ideas, when in fact all that Henry wanted was Lutheran political and military support at a critical juncture in his dealings with Rome.

It soon became obvious this theological enthusiasm for Lutheranism was little more than a temporary political manoeuvre, inspired by Henry's chief adviser, Thomas Cromwell. Unwisely, Cromwell tried to force Henry into a closer alliance with Lutheranism by persuading him to marry Anne of Cleves. Cromwell arranged for Hans Holbein to paint an excessively flattering portrait of this Lutheran princess, whom Henry never met prior to the marriage. On seeing her in the flesh, his enthusiasm for the alliance paled into insignificance. He divorced Anne as soon as it was convenient to do so, and had Cromwell executed.

When it became clear that there was serious opposition within England to his reform measures, Henry backtracked. The 1543 "King's Book" shows every evidence of Henry's desire to avoid giving offence to Catholics. By the time of Henry's death in January 1547, the religious situation in England was somewhat ambivalent. Although Henry had made some concessions to Lutheranism, his own preference appears to have remained for at least some traditional Catholic beliefs and practices. For example, his will made provision for prayers to be said for his soul—despite the fact that Henry had, less than two years earlier, tried to close down the chantries, which existed for precisely this purpose!

From this brief account of the origins of the English Reformation under Henry VIII, it will be clear that there are reasons for supposing that Henry's aims were of critical importance for the genesis of that Reformation. Henry's agenda was political, and was dominated by the desire to safeguard the succession. Through a series of developments, this required a schism with Rome, and an increasingly tolerant attitude toward Lutheranism, both in Germany and England. Yet Henry's tolerance for Lutheranism, which peaked around 1536, does not seem to have been grounded primarily on religious considerations.

This does not mean that Lutheran ideas were without influence in England. Many significant English churchmen were sympathetic to the new ideas, and made it a matter of principle to secure a favourable hearing for them in both Church and society at large. In fact, there are reasons for arguing that at least some degree of popular support for Lutheran ideas led Henry to pursue his policies in certain manners, rather than others. The point being made is that the *origins* of Henry's reform policies were not themselves religious in nature.

In the end, the English Reformation has to be recognized as an act of state. The comparison with the situation in Germany is highly instructive. Luther's Reformation was conducted on the basis of a theological foundation and platform. The fundamental impetus was religious (in that it addressed the life of the Church directly) and theological (in that the proposals for reform rested on a set of theological presuppositions). In England, the Reformation was primarily political and pragmatic. The Reformation of the Church was, in effect, the price paid by Henry (rather against his instincts) in order to secure and safeguard his personal authority within England. It was, however, impossible to isolate issues of religion and politics in the sixteenth century, and Henry's actions were heavily charged with religious implications. Henry's decision to place himself at the head of the English national church, displacing the Pope in this respect, resonated with part of the Reformation agenda—the establishment of national reformed churches, independent of the influence of Rome. And if Henry was sympathetic to this aspect of the Reformation agenda, many reasoned, would he not be equally receptive to others—such as the translation of the Bible into English?

Henry VIII does not appear to have seen things this way. Henry's personal religious views, in so far as these can be established with any degree of certainty, show him to have remained cautious, conservative, and Catholic in his general religious outlook. Nevertheless, the new directions taken by Henry in his relationship with Rome had immense implications. Under pressure from those sympathetic to the Reformation during the 1530s—such as Thomas Cromwell and Thomas Cranmer—Henry gradually found himself moving toward accepting additional aspects of the Reformation agenda. One of those was the increased use of English in matters of religion. Just as Henry had displaced the Pope as the head of the English church, so English came to displace Latin as the language of that church.

In the event, Henry's hand was forced in the matter of Bible translations. Suddenly, without advance warning, a well-produced printed English translation of the New Testament began to circulate in England in early 1526. It caused a crisis. The church authorities immediately set in place measures to block the importation of the book, and to destroy every copy that arrived in England. They knew that, if they could not stop this translation, they would have only one option at their disposal. They would have to produce one themselves, and ensure that it outperformed and outsold its rival.

# 4

## THE FIRST PRINTED
## ENGLISH BIBLES

Having realized the importance of translating the Bible into German, Martin Luther wasted no time in getting on with this task. In September 1522, Luther published his German translation of the New Testament. The work, which represented a translation directly from the original Greek into German, was elegantly produced at the press of Hans Luft in Wittenberg. It was a landmark in European religious history, and was of considerable importance in consolidating the progress of the Reformation in Germany. In the summer of 1523, the same press produced Luther's German translation of the Pentateuch—the first five books of the Old Testament.

There were many who cast admiring glances in its direction, and wondered if it might be possible to equal Luther's achievement in their own native languages. One such admirer was William Tyndale (1494–1536), now widely acknowledged as the most formative influence on the text of the King James Bible.

## THE PIONEER: WILLIAM TYNDALE

WILLIAM TYNDALE WAS born in Gloucestershire, and studied at Magdalen College School in Oxford, from which he went on to attend Magdalen Hall (now Hertford College, Oxford). That Tyndale studied at Oxford, at least, is reasonably clear; what happened next is a little obscure. Traditional accounts represent Tyndale as migrating to Oxford's foremost intellectual rival in England, the University of Cambridge, at which he became a member of the "White Horse" group. Some of the more romantic accounts of this period invite us to imagine Tyndale gathered together with many of the great Cambridge reformers of this era, swapping jokes and biblical texts while quaffing their pewter mugs of ale and plotting the Lutheranization of England.

As is the way with most matters, the real is rather less pleasing than the imagined. We have no documentary evidence to suggest that Tyndale ever attended Cambridge, other than a slightly garbled recollection in John Foxe's *Book of Martyrs*, dating from thirty years later. Far less is known about the "White Horse" group than is generally realized; we are again largely dependent upon some rather nostalgic recollections of John Foxe for our accounts of this group.

Even if it is assumed that Tyndale did indeed leave Oxford for Cambridge, what reasons might have prompted this move? The first, and most obvious, is that by the early 1520s, Cambridge was known to be far more sympathetic to the ideas of the Reformation than Oxford. Luther's books, which had to be imported from continental Europe through the Flemish port of Antwerp, were much more accessible in Cambridge than Oxford. Many of the leading lights of the English Reformation had links with Cambridge around this time— most notably, Thomas Cranmer. It is entirely possible that the reform-minded Tyndale sensed that he might benefit from this more sympathetic atmosphere.

Yet Tyndale's primary concern was with the translation of Scripture—and such translation required knowledge of the three great languages of antiquity—Greek, Hebrew, and Latin. As we have seen, writers such as Erasmus were actively campaigning for the direct engagement with the text of the Bible *in its original languages* as the foundation of Christian theology. Erasmus's opponents had little time for such matters; theology, they held, rested on philosophical analysis. While there is no historical evidence to suggest that they debated over the number of angels that could dance on a pinhead, other important and sophisticated theological questions are known to have engaged their attention. Could God reverse time, and make a prostitute into a virgin? Or could Christ have become incarnate as a donkey, or perhaps a cucumber, rather than a man? While others saw such heady discussions as an intellectual feast, Tyndale regarded them as utterly pointless.

Tyndale himself was more than a little irritated by his experience of theology at Oxford, not least because it seemed to give the study of Aristotle priority over mastering the Bible. In an autobiographical fragment, Tyndale recalled how the Oxford authorities "ordained that no man shall look in the Scripture until he be nooselled ["spoon-fed" or perhaps "nourished"] in heathen learning eight or nine years and armed with false principles with which he is clean shut out of the understanding of Scripture." For him, theology was worthy of its name only when it took its lead directly from the Bible.

Both Oxford and Cambridge were well placed to encourage and sustain the study of Hebrew and Greek. Richard Croke, who served as professor of Greek at Leipzig, had settled in Cambridge in 1518. Cardinal Wolsey established a chair of Greek at Oxford a year later. The tradition of the classical languages continued into the following century. As we shall see presently, both Oxford and Cambridge were able to supply King James I with an ample supply of Greek and Hebrew scholars at the beginning of the next century. Luther taught himself Hebrew using Johannes Reuchlin's 1506 primer *De rudimentis hebraicis* ("On the Basics of Hebrew"); might not Tyndale have done the same? Yet acquiring a knowledge of the biblical languages was perhaps Tyndale's least pressing difficulty at Oxford; the purpose for which he acquired it appears to have been widely ridiculed.

Oxford was not interested in translating the Bible—nor, indeed, any other work—into English. It was the accepted wisdom of the age that Latin—the language of the culture of academia—was the only language worth knowing. Oxford dons might use English in speaking to college servants; otherwise, Latin was the language of choice. This academic commitment to the Latin language proved to be a mixed blessing for the progress of the Reformation in England. It meant that Luther's Latin works could be read at Oxford or Cambridge without difficulty, thus allowing his ideas to be discussed at both universities (though they were received more readily at Cambridge).

Yet part of Luther's agenda was relentlessly populist. Luther wrote works of theology and translated the Bible into his native German, so that *Herr Omnes*—Luther's term equivalent to the English "everyman"—might be empowered and illuminated. Most academics tended to despise this kind of populism, seeing it as academically demeaning. The sophistication of a book was, after all, inversely proportional to the ease with which it could be read. Tyndale's heart lay with Luther's agenda, rather than with the rather stuffy scholarly attitudes he encountered in English academia. So why not go to Germany, and learn the art of biblical translation from Luther himself?

The suggestion that Tyndale went to Wittenberg certainly makes sense. Tyndale would have had access to good libraries, and to scholars of repute, especially in the area of Hebrew. In addition, he would have had the opportunity to learn German, and hence mimic the popular style that Luther used in his vernacular writings. By 1523, Luther had translated both the New Testament and the Pentateuch into German. It is important to note that Tyndale managed to translate *exactly* the same works into English shortly afterward. More than one scholar has hinted that Tyndale's English style and vocabulary may have been influenced by Luther's German.

So did Tyndale visit Wittenberg? Did he sit at Luther's feet? We shall never know for certain. There is no mention of William Tyndale in the registers of the University of Wittenberg, although these are as comprehensive as one might wish. For example, there is mention in the 1525 registers of "Guillelmus Roy ex Londino," a clear reference to "William Roye of London"—Roye being a noted advocate of reform in England at this time. The 1524 registers make reference to one "Guillelmus Daltici." "Guillelmus" is the Latin form of "William"; "Daltici" might *conceivably* be a pseudonym of Tyndale, achieved by playing around with the order of letters in his name, and replacing "n" with "c." But it is not exactly a *neat* explanation.

Yet Tyndale did not need to meet Luther, converse with him, or even study under him to benefit from his German translation of the New Testament. The still-new technology of printing made Luther's translation available throughout Europe, and Tyndale would have been free to benefit from Luther's translation skills wherever he chose.

Tyndale's initial intention had been to translate the New Testament into English while staying in London. He, therefore, sought a patron who might offer him some kind of employment or financial support while he undertook the work. But who could be his patron? He found an answer in one of Erasmus's books, which warmly praised Cuthbert Tunstall, Bishop of London. Tyndale therefore approached Tunstall with a view to obtaining employment in his household.

Sadly, Erasmus seems to have got into the habit of lavishing praise on anyone who might help him in any way, and Tyndale appears to have fallen victim to one of the rhetorical conventions of the age. Tunstall was certainly a religious moderate, by the standards of the age, in that he just burned books, rather than people. He was also sympathetic to the humanist agenda, as can be seen from the generous comments of Thomas More in the opening pages of his *Utopia*.

But Tunstall was a pragmatist, alert to the hidden agendas of monarchs and the subtleties of the winds of change. Tyndale's proposal to translate the New Testament into English was too radical for his liking. He had enough political minefields to negotiate without this complication. Tyndale was disappointed with his rejection, yet realistic enough to realize that he could have no real hopes for such a translation in the England of the 1520s. The translation would have to be undertaken and published outside England.

The evidence available suggests that Tyndale undertook his translation from about May 1524–July 1525. In August of that year, Tyndale settled in the German city of Cologne, with his new assistant William Roye. The translation of the New Testament into English was complete; the task was now to ensure its printing and distribution. They chose to produce the work in the printing house of Peter Quentell. However, Quentell's presses were also producing the works of Johannes Cochlaeus, a noted opponent of Luther, who happened to learn of Tyndale's project. It seems that some of Quentell's printers became drunk in a public tavern one evening, and let slip that three thousand Lutheran New Testaments were being produced in English, right under the noses of the Catholic authorities. Word of this soon reached Cochlaeus, who was no fool, and could see his star rising in the German Catholic firmament if he were to expose and block this project. He arranged for a raid on Quentell's presses.

Tyndale and Roye, however, managed to escape and salvage at least some of their printing, along with the text of the translation. As far as can be ascertained, they had managed to print only ten sheets of paper—making up eighty quarto pages—which took them roughly three quarters of the way through Matthew's Gospel, the first book of the New Testament. Undeterred, they moved their printing operation farther up the Rhine to the city of Worms, and began the tedious process all over again using the presses of Peter Schoeffer. This time, they avoided detection. The work was completed by the end of February 1526.

It had long been assumed that the Cologne quarto sheets of 1525 had been lost. However in 1834, eight of these original sheets were discovered; they had been bound into another work, having been unrecognized for what they really were. These sheets are fascinating, as they help us gauge the influence of Luther upon Tyndale's work. Three factors are of special interest:

1. The pages include a "prologue," which is dependent at points upon Luther's own prologue to his 1522 German New

Testament. This was not included in the 1526 printing of Tyndale's work, although Tyndale subsequently revised and reprinted it as a separate work entitled *A Pathway into the Scripture.*

2. The list of contents of the New Testament follows a convention that existed within Lutheran circles at this stage, which regarded four New Testament works—Hebrews, James, Jude, and Revelation—as being of dubious authenticity. These were placed at the end of the contents, and not numbered. Tyndale appears to have been obliged to follow this convention by Peter Quentell himself. The 1526 printing abandoned this convention.

3. The 1525 printing included marginal notes. The pages that have survived included ninety such notes, suggesting that Tyndale envisaged a high level of comment on the text throughout the New Testament. The general style and tone of these notes is Lutheran. Some are direct cribs of Luther's own notes, provided in various editions of his German New Testament; some, however, are Tyndale's own creation. There are no such notes in the 1526 edition.

## Tyndale's New Testament: Precursor of the King James Bible

THE EDITION OF the English New Testament published at Worms in 1526 must be regarded as a landmark in the history of the English Bible. It is, of course, arguable that the Cologne text—with its explanatory notes—might have had still greater influence. Yet it was the edition of 1526 that was smuggled into England and created irreversible pressure for an English Bible. The book consisted of some seven hundred pages, using the exceptionally clear Schwabacher typeface. While the print run remains unclear, the printing is thought to have been in the region of three thousand.

No copy of the work with its original title page has survived. Only two copies of this work are known today; the first of which lacks a

THE GOSPEL OF ST. LUKE FROM
THE TYNDALE NEW TESTAMENT

title page, and the second missing its first seventy pages. Yet it is
known for certain that the name of William Tyndale was not mentioned on the title page, or at any point throughout the work. Indeed,
there are good grounds for suggesting that no information concerning
the publisher or place of publication was provided at any point. The
work advertised itself simply as a "New Testament," without making
any mention of its translator. Save to those in the know, the origins of
the work lay shrouded in mystery.

The unnamed translator—who, of course, we know to be
Tyndale—made it clear to his readers that he wished to render the
New Testament in "proper English." This is a highly significant phrase,
which is open to several interpretations. For example, Tyndale might
be taken to imply that his concern is to use a form of English that was

"proper" to this task—a judgment involving literary and aesthetic considerations, and suggesting that Tyndale wished his translation to be seen specifically as a work of literature. Although this sense of the word might seem reasonable to a modern reader, Tyndale himself understood it to mean "the right English words." In other words, his criteria were accuracy and clarity. This is made perfectly clear in his own paraphrase of his intentions, in which he affirms his willingness to alter any parts of the translation in which he has "not attained the very sense of the tongue, or meaning of the Scripture, or has not given the right English word." We shall see this theme recurring in our discussion of the King James Bible itself, in which accuracy and clarity were regarded as supreme virtues by the translators.

Certain aspects of Tyndale's translation were instantly perceived as a threat by more conservative English Catholics. Tyndale insisted that the Greek word *presbyteros*, used in Paul's letters to refer to an office within the Christian Church and traditionally translated as "priest," should be rendered instead as "senior." (In 1534, he altered this to "elder.") The English word "priest" should, he argued, be reserved solely for translating the Greek term *hiereus*, used in the New Testament exclusively to refer to Jewish or pagan priests. The Greek term *ekklesia*, traditionally translated as "church," was now translated as "congregation." As a result, many New Testament references that could have been taken as endorsing the institution of the Church were now to be understood as referring to local congregations of believers.

Tyndale's literary achievement is best appreciated by considering two very different types of passages—narratives and arguments. The first passage is one of the parables told by Jesus, which is set in a narrative context. The speaker is Jesus himself.

*Then he said also to him that bade him to dinner: when thou makest a dinner or a supper: call not thy friends, not thy brethren, neither thy kinsmen nor yet rich neighbours: lest they bid thee again, and make thee recompense. But when thou makest a feast, call the poor, the maimed, the lame and the blind, and thou shalt be happy, for they cannot recompense thee. But thou shalt be recompensed at the resurrection of just men.*

*When one of them that sat at meat also heard that, he said unto him: happy is he that eateth bread in the kingdom of God. Then said he to him. A certain man ordered a great supper, and bade many, and sent his servant at supper time, to say to them that were bidden, come: for all things are ready. And they all at once began to make excuse. The first said unto him: I have bought a farm, and I must needs go and see it, I pray thee have me excused. And another said: I have bought five yoke of oxen, and I must go to prove them, I pray have thee me excused. The third said: I have married a wife, and therefore I cannot come. The servant went again, and brought his master word thereof.*

*Then was the good man of the house displeased, and said to his servant: Go out quickly into the streets and quarters of the city, and bring in hither the poor and the maimed and the halt and the blind. And the servant said: lord, it is done as thou commandest, and yet there is room. And the lord said to the servant: Go out into the high ways and hedges, and compel them to come in, that my house may be filled. For I say unto you, that none of these men which were bidden, shall taste of my supper (Luke 14:12–24).*

Even today, the narrative is easily understood. Tyndale uses some words that are strange to modern readers—for example, the archaic "halt" for "lame" or "crippled." But the simple style and vocabulary of the translation can be appreciated without serious difficulty.

A more argumentative passage, taken from Paul's letter to the Romans, shows how Tyndale deals with more complex forms of prose:

*What shall we say then? Is the law sin? God forbid: but I knew not what sin meant but by the law. For I had not known what lust* had meant, except the law had said, thou shalt not lust. But sin took occasion by means of the commandment, and wrought in me all manner of concupiscence. For verily without the law, sin was dead. I once lived without law. But when the commandment came, sin revived, and I was dead. And the very same commandment which was ordained unto life, was found to be to me an occasion of death (Romans 7:7–10).

Paul's argument in this passage makes considerable demands of his readers, and Tyndale's translation conveys the thrust of the argument with a clarity that can still be appreciated today. The translators of the King James Bible appreciated Tyndale's clarity, as can be seen by comparing this later translation with Tyndale's: changes have been made— yet the register of the original remains clearly discernible.

What shall we say then? Is the law sin? God forbid. Nay, I had not known sin, but by the law: for I had not known lust, except the law had said, Thou shalt not covet. But sin, taking occasion by the commandment, wrought in me all manner of concupiscence. For without the law sin was dead. For I was alive without the law once: but when the commandment came, sin revived, and I died. And the commandment, which was ordained to life, I found to be unto death.

Many would argue that Tyndale's translation is to be preferred here, not least because it is more consistent in its translation of the Greek (the King James Bible changed one "lust" into a "covet" with-out good reason), and easier to understand (Tyndale's "I once lived without law" is much more intelligible than the somewhat cryptic "I was alive without the law once").

Some comments are necessary here. First, note the phrase "God forbid!" used here by Tyndale to translate the Greek phrase *me genoito*. A literal translation of this Greek might be "let it not be so!" or "may it not be!" (Incidentally, I still recall with amusement an Oxford undergraduate's adventurous translation of these words: "not bloody likely!"). There is no explicit or implied reference to "God" whatsoever, and Tyndale's translation of this regular Pauline phrase—which was retained by the King James Bible—has perhaps confused some readers.

Second, Tyndale generally avoids Latinate terms, preferring to "English" them. On occasions, this means using words that had only recently been introduced, or coining new words altogether. Yet in this passage, he chooses to use the Latin word "concupiscence," already used in the Vulgate translation of the text, despite the fact that he had already used the English word "lust." The assumption here must be that Tyndale believed that his readers would be familiar with this term, and hence would not encounter difficulty in following the argument.

The impact of Tyndale's translation was immense. There is ample evidence to suggest that many used Tyndale's New Testament to learn to read, as well as to learn about the Christian faith. In what appears to be a recollection of the late 1520s, William Maldon related how, though initially illiterate, he determined to learn to read so that he might have access to Tyndale's New Testament for himself—despite the opposition of his father, who preferred his religion in Latin.

*Divers poor men in the town of Chelmsford in the County of Essex, where my father dwelt, and I born and with him grew up, the said poor men bought the New Testament of Jesus Christ and on Sundays did sit reading in lower end of church, and many would flock about them to hear their reading. Then came I among the said readers to hear them reading of that glad and sweet tidings of the gospel, then my father, seeing this that I listened unto them every Sunday, then came he and sought me among them, and brought me away from the hearing of them, and would have me to say the Latin matins with him, which grieved me very much, and thus did fetch me away divers times, then I see I could*

*not be in rest, then thought I, I will learn to read English, and then*
*I will have the New Testament and read thereon myself.*

Tyndale's translation would prove to be of foundational importance to the shaping of later English translations. Many of the words
and phrases used by Tyndale found their way into the English language. Tyndale was a master of the pithy phrase, near to conversational English, but distinct enough to be used like a proverb. In his
Bible translations, Tyndale coined such phrases as: "the powers that
be" (Romans 13); "my brother's keeper" (Genesis 4); "the salt of the
earth" (Matthew 5); and "a law unto themselves" (Romans 2). These
phrases continue to be used, even in modern English, precisely
because they are so well shaped in terms of their alliteration, rhyme,
and word repetitions.

Tyndale also introduced or revived many words that are still in
use. He constructed the term "Jehovah" from the Hebrew construction known as the "tetragrammaton" in the Old Testament. He invented the English word "Passover" to refer to the Jewish festival
known in Hebrew as *Pesah*. Other neologisms developed by Tyndale
to translate biblical words that had, up to that point, no real English
equivalent include "scapegoat" and "atonement." It should be noted
that this latter word was invented by Tyndale to convey the idea of
"reconciliation." It can be seen immediately that biblical translation
thus provided a major stimulus to the development of the English
language, not least by creating new English words to accommodate
biblical ideas.

Once Tyndale's translation of the New Testament was widely
available, there was no turning back. Tyndale's translation would have
to be authorized—or it would have to be bettered. There seemed to
be no alternative. Reluctant to adopt the former course, Henry's
advisers chose the latter. They would produce their own Bible, and
require it to be used in the public worship of the churches.

A central feature of the Reformation, long resisted, had been forced upon the English church and state. Tyndale can thus be said to have achieved two remarkable successes: first, by producing an excellent English New Testament; and second, by forcing the hand of the English church and state to undertake something that would have been unthinkable only a few years earlier—an officially sanctioned English Bible.

Yet this decision lay some distance in the future. The immediate reaction of the English establishment was not to authorize Tyndale's translation, still less to produce one superior to it. Throughout 1526, a relentless campaign began to suppress the book. The campaign is of considerable interest to our story, as it indicates how many within the English church felt threatened by the new translation. To understand the importance of the fact that the King James Bible was authorized by the English state and church, we must consider what happened to Tyndale's decidedly unauthorized version of the New Testament.

## THE ATTEMPT TO SUPPRESS TYNDALE'S TRANSLATION

TYNDALE'S NEW TESTAMENT was available in London by the end of February 1526. Copies were openly being sold at a number of outlets, including "Master Garrett, Curate of All Hallows in Honey Lane, London." England had few enough printers in the 1520s; none of them would have dared produce such a work in the face of the formidable "Constitutions of Oxford," which explicitly prohibited the production of English Bibles, in whole or in part. The two most important English printers during the 1520s were Richard Pynson and Wynkyn de Worde, responsible for something like 70 per cent of the English book market. They could not compete, however, with the quality of the products of foreign presses in Antwerp, Paris, and Venice. Some 17 per cent of books sold around this time in England were imported from the Continent.

Antwerp was of special importance, not least on account of its geographical proximity to England. At least sixty presses were operational in this Flemish port city during the first decades of the sixteenth century. Some of these appear to have specialized in works destined for the English market, including Jan van Doesborch, Christoffel van Ruremund, and Matthaeus Crom. During the early 1520s, the imported works that sold best included liturgical service books, such as the Latin text of the Sarum rite, and educational textbooks, such as Cardinal Wolsey's *Rudimenta Grammatices* ("Basics of Grammar"), which continued to sell well after its author's fall from power and his death.

Although the English state protected many indigenous industries from foreign competition during the later Middle Ages by the simple means of prohibiting the import of many goods, the import of foreign printed works was tolerated to the point of encouragement. It seems that there was an assumption that English printers were simply not in a position to supply enough works to meet the demands of the market. During this remarkable period of free trade in books, perhaps lasting from 1490–1520, many Flemish printers set up offices in England to ensure a ready supply of their works, many of which were printed in English.

The situation changed radically during the 1520s, for two reasons. First, English printers began to lobby for protection against foreign competition. Antwerp printers had become adept at producing books in English, and were posing a real threat to the livelihood of the English printing industry. The second, however, was of greater importance. Whereas border controls effectively prevented Protestant reformers such as Martin Luther or Huldrych Zwingli from gaining entry to England, it proved impossible to staunch the flow of their published works. The desire to deny the English public ready access to the ideas of the Reformation led to lists of prohibited authors and works being drawn up by an increasingly anxious government. At some point between July 1520 and March 1521, Cardinal Wolsey specifically prohibited the importation or reading of any of Luther's works.

Most official anger was directed against Luther's books. Although there had been public condemnation of Luther's writing earlier in England, hostility toward his writings intensified early in 1526. John Fisher, Bishop of Rochester, preached a public sermon against Luther, and copies of Luther's works—including the German New Testament—were publicly burned. The fact that there was a market for Luther's German language works in a country notoriously poor at foreign languages may seem surprising, but there was a small German mercantile community in London at this time, based at the "Steelyard," which kept itself up to date with the latest religious developments in Germany. It seems that some of Luther's works were initially imported for the personal use of this community. Thomas More organized a raid on the Steelyard in 1526, and it is likely that many of the Lutheran works publicly burned on this occasion had their origins in this community.

More himself was intensely hostile toward Luther. His anti-Luther writings betray a hostility that continues to shock and embarrass those who regard him as a gentle man of letters, given to erudition and elegance. Rabelais himself would have been impressed by the scatological tone of More's comments. Luther, More writes, is "a mad friarlet and privy-minded rascal with his ragings and ravings, with his filth and dung, shitting and beshitted," preoccupied with "privies, filth and dung." More also offers the following rather tasteless pun on the distinction between "prior premise" and "posterior argument" to his readers:

> *Since [Luther] has written that he already has a prior right to bespatter and besmirch the royal crown with shit, we will not have the posterior right to proclaim the beshitted tongue of this practicioner of posterioristics most fit to lick with his anterior the very posterior of a pissing she-mule until he shall have learned more correctly to infer posterior conclusions from prior premises.*

While many of the early critics of Luther used crude language and images in their polemic against him, More's criticisms possess a unique degree of crudity and verbal violence that would later pass into More's critiques of Tyndale himself, as a sycophantic follower of the German heretic. Tyndale's New Testament was treated as a partisan Lutheran work, rather than as a serious and responsible attempt to translate part of the Bible into the English language.

Yet a far more dangerous threat to the English church emerged almost immediately. It was one thing for expatriate German merchants to read Luther's translation of the New Testament in their own language. After all, such a work was not going to galvanize the linguistically challenged English public. It soon became clear, however, that a well-produced octavo English New Testament was in circulation at the same time. At first, nobody had the slightest idea where it had come from. Its title page offered no clues. It then became evident that the work was being imported from Antwerp, the source of many high-quality English-language publications.

Someone pressed the panic button. Cuthbert Tunstall, Bishop of London, worked out—it is still not known how—that the translation was the work of Tyndale and Roye. On October 24, 1526, he issued an injunction against the work. The next day, he summoned London's booksellers—including Francis Byrckman, Peter Kaetz, and Henry Pepwell, all of whom were based in St. Paul's Churchyard—and warned them against stocking or selling the work; two days later, he preached a sermon against the translation, claiming that he had identified two thousand translation errors. Having gathered as many copies of the work as he could find within his diocese, Tunstall arranged yet another public burning of books.

Meanwhile, Wolsey had been busy. After briefing the bishops on the threat posed by the new translation, a decree was promulgated demanding that all "untrue translations" should be burned. On November 21, 1526, Wolsey instructed the English ambassador to the Lowlands to act against any printers or booksellers who were in any way associated with the work. Yet the trade proved impossible to regulate. Books could be—and were—smuggled into England with relative ease. A pirate sextodecimo edition of Tyndale's translation was published at Antwerp by Christoph van Endhoven, further adding to the confusion of the English authorities, and the ease with which the translation circulated.

There are accounts in personal diaries and court records of individuals buying the work, allowing us a good idea of its appeal and cost. John Pykas, a baker from Colchester, bought a copy for four shillings in 1526; Robert Necton sold five to Sir William Furboshore for "seven or eight groats" each, and one copy to Sir Richard Bayfell for 3s 4d. A German merchant offered to sell several hundred copies "of the biggest" (presumably the Worms octavo edition) or "of the small volume" (presumably the Antwerp sextodecimo edition) for 9d. There is no doubt that the work achieved a wide circulation, and that there was little that could be done to prevent it.

England was a mercantile nation, and hence imported a substantial quantity and variety of legitimate goods. Smugglers were thus offered a rich choice of means by which contraband could be clandestinely brought to England. Port officers discovered all manner of means by which books could be concealed. A large cask of salt concealed books and other religious papers. Barrels of oil were built with hidden watertight compartments, and chests constructed with false bottoms. The smuggling of books was made much easier through the practice of supplying unbound books in the form of printed sheets, which could easily be concealed in cargoes of hides, or bales of cloth or other fabric.

Perhaps the most bizarre scheme devised by the English church to stifle the new translation is set out by Edward Hall in his chronicle entitled *The Union of the Two Noble and Illustre Families of Lancaster and York* (1548). In this chronicle, Hall relates how Tunstall, in the course of a 1529 visit to Antwerp, met a merchant by the name of Augustine Packington. Tunstall mentioned how anxious he was to burn as many of Tyndale's New Testaments as possible, upon which

## A Note on Paper Sizes

B ooks dating from this period are often described in terms of the size of its pages. A single large sheet of printing paper would be folded to give pages of various sizes. The simplest procedure was to fold the sheet once. This created two "leaves" of paper, each of which could be printed on both sides to give four printed pages. This is known as a "folio" edition. A "quarto" edition involved folding the original large sheet twice, giving eight printed pages. An "octavo" edition involved folding the original sheet of paper to give sixteen printed pages, and a "duodecimo" edition twenty-four. As the same size of paper was used for each, the overall result was a radical reduction in page size. An octavo edition (whose pages measure roughly 8 x 5 inches) is thus approximately one quarter the size of the full folio edition.

| Name | Number of folds | Leaves per sheet | Number of printed pages |
|---|---|---|---|
| Folio | 1 | 2 | 4 |
| Quarto | 2 | 4 | 8 |
| Octavo | 3 | 8 | 16 |
| Duodecimo | 4 | 12 | 24 |
| Sextodecimo | 5 | 16 | 32 |

Folio-sized works were ideal for placing on lecterns or reading stands of some kind; duodecimo and sextodecimo were easier to carry around, and thus best suited for personal use. They were also easier to smuggle into England.

Packington informed the bishop that he would—for a price—be able to get hold of as many copies as the bishop wanted. He was a personal friend of the merchants involved, and well placed to obtain large quantities of the work. Packington promptly informed Tyndale of the deal. Tyndale was delighted. He would profit from the deal, and be able to invest heavily in producing even more accurate editions of the work. As Hall concluded his story: "forward went the bargain: the bishop had the books, Packington had the thanks, and Tyndale had the money."

The money, if such indeed was its source, was well used. In January 1530, copies of a new work began to appear in England, again smuggled in from Antwerp. The new work was Tyndale's English translation of the book of Genesis, the first section of a translation of the entire Pentateuch. Tyndale's style in this work is robust and colloquial. We read of Pharaoh's "jolly captains" being drowned in the Red Sea (Exodus 15:4), and learn that Joseph was a "lucky fellow" (Genesis 39:2).

Yet the most important product of Tyndale's later period was the 1534 revision of the translation of the New Testament. Some five thousand alterations were introduced, generally to the improvement of the original. Tyndale's final translation of the Parable of the Good Samaritan can still be read today with little difficulty.

*A certain man descended from Jerusalem in to Jericho, and fell in to the hands of thieves, which robbed him of his raiment and wounded him, and departed leaving him half dead. And by chance there came a certain priest that same way, and when he saw him, he passed by. And likewise a Levite, when he was come nigh to the place, went and looked on him, and passed by. Then a certain Samaritan, as he journeyed, came nigh unto him, and when he saw him, had compassion on him, and went to and bound up his wounds, and poured in oil and wine, and put him on his own beast, and brought him to a common inn, and made provision for him. And on the morrow when he departed, he took*

*out two pence and gave them to the host, and said unto him: Take*
*care of him, and whatsoever thou spendest more, when I come*
*again, I will recompense thee. Which now of these three, thinkest*
*thou, was neighbour unto him that fell into the thieves' hands?*
*And he said: he that shewed mercy on him. Then said Jesus unto*
*him: Go and do thou likewise.*

The revision was undertaken in the full knowledge that the religious situation in England was changing, radically and possibly irreversibly. Henry VIII was now alienated from the Pope, and Thomas
More—Tyndale's most severe critic—had resigned as Lord Chancellor
over Henry's refusal to recognize papal authority. Thomas Cromwell
was rising in the royal favour, and was rumoured to be sympathetic to
the cause of the Reformation in general, and a vernacular Bible in particular. With Cromwell as vice-regent, the possibility of further
reform was considerable.

In the end, despite their personal antagonism and totally different
views on matters of religion and biblical translation, More and
Tyndale shared a common fate. Both were executed, victims of the
religious tensions of the period that neither could control, yet each, in
his own way, had helped create. More was executed at the Tower of
London on July 6, 1535, on a charge of high treason. More had
incurred Henry's dislike for a number of reasons, including his continued support for papal authority in England, and his refusal to
attend Henry's wedding to Anne Boleyn in 1533.

Tyndale had fled England, fearing for his safety on account of his
Protestant religious views and his commitment to bringing biblical
translation to England. He settled in the house of Thomas Pointz in
the port city of Antwerp, which by then was beginning to gain a reputation as a place of toleration for Protestant ideas. It was also the centre of an extensive publishing trade, with well-established links with
English booksellers. It was an ideal location for Tyndale to continue
his work of biblical translation. In addition to revising existing translations, he was in a position to extend this work to additional Old

Testament works. Yet Antwerp was close to the staunchly Catholic centres of Brussels and Louvain. There was always a risk that Tyndale would be abducted by those anxious to end his activities.

In the event, Tyndale was betrayed. The motives for the betrayal remain puzzling. Henry Philips, an impoverished Englishman who detested Lutheranism, appears to have been bribed by someone in London to induce Tyndale to leave the safety of Pointz's house on the pretext of inviting him to dinner. While the identity of this person remains unclear, suspicion naturally falls upon certain senior English churchmen, who felt their positions threatened by Tyndale's activities. Tyndale was arrested in May 1535. Vigorous protests from the English government, especially Thomas Cromwell, fell on deaf ears. Tyndale was strangled in October 1536, and his dead body then burned at the stake. Tyndale's fate is an important reminder that biblical translation was more than just a scholarly challenge in the early sixteenth century—it was, in Tyndale's case, illegal, dangerous, and ultimately fatal.

Tyndale might have been eliminated from the scene; yet his New Testament had created pressure for a vernacular Bible that was proving increasingly difficult to resist. The changing religious situation in England meant that there were now many in high places who were more than open to this possibility. Tyndale's biblical translations of the 1520s had opened floodgates that could no longer be closed, such was the force of the torrent flowing through them. It was merely a matter of time before an English Bible was published—but this time, with royal authority. As it happened, the first crack in the establishment appeared a few months before Tyndale's arrest.

In December 1534, the Convocation of Canterbury—representing the clergy of the southern province of the Church of England—petitioned Henry VIII to rule that "the Holy Scripture should be translated into the vulgar English tongue by certain good and learned men, to be nominated by His Majesty, and should be delivered to the people for their instruction." The English clergy had pointedly turned their backs on Tyndale's translation, but they had conceded the need

1536 DEPICTION OF THE EXECUTION
OF WILLIAM TYNDALE

for an officially sanctioned English Bible, which could be freely distributed and read within England. A vital corner had been turned.

## THE FIRST PRINTED ENGLISH BIBLES

THE FIRST COMPLETE English Bible appeared in 1535. This was the work of Miles Coverdale (1488–1569), who based his work largely on existing translations. Coverdale was no great linguist, and was dependent on "five sundry interpreters." One of these is easily identified as the most important influence: Coverdale is clearly dependent on Tyndale's translation of the New Testament and Pentateuch.

Coverdale also consulted two Latin translations of the Bible—the Vulgate (whose errors had been so pitilessly pointed out by Erasmus two decades earlier), and a more recent Latin translation undertaken by the Italian Dominican scholar Sancte Pagnini in 1528. The remaining "sundry interpreters" that Coverdale consulted were Luther's German translation of the Bible, and a variant of this, translated into the Swiss-German dialect of the Zurich region in Switzerland. One of the less felicitous aspects of this use of German translations is that Coverdale seems to have been given to minting new English words that are obviously literal representations of the original German— such as "unoutspeakable" (a clumsy English rendering of the German term *unaussprechlich*).

In one sense, Coverdale's translation is to be treated with some caution. It is not really a "translation" in itself, and is best viewed as a compilation of other people's translations—supremely those of Tyndale—without the sustained critical engagement with the original Greek and especially the Hebrew texts, which one has a right to expect in such a work. Rather than translating the Hebrew and Greek texts directly by himself, Coverdale appears simply to have put together an amalgam of existing translations according to his own personal preferences.

Yet despite this weakness, the work had one immense strength. It was the first complete English Bible to be published, and thus constitutes a landmark on the road to the King James Bible. The translation is rumoured to have found favour with Anne Boleyn, known for her Protestant sympathies. As Henry VIII had divorced Catherine of Aragon in order to marry Anne, her preferences in this matter of Bible translations had no small influence on Henry. Coverdale's translation began to gain the ascendancy. The ground had been laid for an official English Bible, to be sanctioned by royal authority.

Perhaps Thomas Cromwell—a powerful force in the struggle for an authorized English Bible—had hopes that Henry VIII might have given Coverdale's version this coveted status. However, when Anne Boleyn fell from favour and was executed in 1536, Coverdale's translation lost the appeal it once had for Henry. Realizing that Henry would not consent to authorize Coverdale's Bible, Cromwell took another approach. He would encourage a new translation, free from any associations with the unfortunate Anne Boleyn, and wait for an opportune moment to persuade Henry of its merits.

He would not have to wait long. The English printer and entrepreneur Richard Grafton had been busy for some years working on the production of an English Bible. The text was edited by John Rogers, an associate of Tyndale's. The work, published in 1537, is often known as "Matthew's Bible," from the pseudonym adopted by Rogers to protect his identity. The translation was produced and printed in Antwerp, from where it would be exported to England. Although Matthew's Bible was based partly on Coverdale's work, it is clear that the most important influence was the translations of Tyndale, including some Old Testament material that Tyndale had translated but never managed to publish, and which had remained in Antwerp after his execution. In addition to the text of the Bible, the work included marginal notes based upon the French biblical translation of Pierre-Robert Olivétan (c. 1506–38).

Grafton kept both Thomas Cromwell and Thomas Cranmer informed of the progress of the work, aware that the influence of these senior figures was such that they might be able to secure Henry's active support for the project. By August 4, 1537, Cranmer had secured an advance copy of the work, and was favourably impressed with what he read. He sent the copy on to Cromwell, expressing the hope that it might gain royal favour. Whether by accident or design, Cranmer seems to have caught Henry VIII in an unusually good mood. On August 13, Cranmer wrote again to Cromwell, this time expressing his delight and thanks that the Bible had been presented to the king, and had received a favorable reception. The Bible had been given royal approval, and was authorized for general sale. Henceforth, the title page of the Bible bore the words "Set forth with the king's most gracious licence." Given the extent of the dependence of this version upon Coverdale's, the royal license was subsequently extended to include later printings of Coverdale's Bible.

1546 PORTRAIT OF THOMAS CRANMER
BY GERLACH FLICKE (ACTIVE 1545-58)

Pressure now began to develop for an English Bible to be placed in every parish church in England. In part, this reflected a growing consensus that, as a matter of principle, the people of England should be allowed to hear the Bible read to them in their own language. Yet another unstated concern may be discerned as lurking in the background. The most effective way of countering the influence of potentially seditious unauthorized translations was to flood the country with reliable and safe translations, and insist that these be read out loud during regular public worship. On September 3, 1538, an injunction, published in the name of the king, charged the clergy of the church as follows:

*That ye shall provide, on this side of the feast of All Saints next coming, one book of the whole Bible of the largest volume in English, and the same set up in some convenient place within the said church that ye have cure of, whereas your parishioners may most commodiously resort to the same and read it. The charges of which book shall be rateably borne between you, the parson and the parishioners aforesaid, that is to say, the one half by you and the other half by them.*

The king may have authorized the use of such a Bible; he was most emphatically not prepared to pay for it.

The reference to the "largest volume" immediately suggested that Matthew's Bible was the text of choice for this purpose. Coverdale's translation took the form of a quarto edition, which was too small to be used properly on most church lecterns. Matthew's Bible was published in the larger folio edition, ideally suited for church use. Its future seemed assured; Grafton would surely become a rich man. Henry might have authorized the book; it remained, however, the product of private enterprise and entrepreneurship.

## AN OFFICIAL ENGLISH BIBLE:
## THE GREAT BIBLE OF 1539

GRAFTON WAS TO be disappointed. A feature of Matthew's Bible that he believed to be a selling point became instead a sticking point. Grafton had included a large number of marginal notes in his Bible, following a precedent set by a highly successful French Protestant translation of the Bible produced earlier in Geneva. Perhaps it was inevitable that the notes accompanying the text reflected the strongly Protestant outlook of Pierre-Robert Olivétan, who had originally written them. They might well have won universal favour in Protestant Geneva; England, however, was simply not ready for such strong Protestant meat. While Rogers's translation was broadly acceptable across theological divisions within the English church, being seen as neither especially Protestant nor Catholic, the notes caused difficulties for some senior English clergy. They were still nervous about allowing the laity to read the Bible in English; the marginal notes could well lead to the Bible being read in a radical Protestant manner.

This perception of a strong Protestant bias was reinforced by an additional factor. The ordering of the books of the New Testament in Matthew's Bible followed the early Lutheran practice of placing Hebrews, James, Jude, and Revelation at the end of the New Testament, in a category of their own. This reflected Luther's personal doubts concerning their canonicity—doubts not shared by other reformers, such as John Calvin, or by the Catholic opponents of the Reformation. If a Bible was to be authorized for public use in church, it was argued, it must treat all the New Testament works as canonical.

Matthew's Bible failed to gain the acceptance that Grafton had expected. Thomas Cromwell realized that a new translation was needed. To begin from scratch would have taken an enormous amount of time, whereas the political situation demanded the rapid production of a completed text. The simplest solution was adopted. Cromwell asked Coverdale to revise Matthew's Bible, with such changes as were required to keep influential churchmen happy. The new translation—which contained no offensive marginal notes—appeared in April 1539 from the presses of Richard Grafton and Edward Whitchurch, and rapidly became the favoured Bible for use in churches. It was this Bible that became known as "the Great Bible." It included both the canonical and apocryphal books, mistakenly referring to the latter as the "Hagiographa." The New Testament works were printed in the order set out by Erasmus in his 1516 Greek New Testament, with the four works regarded by Luther as being of doubtful authority—Hebrews, James, Jude, and Revelation—fully integrated into the text. The pattern set by the Great Bible became normative for English Bibles, and is reflected in the presentation and ordering of the text in both the Geneva Bible and the King James

Bible. The work was reissued with revisions in April 1540, and included a new preface by Thomas Cranmer, Archbishop of Canterbury.

The translation of the text offered by the Great Bible is best seen as a judicious blend of Tyndale and Coverdale, with the offending notes of Matthew's Bible removed. Although Coverdale intended to include an appendix of "certain godly annotations," it seems that this was omitted at a late stage; Coverdale's Protestant views, however moderately couched, would inevitably have offended some in England, and reduced the appeal of the Bible. The lesson to be learned from the failure of Matthew's Bible was that Protestant annotations were unacceptable—for the moment, at any rate.

The title page of the work is itself a remarkably revealing piece of reformist iconography, and is worth studying carefully (see the illustration on page 96). It represents a powerful visual statement of the place of the Bible in Tudor England, and brings out the close link between church and state that existed throughout this important period in English history. It also firmly identifies Thomas Cromwell and Thomas Cranmer as the central figures, apart from Henry VIII, in the production of the English Bible.

The central figure of the illustration, located directly above the work's title, is Henry VIII. At his right hand is Thomas Cranmer, along with his fellow bishops. Cranmer is depicted as gratefully receiving the Bible from the king, thus stressing the mutual commitment of church and state to the Christian gospel, and especially to the Bible as the textual embodiment of that gospel. Immediately beneath, we see Cranmer passing the Bible on to a priest of the Church of England. Cranmer's coat of arms is placed alongside this scene, to allow easy identification of the central figure of this cameo. In the cameo immediately beneath this scene, we see the same clergyman preaching to his congregation. To emphasize the harmonious relation of church and state, the pulpit is inscribed with the words *Vivat Rex!* "Long live the king!"

The other side of the title page deals with the secular aspects of the matter. Henry VIII is here depicted as passing a copy of the Bible

THE TITLE PAGE OF THE GREAT BIBLE.
NOTE HOW THE ARMS OF THOMAS CROMWELL
HAVE BEEN ERASED, FOLLOWING HIS FALL
FROM ROYAL FAVOUR.

to Thomas Cromwell, the Vice-Regent, in the presence of members of the Privy Council. The cameo immediately below this depicts Cromwell distributing the Bible to members of the laity; Cromwell's coat of arms accompanies this illustration. Finally, another group of laity are depicted below this, apparently milling around in a rather aimless way—in contrast to the rapt attention with which the group on the right are listening to a sermon.

The title page of the Great Bible is a classic example of image-making. The image projected is that of a unified nation, united under the monarch and the Bible, in which church and state work harmoniously together. The church upholds the monarchy—recall the *Vivat Rex!* of the pulpit—and the monarchy defends true religion. It is an icon of a godly state and church under their supreme head, who in turn acknowledges his obligations to God, expressed in the Bible. The social ordering of England was thus affirmed every time the Great Bible was opened on a church lectern.

This was an icon that, despite its confident and harmonious portrayal of the English state and church, could not entirely mask the real, and rather more fragile, state of affairs. After Cromwell's spectacular fall from grace in 1540, one central theme of the title page was now problematic. If Cromwell was no longer *persona grata*, how could his image be removed from the design? The simple expedient was to remove his coat of arms, so that the third and subsequent editions displayed a blank space. This allowed the identity of the figure to whom Henry passed a copy of the Bible to remain vague—perhaps a senior government figure? The massive disruption to the English state and church caused by the radically different religious and political agendas of Edward VI, Mary Tudor, and Elizabeth I made something of a nonsense of the idealized scheme portrayed by the Great Bible.

But there is little doubt that the scheme that it depicted corresponded well with the self-understanding of a later monarch—James I. For James, political and religious unity were to be achieved through the person of the monarch, and a single version of the Bible, issued with royal authority. With serious religious tensions growing in

England at the time of his accession to the throne (1603), the image of the king giving the Bible to his people was more than a piece of religious theatre; it was the essential means by which national unity might be secured at a time of potential fragmentation.

The importance of this point was brought home to James I, as it was to many others in earlier years, by a new translation of the Bible, which demonstrated the power of a printed Bible to evoke demands for religious and political change. The Geneva Bible broke new ground and set new standards in biblical translation, illustration, and layout. Its numerous features—such as the marginal comments—propelled it to the forefront of English Bible translations. By the time the King James Bible was published, the Geneva Bible was the undisputed market leader. The Great Bible and its officially inspired successors were powerless to meet the challenge posed by this new translation, which was the product of private enterprise and religious enthusiasm on the part of a small group of English Protestant exiles in the city of Geneva.

From the moment of its publication in 1611, the major challenge faced by the state-sponsored King James Bible was to displace its older and privately produced Geneva Bible.

# 5

## EXPLAINING
## THE "HARD PLACES":
## THE GENEVA BIBLE

The English translation of the Bible that did more than anything to shape English religious thought throughout the long reign of Elizabeth I was produced in the city of Geneva in 1560. This immensely influential translation is the source of the many allusions to the Bible that are found in the works of Shakespeare. Perhaps the greatest—and certainly the most curious—tribute to the popularity of the Geneva Bible is the remarkable fact that, when citing from the Bible, the preface to the King James Bible itself chose to use the Geneva translation rather than the new translation that the preface was intended to introduce and commend. The greatest obstacle faced by the King James Version as it sought to establish itself in the seventeenth century was the continuing popularity of the Geneva Bible.

As we shall see, the Geneva Bible did rather more than offer an acceptable English translation of the entire Bible, including the Apocrypha. It offered comments on the text, which often expressed the radical Protestant ideas associated with Geneva at this time. The title page of the Great Bible depicted the close relationship between church and state, monarch and people, which it envisaged as being authorized and encouraged by the Bible. Geneva was a republic, and had a strong interest in spreading its republicanism, as much as its Protestantism, throughout Europe. The Geneva Bible threatened to undermine the entire structure of church and state that had been set up under Henry VIII, and continued more or less unchanged under Elizabeth I.

So how did this enormously influential Bible come into being? Why was the household Bible of Elizabethan English Protestants produced in Geneva? What conceivable reason might there be for a book intended for distribution in England to be produced in a far-off French-speaking city? The answers to these questions are fascinating, and merit close attention.

## THE REFORMATION OF GENEVA

THE ORIGINS OF Geneva go back to a settlement established in Roman times. Its geographical location helped it become one of the many crossroads of Europe, at which traders from northern Europe met their colleagues from the south, especially Italy. Four international trade fairs were held annually from 1262. So important was Geneva as a trade centre that the immensely wealthy Medici family even reckoned it worth establishing a bank in the city. Yet Geneva was not a free city, enjoying the privileges of the great "imperial cities," such as Strasbourg. It was part of the duchy of Savoy, a territory high up in the French Alps. Its affairs were directed from the city of Annecy, some distance to the south. The citizens of Geneva did not like this arrangement, but there was little that they could do about it.

Yet many in Geneva were looking enviously to the east, where the Swiss Confederation was growing in power and prosperity. The Swiss Confederation came into being in the fourteenth century, as a means of defending the political and economic liberties of the region against the Austrians. By the early sixteenth century, the Swiss cities of Zurich, Basel, and Berne had established themselves as important regional centres of economic growth and political influence. Many in Geneva became interested in developing closer links with the Swiss Confederation, which was not far to the east of Geneva. This seemed to offer the hope of economic and political liberalization.

It was not, however, something that Geneva's masters in Savoy were prepared to allow. When some leading citizens of Geneva arranged an alliance with the Swiss city of Fribourg in 1519 without permission from their political masters, the pact was promptly annulled by Savoy. The leader of the delegation that negotiated the pact was publicly executed shortly afterwards.

But this merely increased many Genevans' longing for independence, and gave new momentum to finding ways of breaking free from foreign control. In 1526, Geneva—again, without Savoy's permission—entered into a pact with the Swiss city of Berne. This was a major development. Not only was Berne a major economic centre, it also possessed a large standing army, which it was perfectly prepared to deploy in support of its allies.

Religious matters had not played any significant role in the life of Geneva up to this point. The situation changed radically in 1528. After a public debate, the hitherto Catholic city of Zurich had accepted the Protestant Reformation in 1523, largely through the efforts of the leading Swiss reformer Huldrych Zwingli (1484–1531). From Zurich, the Reformation rapidly spread to other Catholic cities in the region. Typically, a public disputation was arranged by the city councils, with representatives of the Reformation being pitted in debate against their Catholic opponents. A binding vote was then taken within the city's ruling body as to whether the city should accept the principles of the Reformation. In 1528, Berne voted to accept the Reformation.

Geneva now found itself in an interesting position. The Berne it had allied with in 1526 was Catholic; in 1528, it became Protestant. More than that; it actively campaigned for its allies to accept the Reformation. The winds of religious change began to blow through Geneva. Berne was a German-speaking city, whereas the dominant language of Geneva was French. Berne, therefore, recruited a small group of French-speaking reformers and sent them to Geneva. Their brief was simple: win over the Genevans to the Reformation. In 1534, a public debate took place within Geneva. Although the result was not clear-cut, the city lurched decisively in a Protestant direction. In 1535, the city declared its independence from Savoy, and its public adoption of the principles of the Reformation. Coins were minted, proudly bearing the slogan of the new republic: *post tenebras lux*— "after the shadows, light!"

Savoy was alarmed, and promptly sent an army to sort out their rebellious colony. By January 1536, the city was surrounded and cut off from its neighbours. Capitulation seemed inevitable. However, Berne was determined to support its ally, and simultaneously extend its own influence in the region. By February, Bernese armies had swept westward, occupying every Savoyard possession in their path. Geneva was now free from the rule of Savoy; in practice, it would remain a vassal of Berne for years to come.

By the summer of 1536, Geneva was settling down to its new status as a Protestant republic. There had been a massive outflow of Catholic professionals in the aftermath of the revolution of 1535 and the siege of January 1536. The city needed lawyers. It also needed help with the consolidation of the Protestant revolution initiated the previous year. It was at this point that the link between Geneva and one of its most famous inhabitants was created.

## JOHN CALVIN AND GENEVA

JOHN CALVIN (1509–64) is one of the most significant players in the great religious debates and developments of the sixteenth century. Jean Cauvin—to use his French name for the moment—was born in the French city of Noyon, about seventy miles northeast of Paris. His father was involved in the financial administration of the local diocese, and could rely on the patronage of the bishop to ensure support for his son's career. At some point in the early 1520s (probably 1523), the

PORTRAIT OF JOHN CALVIN
(ARTIST UNKNOWN)

young Calvin was sent up to the University of Paris. From now on, he would be known by a Latinized form of his name—John Calvin.

After completing his undergraduate studies at Paris, Calvin moved to Orléans to study civil law. Although Calvin's father had originally intended that his son should study theology with a view to entering the priesthood, he changed his mind shortly after Calvin began his studies. The study of law generally makes people—and their relatives—rich, Calvin later remarked caustically. It is also possible that Calvin's father may have lost the patronage of the local bishop on account of a financial wrangle back at Noyon. If Calvin was to have a brilliant career in the Church, he would need powerful patrons—and Calvin's father appears to have alienated those who might otherwise have supported him.

Soon after graduating in law at Orléans, Calvin returned to Paris to continue his scholarly work. During this period, he became increasingly sympathetic to the reforming ideas that were then gaining an excited hearing in that city. Parisian academic culture found itself both fascinated and revolted by Luther, and his ideas were widely discussed by students. On November 2, 1533, Calvin was obliged to leave Paris in some haste. The rector of the University of Paris, Nicolas Cop, had delivered a university address in which he seemed to endorse some aspects of Luther's reform programme. A copy of Cop's sermon has survived in Calvin's handwriting, prompting some to speculate that Calvin might have been the author of this piece of reform rhetoric.

The Parisian authorities immediately took action against Cop and his circle—which included Calvin—and set about rounding them up. Calvin, realizing that he was a marked man, fled Paris, fearful for his safety. During the following year, he settled in the Swiss city of Basel, known as a place of political and religious asylum, safe from any threat from the French authorities.

Calvin was now firmly committed to the cause of the Reformation, and felt a special responsibility for advocating its ideas in his native France. While in exile in Basel, he wrote a short book, dedicated to the king of France, in which he set out clearly the main ideas of the French reform constituency. Calvin's intention was both to refute its many critics within France, and to set out clearly and attractively the leading themes of Protestant theology. The work was published in Latin in May 1536, with the title *The Institutes of the Christian Religion*. It became one of the most influential books of the sixteenth century, and established Calvin as a leading Protestant intellectual.

Calvin seems to have had no real idea what to do next. As it happened, others would make that decision for him. After a period of restless wandering, Calvin decided to settle in the great German city of Strasbourg, which had become a citadel of Protestantism in the early 1530s. After settling some family business, Calvin began his journey to Strasbourg in the summer of 1536. The activities of French and German armies caused him to take an indirect route to his destination, passing through the city of Geneva. Calvin intended to spend a night there, resuming his journey in the morning. Fate—or, Calvin would say, divine providence—intervened. He was recognized by Geneva's Protestant leaders as the author of the *Institutes*. They demanded that he stay and help consolidate the Reformation in Geneva.

So began the association between Calvin and Geneva that is one of the fixed reference points of sixteenth-century intellectual history. The relationship was often troubled and stormy, especially in its early stages. Calvin's rather rigorous conception of reform gave rise to much opposition within the city. Genevans did not particularly like being forced to attend long sermons. More seriously, Calvin allowed it to be known that he was critical of Geneva's political dependence on Berne, particularly in matters of religion. For example, the Bernese churches celebrated Holy Communion four times a year, while Calvin wished to celebrate communion monthly. Not wanting to alienate their powerful ally, the Geneva city council insisted that Geneva fall into line. What Berne wanted, Berne would get. Calvin protested, and was thrown out of Geneva in April 1538.

Calvin spent the period 1538–41 in exile in Strasbourg. It was no great hardship for him. His original intention, two years earlier, had been to settle in this great city, and get on with a life of scholarship. In the event, Calvin was called back to Geneva in 1541. Political and religious instability had broken out in his absence, and the city council had reluctantly decided that they would prefer to have Calvin than chaos. The anti-Calvin faction at Geneva had been fatally wounded by a scandal over Bernese treaty obligations, which had seen their credibility evaporate virtually overnight. They wanted Calvin back.

The treaty between Berne and Geneva, signed after Berne had routed the Savoyard besiegers of the city in February 1536, contained several obscure clauses that became the subject of some tension between the cities in 1539. A delegation of four Genevans travelled to Berne to negotiate a satisfactory resolution of the difficulties. The negotiations were conducted in Swiss German, the language of Berne.

The Genevan negotiators presented themselves as international statesmen, who were perfectly capable of negotiating in languages other than their native French. They returned home to popular acclaim, well satisfied with their achievements.

A few months later, however, the Bernese thoughtfully provided Geneva with a full French translation of the articles negotiated at Berne. These were received with disbelief, then outrage. The Geneva negotiators had clearly failed to understand the terms they had allegedly "negotiated." Geneva immediately repudiated the articles, and ordered their negotiators back to Berne to sort out the mess. Their refusal to do so was viewed as tantamount to treason. The pro-Bernese faction was discredited, being seen as little more than a Bernese fifth column within Geneva. In the next round of city elections, the faction was swept from power, and the way cleared for Calvin to be invited to return to Geneva. He accepted their invitation. Calvin would remain in the city until his death in 1564.

Calvin was a man of vision, and recognized the importance of printing as a means of spreading the ideas of the Reformation throughout Europe. The printing presses of Geneva would produce copies of his works, both in Latin and French, which would actively promote the cause of reform within his native France. Yet Calvin was also aware of another means by which the Protestant cause could be advanced. As Calvin's ideas gained influence throughout Europe, especially in the late 1540s and early 1550s, many religious refugees from France, England, and Italy began to arrive in Geneva. Not only would the city offer them asylum from their enemies, it would allow them to absorb Calvin's ideas and methods at firsthand. Every refugee was a potential Protestant missionary to his country of origin.

Calvin realized that Geneva's unique situation allowed it an un-rivalled position as a catalyst for Protestant revolution throughout Europe. Geneva could produce both Protestant books and highly motivated individuals who would be able and willing to spread the ideas of the Reformation. Although Calvin's primary concern would always be for his native France, he was not unaware of the critical role that educated English Protestant émigrés might play in bringing about a Protestant revolution in England.

As events made clear, this point was not lost on a group of English refugees who sought asylum in Geneva, while they plotted the conversion of their native land to Calvin's cause.

## RELIGIOUS REFUGEES AND THE GENEVAN ECONOMY

UNDER CALVIN, GENEVA became a symbol of the Protestant Reformation. The biblical image of a "city on a hill," whose light could not be hidden, was widely applied to the fledgling Protestant republic, which achieved almost iconic significance to Protestants throughout Europe in the late 1540s and early 1550s. As the religious persecution of Protestants gained momentum in Calvin's native France, many wealthy French Protestants took a momentous decision: they would seek refuge in Geneva. They believed they would be welcomed there on account of their religious beliefs, and knew that they would be useful on account of their wealth and professional skills. They included printers (such as Robert Estienne), watchmakers (Geneva's association with watches dates from this period), and armourers.

The population of Geneva around 1500 is estimated to have been about 5,000. By 1550, it had climbed to 13,100; by 1560, it had reached 21,400. The main reason for this massive growth in its population was the influx of religious refugees, mainly from France. As these refugees were attracted to Geneva on account of its reputation as a bulwark of Protestantism, it is hardly surprising that the refugees were generally strongly supportive of Calvin's religious ideas and policies.

Yet it was not only French Protestants who sought refuge in Geneva. From the point of view of our story, the most important of these asylum-seekers was a group of "Marian exiles"—that is, English Protestants who fled to Europe to escape the repressive religious

PORTRAIT OF EDWARD VI AS PRINCE OF WALES,
ATTRIBUTED TO A FOLLOWER OF
HANS HOLBEIN THE YOUNGER

policies of Mary Tudor, who came to the English throne in 1553. Edward VI, who reigned from 1547–53, was heavily influenced by a group of senior figures who were openly Protestant in their sympathies. During his reign, a number of continental Protestant divines were welcomed to England to assist with the theological consolidation of the English Reformation. Edward VI appointed the Strasbourg reformer Martin Bucer as Regius Professor of Divinity at Cambridge, and Peter Martyr Vermigli to the Regius chair at Oxford. It seemed that it was only a matter of time before England consolidated its position as a Protestant nation.

But Edward's early death in 1553 put an end to these Protestant experimentations. Mary Tudor was determined to re-establish Roman Catholicism within England, and systematically eliminated those who stood in her way. Mary's accession to the English throne marked a radical reversal of the Protestant policies openly pursued under Edward VI. Those whose religious views had endeared them to one monarch alienated them from his successor. Some were banished; others deemed it prudent to escape before a worse fate overtook them.

Those English Protestants who could afford to do so went into exile in the Protestant cities of Europe—such as Geneva or Zurich—to await a change in the religious climate. According to John Foxe (1516–87), "well near to 800 persons, students and others together" fled England for refuge within the Protestant havens of Europe in the first few years of Mary's turbulent reign. It can be estimated that more than half of this figure of 800 was male—perhaps 450. Of these, Foxe estimated that 148 were gentry, 74 clergy (including four bishops), and 99 were students of divinity.

So where did these émigrés—who have come to be known as the Marian exiles—settle while they waited for Mary to die? The favoured sites of exile were the Swiss cities of Aarau, Basel, and Zurich; the German cities of Emden, Frankfurt, and Strasbourg; and the independent city of Geneva. Some were wealthy enough to support themselves in exile; others received discreet financial support from well-wishers back home, particularly from wealthy Protestant mer-

JOHN MASTER'S 1544 PORTRAIT OF MARY TUDOR
AT THE AGE OF 28

chants who already had extensive trading links with the cities in which their protégés sought refuge. It proved to be a relatively easy matter to link business deals with merchants in Strasbourg, for example, with covert support for their exiled colleagues.

The Marian exiles appear to have regarded their time in the cities of Europe as paralleling a biblical event that took place two thousand years earlier—the exile of the people of Jerusalem in Babylon. Was not this time of exile to be a time of purification and preparation for a return to their native land? And would not the returning exiles bring a purer form of religion with them? In the event, the period of the Marian exile was a mere six years, in comparison with the fifty of their biblical counterpart. Yet it was a period the exiles saw as one of schooling, in preparation for their return. Their time of exile allowed them firsthand experience of successful working Protestant churches and communities, and provided them with role models that would shape their vision of the new reformed Church of England, which they proposed to establish on their return. The anticipation of a new era of Protestant renewal and reform in England sustained the English Protestant communities during their exile.

The period of exile was difficult for many reasons, not least in that nobody had any real idea how long it would last. Economic hardship was widespread in the small English communities; the exiles were often treated with disinterest or hostility by their host cities. Serious divisions arose over issues of liturgy and theology within the exiled English Protestant communities in Basel, Emden, and Frankfurt, causing embitterment and demoralization. An exception to this was provided by Geneva—attracting approximately one quarter of the émigrés—which was hailed by John Knox as "the most perfect school of Christ," the finest embodiment of a Christian society since the time of Christ. The English community in Geneva proved to be especially important in forging attitudes among the exiles that would be of particular importance in shaping the debates and tensions of Elizabethan Protestantism.

When they were not fighting each other, the Marian exiles continued the struggle for the establishment of a Protestant national church in England. They realized that one of the most effective weapons at their disposal was the printing press. The works they produced can be divided into two broad categories:

1. Works published in Latin, intended to be read by a broad European readership, intended to justify the principles of the English Reformation to the intellectual elite of the region. Latin was the only language that the English exiles had in common with their hosts in the cities of Europe. Roughly forty works are known in this category.
2. Works published in English, which were intended to be smuggled into England, where they were expected to find a ready readership among the religiously oppressed population. Roughly 120 works are known in this category.

One of the most prolific of the Marian exiles was John Foxe, who settled in the Swiss city of Basel. Foxe's experience of exile led him to write about the English Lollards, whom he regarded as heroic forerunners of the English Reformation. However, it is clear that Foxe had a much grander work in mind, one that would take in a much wider range of historical events.

What triggered his decision to write a much larger work in English was the launch of a vigorous official wave of persecution against England's Protestants in January 1555. This may be said to have changed Foxe's whole agenda. Prior to this he had written about Lollards, the fourteenth-century followers of John Wycliffe, often regarded as a forerunner of the Reformation. The people that Foxe would now write about were people whom he had known personally. In 1559, he produced an expanded edition of the work, including accounts of those who were martyred under Henry VIII and Mary Tudor. The resulting work—known as the *Book of Martyrs*—achieved a wide readership, shaping and hardening Protestant attitudes to the

Catholicism that Mary attempted to restore, and it remains an important source for historians.

The most important single literary production of the Marian exiles was the English translation of the Bible undertaken in Geneva, which has simply come to be known as "the Geneva Bible." There is no doubt that the success of this volume contributed to the decision of James I of England to authorize a new English translation of the Bible. At the Hampton Court Conference of 1604, James expressed his grave concern over the Geneva Bible. It was, he remarked, the worst English translation he knew. In fact, this judgment needs careful scrutiny, in that James's comments appear to apply to the marginal notes that accompanied the English translation, rather than the translation itself—notes that James deemed to be "very partial, untrue, seditious, and savouring too much of dangerous and traitorous conceits."

So how did this translation come into being? And why did it prove so popular? To understand the issues, we must first consider a serious difficulty that had arisen earlier in the Reformation—the need for reliable biblical interpretation.

## THE BIBLE:
## TRANSLATION AND INTERPRETATION

THE REFORMATION URGED all Christians to read and value the Bible, and act on what they found within its pages. The traditional response of the opponents of the Reformation to this proposal was that the Bible—which all agreed, although with markedly varying degrees of enthusiasm, was ultimately the foundation of Christian life and thought—was difficult to understand. People needed help to make sense of it. Not only was it written in a language few could understand, its ideas were complex, and needed explanation for the people. The Church, of course, was more than willing to provide such an explanation. Luther, however, argued that the interpretation offered by the Church merely reinforced its own position. The Bible was not, as a matter of principle, allowed to critique either the teachings or practices of the medieval Church. For Luther, it was axiomatic that every Christian had the right to read and interpret the Bible for herself.

As the Reformation progressed, it became clear that making sense of the Bible was not perhaps as straightforward as some had thought. There were "hard places"—to borrow a phrase that would be used by the Geneva Bible—that puzzled and perplexed readers. Translation of the Bible was not enough; this needed to be supplemented by *explanation*. A work that offered the benefits of both accurate biblical translation and interpretation had the potential to be hugely influential. It could also be a best-seller, no small consideration for the entrepreneurs who might be tempted to invest in such a project.

This is precisely what was provided by the Geneva Bible of 1560, which offered both the best English translation of the biblical text then available, along with copious English marginal notes, designed to allow its readers to make sense of what they read in the biblical text itself. The immense success of this work—which is beyond dispute—clearly shows that the work met a real need, and met it effectively.

## THE GENEVA BIBLE

THE GENEVA BIBLE is generally agreed to have mainly been the work of William Whittingham (c. 1524–79), who was assisted by Anthony Gilby and Thomas Sampson. It is also thought that Miles Coverdale, John Knox, and Laurence Tomson were involved, although the extent and nature of their contribution is far from clear. Whittingham was elected a fellow of All Souls' College, Oxford, in 1545. His Protestant views led him to flee England under Mary Tudor, and settle in the city of Frankfurt. The English congregation in Frankfurt had been established in April 1554 by a group of French Protestants, originally based at Glastonbury, who had fled England. The minister of this church, Valerand Poullain, urged his congregation to welcome any others who would flee England on account of their religious beliefs.

A few weeks later, a group of English Protestants arrived, and were allowed to use the French church for their own worship. To avoid language difficulties, it was agreed that the English-speaking congregation should worship on its own. But what form of service would they use? A ferocious debate broke out over whether the 1552 Prayer Book of Edward VI should be used or not. The debate split the congregation, and led to continued bitterness over issues—including both matters of liturgy and theology—and would erupt again in England during the reign of Elizabeth and beyond. Whittingham and Gilby were both involved in what came to be known as the "troubles of Frankfurt," siding with those who wanted to avoid using the Prayer Book. When it became clear that they were losing the debate, they decided to move on.

Following the Frankfurt controversy, Whittingham and Gilby settled in Geneva, under John Knox as the pastor of the English church in the city. Calvin's Geneva provided a place of safety for the refugees; Geneva's Calvin provided them with the biblical commentaries and works of theology that ensured the academic excellence of their translations and annotations. Whittingham's relationship with Calvin went considerably beyond that of the appreciative theological apprentice; he appears to have married Calvin's sister (or perhaps sister-in-law). The English Protestant community in Geneva proved to be especially close-knit, and avoided the divisions and bitterness of émigré communities in other European cities. This close-knit community of entrepreneurs and theologians became the womb within which the Geneva Bible was conceived and nurtured.

Whittingham's first major contribution to the "Englishing" of the Bible was his English New Testament published in 1557. This work was largely derivative, being based primarily on Tyndale's English translation of a generation earlier. However, significant modifications were introduced. Calvin's colleague Theodore Beza had published a new

THE SO-CALLED "ARMADA PORTRAIT"
OF ELIZABETH I BY AN UNKNOWN ARTIST
OF THE ENGLISH SCHOOL, C. 1588

Latin translation of the New Testament in 1556, which was available to Whittingham; it is clear that this influenced his English translation at certain important points. The work was published by Conrad Badius, the son-in law of leading Geneva printer Robert Estienne. Whittingham was quite clear concerning his proposed readership. The translation was, according to Whittingham, aimed at "the simple lambs, which partly are already in the fold of Christ, and so hear willingly their shepherd's voice, and partly wandering astray by ignorance, tarry till the time the Shepherd find them and bring them unto his flock."

The translation is of note in a number of respects, particularly in that it may be regarded as establishing some of the characteristic vocabulary of the King James Version. For example, Whittingham chose to abandon the use of the English term "congregation" to translate the Greek term *ekklesia*, and replace it with the more nuanced term "church." Earlier English translations of the New Testament had referred collectively to the letters of James, Peter, John, and Jude as the "Catholic Epistles"; Whittingham established the practice of referring to them as the "General Epistles." Interesting though this work was, it must be judged to be little more than an anticipation of the greater work we shall consider presently.

In 1558, Mary Tudor died. A surge of relief was experienced throughout English Protestant émigré communities. When it became clear that her successor, Elizabeth, appeared sympathetic to Protestantism, the Marian exiles realized that their moment had come. They would return to England. The Elizabethan "Settlement of Religion" of 1559 seemed to guarantee the position of Protestantism within England, and offer the possibility of it gaining the ascendancy as time went on. There was work for Protestant activists to do at home, and an abundance of opportunities to use the experience they had gained in exile. Most of the Marian exiles returned to England late in 1559 or early 1560. Whittingham, however, chose to remain in Geneva until his major new translation of the Bible was published late in 1560.

The title page of Whittingham's translation of the Bible read as follows:

*The Bible and Holy Scriptures, contained in the Old and New Testament. Translated according to the Hebrew and Greek, and conferred with the best translations in divers languages. With most profitable annotations upon all the hard places, and other things of great importance as may appear in the "Epistle to the Reader." "Fear not, stand still, and behold the salvation of the Lord, which he will show to you this day." Exodus xiv.13. At Geneva. Printed by Rowland Hall. M.D.LX.*

The reference to Geneva in this title page explains why this came to be known as the "Geneva Bible."

The work was printed in the fashion that had gained the ascendancy at Geneva since its revolution of 1535. The Geneva printers Robert Estienne and Jean Girard had produced Bibles in roman, rather than "Black Letter," type since 1534. The old, Germanic appearance of the "Black Letter" Bibles—such as that of Gutenberg— thus gave way to a more modern style. The older "Black Letter" type was modelled on written script, and was not especially easy to read. The roman type, in contrast, was much clearer, making reading— whether public or private—a considerably more pleasant and less-demanding process. Increasingly, the older "Black Letter" type began to be regarded as archaic in England.

In addition, in a New Testament published in 1551, Estienne introduced the practice of numbering individual verses, and dividing the passages in those verses. In effect, each verse, therefore, begins on a new line—a development that seriously interrupted the flow of the text, and failed to take account of the frequently unsatisfactory division of the text into verses. The technique also made it impossible to distinguish between prose and poetry, in that both were presented in precisely the same manner. Two years later, Estienne issued a complete French translation of the Bible, the first to use the chapter-and-verse division throughout. The basic format that would be followed by the English translation of 1560 was, therefore, in place by 1553.

The considerable costs of producing the work were met by the exiles themselves, or by their covert supporters back in England. Although it is clear that the fundamental motivation for the new translation was a concern to make the Bible accessible and intelligible to a lay English readership, the financial aspects of the project could hardly be overlooked. If the new Bible caught on, fortunes were waiting to be made. With the death of Mary and the accession of Elizabeth, it was widely anticipated that there would be a surge in demand for English translations of the Bible. The best would win—

and the supporters of the Geneva Bible were convinced that it out-performed the competition on every point.

One of the former Marian exiles in Geneva who stood to benefit most from this was John Bodley, who secured a licence to print the Geneva Bible (under episcopal supervision) for a period of seven years. The Archbishops of Canterbury and York indicated that they were prepared to extend this for a further twelve years, under certain conditions. Confident of its adoption in England, John Bodley arranged for a folio edition of the work to be published, this much larger size being suitable for use on lecterns in churches.

It might thus at first seem that the commercial and spiritual prospects for the Geneva Bible were excellent. The 1560 edition was produced relatively cheaply (bringing it within the reach of many families). It was handsomely printed in an attractive typeface, and its relatively compact size—quarto rather than folio—made it convenient for personal and family use. The English translation itself was perhaps the best of its day. The biblical text was broken down into individual verses; words that were introduced into the text, yet had no direct equivalent in the original, were printed in italics. It was important to Whittingham to indicate which parts of the text were the word of God, and which the necessary additions of the translator.

Yet its most important and attractive features were its illustrations, prefaces, annotations, and marginal notes. The illustrations were added to enable the reader to make more visual sense of some difficult passages (for example, the vision of Ezekiel), to offer maps to accompany descriptions of lands or journeys, and to depict scenes from biblical narratives (such as the "garments of the High Priest," described in Exodus 28). Those who created the Geneva Bible had absorbed Calvin's famous maxim concerning the need to "accommodate to the ability of the individual." If God "accommodated himself to human capacity" in communicating with humanity—for example, by using visual images, such as "God as shepherd"—why should not Bibles follow this excellent precedent? The divine sanction for explanation and illustration underlies the distinctive approach of the entire

Geneva project, which aims to make the engagement with Scripture as simple as possible for the reader. As the preface to the Geneva Bible put it:

> *Whereas certain places in the books of Moses, of the Kings and Ezekiel seemed so dark that by no description they could be made easy to the simple reader; we have so set them forth with figures and notes for the full declaration thereof that they . . . as it were by the eye may sufficiently know the true meaning of all such places. Whereunto we have added certain maps of cosmography which necessarily serve for the perfect understanding and memory of divers places and countries, partly described and partly by occasion touched, both in the Old and New Testament.*

It may be noted that not all these illustrations were composed specifically for the Geneva Bible; Robert Estienne had amassed a considerable number of biblical illustrations for other Bibles, and was able to draw on these for this new work.

The prefaces aimed to explain what the individual books taught, allowing their readers to see the purpose of the book within the Bible as a whole. For example, consider the preface to Genesis (which is here treated as having been written by Moses himself):

> *Moses in effect declares three things, which are in this book chiefly to be considered: First, that the world and all things in it were created by God, and to praise his Name for the infinite graces, with which he had endued him, fell willingly from God through disobedience, who yet for his own mercies sake restored him to life, and confirmed him in the same by his promise of Christ to come, by whom he should overcome Satan, death and hell. Secondly, that the wicked, unmindful of God's most excellent benefits, remained still in their wickedness, and so falling most horribly from sin to sin, provoked God (who by his preachers called them continually to repentance) at length to destroy the whole world.*

*Thirdly, he assures us by the examples of Abraham, Isaac, Jacob and the rest of the patriarchs, that his mercies never fail those whom he chooses to be his Church, and to profess his Name in earth, but in all their afflictions and persecutions he assists them, sends comfort, and delivers them, so that the beginning, increase, preservation and success of it might be attributed to God only. Moses shows by the examples of Cain, Ishmael, Esau and others, who were noble in man's judgment, that this Church depends not on the estimation and nobility of the world: and also by the fewness of those, who have at all times worshipped him purely according to his word that it stands not in the multitude, but in the poor and despised, in the small flock and little number, that man in his wisdom might be confounded, and the name of God praised forever.*

The prefaces thus served the purpose of introducing readers to the leading theological themes set out in the books in question. No other work had such a useful feature—a feature that, it need hardly be added, was easily adapted to stressing and defending Protestant doctrines, and critiquing Roman Catholic teachings.

It was the marginal notes that proved to be of supreme importance in the great religious controversies of Elizabethan and Jacobean England. Whereas William Tyndale had assumed—hopelessly optimistically, as it proved—that the Bible, once translated, could easily be understood by any ploughboy, the Geneva Bible explicitly recognized that there were "hard places"—that is, passages of the Bible that needed explanation.

As we shall be exploring some of the Geneva marginal comments in this section, it is appropriate to explain how the text is presented. The biblical text is printed first, along with the note indicators in brackets. These may take the form of letters or numbers, which refer to the annotations that follow. For example, consider the complex argument concerning justification by faith in Paul's letter to the Galatians. Aware that many readers would find difficulty in following

# THE
# NEWE TESTAMENT
## OF OVR LORD
### IESVS CHRIST,

Conferred diligently with the Greke, and beſt appro-
ued tranſlacions in diuers languages.

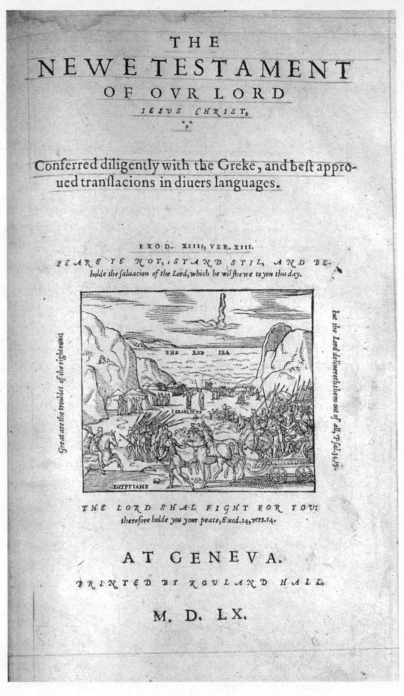

EXOD. XIIII, VER. XIII.

FEARE YE NOT, STAND STIL, AND BE-
holde the ſaluacion of the Lord, which he wil ſhewe to you this day.

Great are the troubles of the righteous:

THE RED SEA

but the Lord deliuereth them out of al, Pſal.34.19.

ISRAELITES

EGYPTIANS

THE LORD SHAL FIGHT FOR YOV:
therefore holde you your peace, Exod.14, vers.14.

# AT GENEVA.

PRINTED BY ROVLAND HALL

# M. D. LX.

THE TITLE PAGE OF THE GENEVA
NEW TESTAMENT

the argument—and hence were likely to misunderstand Paul at critical points—the Geneva Bible offered detailed comments on critical verses; or, to use its own phrase, "most profitable annotations upon the hard places." A good example is provided by Galatians 2:17.

> {4} *But if, while {s} we seek to be justified by Christ, we ourselves also are found sinners, is therefore Christ the minister of sin? God forbid.*
>
> *(4) Before he goes any further, he meets with the objection which abhorred this doctrine of free justification by faith, because, they say, men are by this means withdrawn from the performing of good works. And in this sort is the objection: if sinners should be justified through Christ by faith without the Law, Christ would approve sinners, and should as it were exhort them to sin by his ministry. Paul answers that this conclusion is false, because Christ destroys sin in the believers: for so, he says, do men flee to Christ through the terror and fear of the Law, that being acquitted from the curse of the Law and justified they may be saved by him. And in addition he together begins in them by little and little that strength and power of his which destroys sin: to the end that this old man being abolished by the power of Christ crucified, Christ may live in them, and they may consecrate themselves to God. Therefore if any man give himself to sin after he has received the Gospel, let him not accuse Christ nor the Gospel, but himself, for he destroys the work of God in himself.*
>
> *(s) He goes from justification to sanctification, which is another benefit we receive from Christ, if we lay hold of him by faith.*

It can be seen immediately that the marginal notes anticipate the difficulties that might be encountered by readers, and provide clarification to ensure that misunderstandings did not arise. By providing such explanations in plain English, the Geneva Bible secured its position as the market leader—assuming, of course, that there was to be an open market for translations of the Bible in England.

## THE INITIAL ELIZABETHAN RESPONSE
## TO THE GENEVA BIBLE

THE RELIGIOUS REFORMS introduced by Elizabeth I in 1559 included explicit demands both that an English Bible should be set up in every parish church and that no person should be inhibited from reading such Bibles. But which version? The Great Bible, which appeared in 1539, was last printed in 1553, shortly before Mary Tudor's accession, and it seems that many copies of this printing survived Mary's reign. There is ample documentary evidence that this version was initially installed in churches; demand was such that it was reprinted in folio editions in 1562 and 1566. Aware of the importance of the religious reforms introduced by Elizabeth, Whittingham included a dedicatory epistle to the English monarch, praising her explicitly for her many religious virtues. The none-too-subtle subtext of this dedicatory epistle could hardly be missed: Whittingham wanted his to be the Bible of choice for use in churches.

Yet, despite its obvious popular appeal, the Geneva Bible was studiously ignored by the authorities of the Church of England. The truth of the matter is that they felt threatened by it. It was clear that Archbishop Matthew Parker (1504–75) disliked the Geneva Bible, not on account of the translation it offered, but because of the notes that accompanied it. Like Matthew's Bible before it, the Geneva Bible alienated the establishment on account of its marginal notes.

In a letter to William Cecil, dated March 9, 1565, Parker commented that it would "do much good, to have diversity of translations and readings." Parker devised a way to destroy both the sales and influence of the Geneva Bible. He would produce a translation of the Bible, based on the Great Bible, which would be much more acceptable to the authorities of the Church of England. The translators were given strict instructions: they were only to depart from the Great Bible translation when strictly necessary, and they were to avoid any form of polemical or controversial annotations to the text. It is here that we can see Parker's real concerns about the Geneva Bible.

Writing to Elizabeth I in 1566, Parker complained bitterly about the "diverse prejudicial notes" of earlier translations—a clear reference to the annotations of the Geneva Bible. What Parker disliked, of course, was much appreciated by his many critics—and the reading public, who obstinately kept on buying the Geneva Bible.

Parker's anxiety was that the Geneva Bible's annotations in effect offered an interpretation of certain biblical passages that contradicted those found in the *Books of Homilies*—in effect, a collection of "authorized sermons," dating from the reign of Edward VI, which were intended to be read aloud in churches. Concerned about maintaining control over what was taught in the churches throughout the realm of England, Parker intended to ensure that the Bibles set up in churches for the purpose of reading aloud, and sermons preached upon themes or biblical passages, were in line with the teachings of the newly established Church of England.

The Elizabethan Settlement of Religion was a delicate creature. This Settlement of Religion can perhaps best be thought of as reaching a judicious compromise between the various religious factions within England at the time. The English national church would have an essentially Catholic structure—for example, retaining clerical robes and bishops—while adopting a basically Protestant set of beliefs, as would be set out in the Thirty-Nine Articles of Religion in 1563. These articles, issued under Elizabeth I, would be bound into prayer books to ensure that clergy were familiar with them. The Settlement was a compromise, and was widely recognized as such. Protestants were inclined to accept it on the basis of the hope that the concessions made to them were merely the first phase in a process that would lead to other, more significant victories later. As it happened, these hopes—which had been encouraged by Elizabeth as a means of securing assent to her proposals—were to prove unfounded. In private, Elizabeth initially seems to have seen religion as a matter of no great importance, provided that it did not interfere with national life. She declined to "make windows into men's souls," and argued that "there is only one Jesus Christ and all the rest is a dispute over trifles."

External conformity suited her purposes well. Many historians have argued that Elizabeth's Settlement of Religion probably spared England a religious war, such as that which ravaged France in the second half of the sixteenth century.

Elizabeth had indeed introduced some Protestant ideas into the Church of England. The Thirty-Nine Articles of Religion, for example, took a strongly Protestant position on matters of doctrine, rejecting many traditional Catholic teachings. Yet Elizabeth wanted to reassure Catholics within England, not least because she feared the possibility of a civil war that might end up by dragging England into conflict with its powerful Catholic neighbours, such as Spain. She, therefore, retained many more traditional Catholic practices and institutions, including bishops and the requirement that clergy should wear robes. It was an uneasy balance, which tried to achieve peace by placating both Protestants and Catholics. Inevitably, it was an unstable situation, which could easily fall apart if controversy were to break out.

Like an ecosystem, the Elizabethan Settlement of Religion included complex checks and balances to ensure that no religious party could gain control of the church or plunge it into the bitter religious controversies of an earlier period. As Parker well knew, England needed religious stability. The Geneva Bible, by offering an attractive and coherent commentary on the Bible, based on a strongly Protestant theological position, could easily undermine that stability. Those who wanted to direct the Church of England in a much more specifically Protestant direction would find ample ammunition for their campaign in the marginal notes of the Geneva Bible.

That Parker's anxieties over the Geneva Bible were well founded can be seen from the behaviour of its chief translator, William Whittingham, on his return to England from Geneva. In 1563, Whittingham was appointed Dean of Durham. His attempts to introduce the radical Protestantism he knew from Geneva to this traditionally conservative northern cathedral met with resistance and controversy, eventually forcing the Archbishop of York to intervene in 1578. Whittingham had shown that the fragile truce between the warring religious factions in

England could easily be blown apart, leading to tension and anger. The archbishop knew that he had to act to preserve religious stability; his only option was to sack Whittingham.

As things worked out, the archbishop's efforts to remove him from office ultimately proved unnecessary. Whittingham died in 1579. Yet the precarious nature of the Elizabethan Settlement had been more than adequately demonstrated through the episode. From now on, anything that might destabilize the Elizabethan equilibrium was vigorously resisted by the church establishment.

## THE TRIUMPH OF THE GENEVA BIBLE

BUT OFFICIAL OPPOSITION to the Geneva Bible could not prevent it from becoming the most widely read Bible of the Elizabethan, and subsequently the Jacobean, era. It may never have secured official sanction, yet it needed no such endorsement by the political or religious establishment to gain enthusiastic and widespread acceptance. Even though the book initially had to be imported from Geneva— English printings of the work having been prohibited by nervous archbishops—it still outsold its rivals. Throughout his long period as Archbishop of Canterbury, Matthew Parker (1559–75) was able to block any efforts by the Stationers' Company (The Worshipful Company of Stationers was a professional guild that controlled the publishing of manuscripts, and later printed books, in England) to print the Geneva Bible, and ensured that the monopoly for printing an officially approved translation (the Bishops' Bible of 1568) remained with Richard Jugge.

Parker was succeeded as archbishop by Edmund Grindal, with important consequences for the monopoly on Bible productions. Up to this point, Jugge, who held the office of "Queen's Printer," had been able to rely on the support of the ecclesiastical establishment for his monopoly on the printing of English Bibles. With Parker's death, power shifted within the court. Sir Francis Walsingham—Elizabeth's Secretary of State—and Grindal conspired to undermine Jugge's stranglehold on the market for Bibles. While allowing Jugge to retain his monopoly on large (e.g., folio) Bibles, Grindal allowed others to produce smaller (e.g., quarto) Bibles. Christopher Barker had produced a version of the Geneva Bible in duodecimo in 1575; he now published editions in quarto and folio, ensuring that the Geneva version was available in formats suitable for both private devotion and public worship in churches. The basic format of the original Geneva edition was generally followed, although later English and Scottish printings occasionally used "black letter" rather than roman type, perhaps reflecting the more conservative taste of a British readership. On Jugge's death in 1577, his monopoly passed to Barker. There was now no possibility that the Geneva Bible could be toppled from its position.

One of Barker's more significant innovations was the production of a composite version of the Geneva Bible, which included modifications to the translation of the New Testament, based on the work of Laurence Tomson, a member of the English community of Marian exiles, and his notes to the New Testament, which were in turn based on commentaries by the Genevan theologian Theodore Beza. The first such composite Bible appeared in 1578, and was followed by many editions over the period 1587–1616. Tomson produced few annotations and marginal notes to the Book of Revelation, and remedied this deficiency in 1594 with a set of notes to this book based on the writings of the Huguenot writer Franciscus Junius. By the turn of the century, there were, therefore, a number of variants of the text, all entitled to style themselves "the Geneva Bible."

Barker's publishing extravaganza came to an end with the death of Grindal (1583). Anxious because of the growing influence of the Geneva Bible, which was now readily available in several formats, Grindal's successor John Whitgift ordered Barker to begin publishing more compact editions of the Bishops' Bible. Whitgift further commanded that only the Bishops' Bible was permitted to be used in the public services of the churches. Yet Whitgift's decrees had limited impact. Between 1583 and 1603, fifty-eight editions of the Bible were published in England—seven of the Bishops' Bible and fifty-one of the Geneva edition. There was no doubt about which version had secured the loyalty of English Protestants, whatever senior church figures had to say about it. Paradoxically, the translation was so good that even establishment figures found themselves drawn to it. Having done all he could to limit the influence of the Geneva Bible, Archbishop Whitgift found himself using the Geneva Bible in his heated controversy with the Puritan writer Thomas Cartwright. The irony of this was lost on neither writer.

By 1600, the Geneva Bible had become the Bible of choice of English-speaking Protestants. It was entirely natural that John Knox, the moving light of the Scottish Reformation, should have pressed for the introduction of the Geneva Bible as the authorized version of the reformed Church of Scotland. Had not this Bible been translated in Geneva, by people he knew and trusted? And did not its marginal notes offer a theology of which he thoroughly approved?

As England's reputation as a Protestant nation became a matter of national pride, especially following the defeat of the Spanish Armada, the views of the Geneva Bible came to resonate ever more closely with the consciously Protestant national identity. England was a Protestant nation, and the Geneva Bible was its sacred book. It was natural that England's greatest living playwright, William Shakespeare, in penning his dramas, should make use of the Geneva Bible, rather than the official translations urged on the English people by the church authorities.

When James I came to the throne of England in 1603, having previously ruled a fiercely Protestant Scotland, many believed that the sales and influence of the Geneva Bible could only increase, eventually leading to radical changes in the English church and state. Perhaps the new king of England might even authorize the Geneva Bible, giving it the royal seal of approval? Might not the Geneva Bible become the King James Bible?

In fact, the new king of England had no interest in promoting the Geneva Bible. His secret agenda was to destroy, discredit, or displace it—whichever could be achieved most rapidly.

# 6

# A PURITAN KING?
# THE ACCESSION OF
# KING JAMES

When Elizabeth I died in 1603, she left a nation that had been propelled to global greatness by the events of her long reign. England's rise to international power, which dates from the second half of the sixteenth century, is widely attributed to the national stability that developed under the long reign of Elizabeth I (1558–1603). Religious stability was an essential element of Elizabeth's programme of national reconstruction.

Elizabeth came to the throne of England in the aftermath of the disastrous reign of Mary Tudor, which had seen widespread persecution of Protestants in England. The assassination of the Protestant statesman William of Orange by Roman Catholics led many to fear that Elizabeth would suffer the same fate. In 1570, the Pope had specifically released Elizabeth's subjects from any allegiance to her— in effect, offering them a licence to depose her, and replace her with someone more sympathetic to Rome. The obvious replacement was Mary, Queen of Scots, who was the focus of assassination plots against

Elizabeth, including the Babington Plot of 1586. At Parliament's insistence, Elizabeth ordered Mary's execution in February 1587.

The most important event to secure England's Protestant identity was the decision of Philip II of Spain to defeat English Protestantism, and reconvert England to Roman Catholicism—in effect, to restore the situation as it was under Mary Tudor, to whom Philip had briefly been married. A huge armada—the Spanish word simply means "fleet"—of some 130 ships was assembled in Portugal, and sailed for England in the final days of May 1588. The original intention was to link up with the army of the Duke of Parma at Calais, and then to proceed across the English Channel to invade southern England.

The plan went catastrophically wrong. The armada was intercepted long before Calais, and was harassed by English warships until it finally reached Calais. The Duke of Parma failed to show up with his army. On July 28, English fire ships caused havoc among the anchored Spanish warships. They put to sea, and were engaged at the Battle of Gravelines the following day. Routed, the Spanish decided to abandon any attempt to invade England, and returned home by a circuitous route that took them around the north coasts of Scotland and Ireland. Both severe weather and English attacks took their toll, and the survivors limped home, as defeated as they were demoralized.

The outcome was seen as confirming England's credentials as a Protestant nation. It was also seen as marking a decisive shift of power in Western Europe. Up to that point, Spain had been widely considered as the dominant naval and military power in Europe. The English victory was thus a landmark in English self-confidence. Elizabeth's reign would be celebrated as a golden age, with the queen herself as a symbol of English pride. The names by which she was known—"Good Queen Bess," "the Virgin Queen," and "Gloriana"—pointed to her potent symbolic role as the head of a powerful emerging nation.

Alongside the economic growth, military successes, and increasing sense of national identity and pride that developed under Elizabeth, a new confidence in the English language began to emerge. Elizabeth's reign witnessed the emergence of a major body of English literature. Writers such as Ben Jonson, Christopher Marlowe, Edmund Spenser, William Shakespeare, and Sir Philip Sidney gave the English language some of its most important works of literature.

Yet things were not quite as straightforward as they might seem. Beneath the image of a unified Protestant nation lay serious tensions, of major importance to the origins of the King James Bible.

## THE FAULT LINES: TENSIONS WITHIN LATE ELIZABETHAN PROTESTANTISM

ALTHOUGH HERSELF WISHING religious peace, Elizabeth rapidly found herself caught up in the religious controversies of the age. Many of the English Protestants who had sought exile in the cities of Europe—including Geneva—returned on learning of Mary's death, and began to press for England to become much more explicitly Protestant. Yet England's Roman Catholics had enjoyed the ascendancy during the reign of Mary Tudor, and were not inclined to give up their privileges easily. There was a serious threat of religious strife within England, which could easily lead to foreign invasion—for example, from France. Elizabeth determined to settle the religious question as quickly as possible, and managed to achieve a compromise that offered something to both her Protestant and Catholic subjects. It was, however, an uneasy situation, which could easily become destabilized.

The Elizabethan period was noted for growing religious tensions, arising directly out of the expediencies of the Elizabethan Settlement of Religion. These differences may have been suppressed; nevertheless, they existed, and grew in importance and bitterness as the reign proceeded. As we have seen, Elizabeth's concern was primarily to establish religious peace within her realm, and she was perfectly prepared to compromise over matters she regarded as being of little importance.

The difficulty was that the matters she deemed trifles were

viewed as major issues by others—especially by those Protestants who were dissatisfied with her religious reforms to date. The Puritans were by then emerging as a radical Protestant protest movement, dissatisfied with the compromises which Elizabeth I had forced on her national church. Many in the growing Puritan movement saw issues such as the use of the Prayer Book and clerical dress as being controversial, and were prepared to make them into issues of contention. This point is illustrated by the group of Marian exiles in Geneva, including Thomas Sampson, who were responsible for the Geneva Bible. Sampson returned to England in 1559, and was appointed Dean of Christ Church, Oxford.

Elizabeth laid down the rule that clergy should wear vestments at public church services. In effect, this meant returning to something like the form of dress worn by clergy before the Reformation. For Elizabeth, this was not an issue of great importance, yet one that she believed would help reassure Catholics within England—whose support she might need in the event of a national emergency. The returning Marian exiles saw it as a symbol of Roman Catholicism, which they regarded as totally out of place in a reformed church. Matthew Parker, Archbishop of Canterbury, tried to negotiate a compromise in 1564. When this failed, he issued a series of precise instructions for clerical dress, which insisted that clergy should wear vestments, such as a surplice.

For Sampson, this was nothing less than a degeneration into superstition and idolatry. He wrote to his Protestant colleagues in Zurich, seeking guidance. Peter Martyr Vermigli—formerly Regius Professor of Divinity at Oxford—had no doubts. Sampson should denounce the vestments, yet wear them if they were made a condition of office. Otherwise, those hostile to the Reformation would be promoted over him, and he would lose any chance of affecting English religious life from a position of influence.

This was but one of the many expressions of discontent over the Elizabethan Settlement. Puritans found the use of the Prayer Book objectionable. It obliged the clergy to say and do certain things that

Puritans found to be incompatible with the Bible—such as kneeling to receive the bread at communion, or making the sign of the cross at baptism. They had serious difficulties with the idea that the monarch was the supreme governor of the church. The more the Zurich Protestants learned of Elizabeth's religious measures, the less they liked them. Heinrich Bullinger wrote in anger to sympathize with his English colleagues. The demands to wear vestments and other such outrageous things were, he declared, "fabricated in the school of anti-Christ"; they were "the restored relics of a new popery."

Tension grew. The radical Protestant party might well have been defeated politically through measures introduced in the final decade of Elizabeth's reign by Archbishop Whitgift; theologically, however, Puritanism was clearly becoming an increasingly powerful and sophisticated presence in England. By the end of Elizabeth's long reign, the most serious religious tensions within England no longer had anything to do with those between Protestants and Catholics. The new battles concerned two different styles of English Protestantism—Anglicanism and Puritanism.

Anglicanism stressed the close link between the church and the monarch, and valued the role of the queen as the "supreme governor" of the Church of England. It affirmed the importance of the Prayer Book as a means of enforcing religious uniformity throughout England, and hence ensuring national unity. This approach was strongly defended by John Whitgift, who became Archbishop of Canterbury in October 1583. In one of his most important early sermons, Whitgift affirmed the principle of royal supremacy and the necessity of obedience to those in authority—including princes, bishops, and magistrates. He was perfectly prepared to enforce conformity to the teachings and practices of the state church in the courts. Anglicanism was the state religion of England. English national identity, in Whitgift's view, could be sustained and guaranteed only by the English national church.

The Puritans thought otherwise, and longed for a radical overhaul of the English church. They looked to Geneva, rather than

Canterbury, for inspiration and guidance. It must be appreciated that "Puritanism" was a diverse movement in the late Elizabethan period. Some Puritans were content to put up with clerical dress and the use of the Prayer Book, provided that they were allowed to adopt a Calvinist theology and develop a preaching ministry. Others believed that the Protestant religion, as they understood it, demanded a total reform of the church to bring it into line with Genevan practice and the abolition of the monarchy.

In the 1580s, Geneva became for Elizabethan Puritans what Moscow was to British communism during the 1930s—a symbol of their aspirations, and a source of the ideas and support that might bring them about. The Geneva Bible thus came to be a potent symbol of the reform that they believed lay ahead. If Elizabeth would not allow them their demands, what of her successor? She could not live forever. It was just a matter of time before an opportune moment for radical change would arrive.

Elizabeth might well have suppressed serious religious dissent within her realm. But what would happen after her death? Was there not a serious danger of radical religious upheaval just over the horizon? This was certainly what many members of the Anglican establishment feared; it was also, of course, precisely what many Puritans were hoping for. When it was announced that Elizabeth would be succeeded by James VI of Scotland, English Puritans believed their moment had come. To understand why, we need to consider the question of the succession in a little more detail.

## THE SUCCESSION:
## FROM ELIZABETH I TO JAMES I

THE STABILITY AND prosperity of England seemed to many to be a direct result of the wise rule of Elizabeth. It was no accident that the date of her accession was celebrated as a national holiday in England for two centuries. But who would succeed Elizabeth on her death? Elizabeth had never married, and died childless. Henry VIII had gone to immense pains to ensure a smooth transition of power to his children after his death. But with the death of the last of his children, the benefits of Henry's careful planning came to an end. As England's peace and prosperity were so closely linked with the person of the monarch, the question of her successor was of critical importance. As Elizabeth had no children, it was not clear who her successor would be.

The eyes of many fell upon the son of Mary Queen of Scots, who had ascended the Scottish throne in 1567. James VI had shown himself to be a staunch supporter of Protestantism in Scotland, and could be relied upon to safeguard Elizabeth's Protestant legacy. Other possible contenders for the English throne were regarded with mistrust on account of their more Catholic religious beliefs.

In one sense, James was the obvious choice to succeed Elizabeth. None of the children of Henry VIII had produced children; it was, therefore, necessary to seek the heir to the English throne from the descendents of Henry VIII's father, Henry VII. As the senior living descendent of Henry VII, James was strategically placed for the succession. Henry VII's elder daughter, Margaret Tudor, had married James IV of Scotland, and James VI was descended from this line through his mother, Mary Queen of Scots.

Yet there were complications. Henry VIII's will, which had established the rules for his successors, had laid down that no alien could succeed to the throne of England. As James was born in Scotland—and hence was an "alien" by the terms of Henry's will—he was apparently disqualified from the succession. Furthermore, that same will had given priority to the descendents of Henry VII's *younger* daughter—Mary Tudor—over those of his elder daughter, Margaret Tudor. Yet the descendents on this side of the family were conspicuously unpromising, not least on account of a string of questionable marriages and children of dubious legitimacy.

In the end, James succeeded to the English throne because he was the only obvious viable candidate. He was male, Protestant, and possessed both rank and experience of government. James had a strong

PORTRAIT OF KING JAMES I BY
CORNELIUS JOHNSON (1593–1661),
ENGRAVED BY R. WHITE

hereditary claim to the English throne, and already had children—so the question of who would succeed James would not be as difficult as in the case of the childless Elizabeth.

One of Elizabeth's earliest appointments had been William Cecil—later Lord Burghley—as her Secretary of State. Such was the level of confidence that Cecil enjoyed with the queen that it was widely assumed that he would determine the queen's choice of her successor. However, Cecil died in August 1598. An immediate power vacuum resulted. A struggle for power broke out between Cecil's younger son and presumed political heir, and Elizabeth's favourite, the Earl of Essex (Robert Devereux). Initially, Essex seemed well placed to ensure that his candidate for the succession would gain the upper hand. He had already approached James VI of Scotland, and had pressed Elizabeth to name him as her successor. So far Elizabeth had declined to listen to him, but he was confident that she would eventually yield on this point.

In 1599 Essex accepted the position of Lord Lieutenant of Ireland, which gave him command of the queen's army in Ireland at a time when rebellion had broken out. This proved to be an unwise move, in that it took him away from court at a critical time. In his absence, Robert Cecil was able to secure his hold on power. Realizing his error, Essex returned to London without permission, and began to organize a rebellion against Elizabeth.

James VI realized that Essex's rebellion could destroy his chances of succeeding to the English throne; there were rumours that James and Essex were in collusion over a possible military solution to the question of the succession. Noting that power was now firmly in the hands of Robert Cecil, James sent his close friend, the Earl of Mar, to London to secure Cecil's support. It seems that Cecil concluded that his own position would be best served if James were to succeed Elizabeth, and agreed to support James when the time came. Cecil was as good as his word, and in 1603 secured James's accession to the throne as James I of England. James created Cecil a baron in 1603, a viscount in 1604, and finally made him Earl of Salisbury in 1605.

The news that James VI would become king of England galvanized English religious activists, both Protestant and Roman Catholics. Their agenda had been consistently ignored by Elizabeth. They now saw an opportunity to press for radical changes in the English religious situation. Was not James VI of Scotland the monarch of a Protestant nation? And might not the situation be ripe for religious change? Might not the new king allow the implementation of a more radical Protestant agenda that Elizabeth had so carefully evaded?

In fact, things were not quite so straightforward, as we shall see.

## THE NEW KING:
## A CRITIC OF PURITANISM

JAMES VI HAD previously reigned over Scotland, in which the religious ideas that had been championed at Geneva had gained the ascendancy. English Puritans looked enviously north of the border to the happy situation enjoyed by their Scottish brethren. The triumph of Calvinism in Scotland seemed to them to be an ideal to which they could only hope to aspire during the long reign of Elizabeth I. The death of Elizabeth and the announcement that James VI of Scotland was to succeed her caused undisguised delight in Puritan circles in England. Their hour had come. England seemed set to become a properly Protestant nation, in which the compromises of the Church of England would be put to an end.

Yet the reality of the situation was very different. James disliked Presbyterianism, believing passionately that his royal authority was dependent upon bishops. "No bishops, no king" summarized admirably his view of the interrelationship of church and state. It is true that the Scottish church (or "kirk") had adopted the Presbyterian system of church government, developed by Calvin in Geneva, under reformers such as John Knox and Andrew Melville. Yet whatever his public obligations may have been to support this system, in private James VI had serious misgivings about Presbyterianism, which had no place for any bishops. He lobbied for the retention of episcopal government of the Scottish church. James believed that Presbyterianism was linked with egalitarianism and republicanism—after all, had not the city of Geneva declared itself to be a republic after overthrowing its former rulers? He preferred an episcopal system, not least because of its more positive associations with the monarchy.

His views on this matter were shaped to no small extent by some unpleasant experiences with Scottish presbyteries, particularly under Andrew Melville, a Scottish presbyterian who had taught at the Genevan Academy, and formed a close personal friendship with Calvin's protégé, Theodore Beza. At a heated encounter between the king and senior churchmen at Falkland Palace in October 1596, Melville had physically taken hold of James, and accused him of being "God's silly vassal." Melville pointedly declared that while they would support James as king in public, in private they all knew perfectly well that Christ was the true king in Scotland, and his kingdom was the kirk—a kingdom in which James was a mere member, not a lord or head. James was shaken by this physical and verbal assault, not least because it suggested that Melville and his allies posed a significant threat to the Scottish throne.

The simple fact of the matter is that James had not the slightest intention of promoting a Puritan or Presbyterian agenda in England. He thoroughly detested what he had seen in Scotland, and did not wish to encounter the same difficulties in England. He much preferred the Anglican system of church government, seeing the institution of episcopacy as a safeguard to the monarchy.

English Puritans, who were not aware of James's strong views on this matter, naturally assumed that they were about to receive a monarch who would not merely take them seriously, but would actually be sympathetic to their agenda. It would take some time before the real state of affairs became clear—and James made the most of that window of opportunity to neutralize the Puritan threat, while pretending to honour its concerns.

Yet James's dislike of Scottish Presbyterianism extended beyond its ideas and personalities, and embraced the translation of the Bible that had become the favoured translation of the Scottish church. The translation in question? The Geneva Bible.

## THE NEW KING:
## AN ENEMY OF THE GENEVA BIBLE

BY THE END of Elizabeth's reign, the position and influence of the Geneva Bible seemed to have become unassailable. It was the Bible of choice of England's increasingly confident Protestants. Yet with the accession of James I, a new and unexpected factor entered into the situation. By January 1604, it had become clear that James had taken an intense personal dislike to this Bible. The reason for his dislike is not difficult to discern.

As we saw earlier, the marginal notes to the Geneva Bible did more than provide theological elucidation at points of difficulty—the "most profitable annotations upon the hard places" mentioned on the title page of the work. They offered political comments on the text, which could easily be applied to the political situation under James I—and James cordially detested what he found in those notes.

The ultimate grounds for James's hostility toward the Geneva Bible was the challenge its marginal notes posed to his passionate belief in the doctrine of the "divine right of kings." While the ultimate origins of the theory of the divine right of kings can be traced back to the mists of the early Middle Ages, it had received a new sense of direction under James I. While still James VI of Scotland, James had written some works that showed a keen interest in the divine validation of royal authority, subject to certain limitations. These ideas were set out especially in his *True Law of Free Monarchies* (1598), but can be summarized neatly in the opening sonnet of his *Basilikon Doron* (also 1598):

> *God gives not Kings the style of Gods in vain,*
> *For on his throne his Sceptre do they sway;*
> *And as their subjects ought them to obey,*
> *So Kings should fear and serve their God again.*

The language and imagery of this work suggest a God-King who is endowed with divine authority for his work on earth. The language is at times quite extravagant, such as the references to kings as "the breathing images of God," or the suggestion that even God himself pleases to refer to kings as divine. It is perhaps worth recalling that this work was written at a time when James VI felt himself under severe pressure from radical Presbyterian critics, when it was felt that a none-too-subtle appeal to divine validation might help stem such criticisms.

The theory was widely welcomed by Anglicans, who saw it as a means of ensuring the stability of the monarchy, and hence the position of the established church within England. The theory neatly locked church and king together into a robust circle of mutual support and reinforcement. It was, however, a theory that Puritans regarded as nonbiblical, and looked to the notes of the Geneva Bible for its refutation. They found ample ammunition in those annotations, as will become clear from what follows.

The book of Daniel relates the experience of Daniel and his colleagues, who are portrayed as faithful to God in an alien environment, dominated by a powerful king. Much of the narrative of the book concerns the tensions between the integrities of faith and the realities of life under an autocratic monarch. It is, therefore, little cause for surprise that the Geneva Bible picked up on the importance of this work in relation to the English situation. For example, the sixth chapter deals with Daniel and his companions being thrown into the lions' den for disobeying the king's orders. The text and marginal notes, as set out in 1599, read as follows:

*Daniel 6:22 My God hath sent his angel, and hath shut the lions' mouths, that they have not hurt me: forasmuch as before him {h} innocency was found in me; and also before thee, O king, have I done {i} no hurt.*

*(h) My just cause and uprightness in this thing in which I was charged, is approved by God.*

*(i) For he disobeyed the king's wicked commandment in order to obey God, and so he did no injury to the king, who ought to command nothing by which God would be dishonoured.*

The implications of these annotations would be lost to none. The commandments of kings are to be disobeyed when they conflict with the will of God.

Further comment on the place of a tyrant king can be found in the comments on Daniel 11:36, which speaks of such a king oppressing his people.

*And the {s} king shall do according to his will; and he shall exalt himself, and magnify himself above every god, and shall speak marvellous things against the God of gods, and shall prosper till the indignation {t} be accomplished: for that that is determined shall be done.*

*(s) Because the angels purpose is to show the whole course of the persecutions of the Jews until the coming of Christ, he now speaks of the monarchy of the Romans, which he notes by the name of a king, who were without religion and condemned the true God.*

*(t) So long the tyrants will prevail as God has appointed to punish his people: but he shows that it is but for a time.*

The point being made is that God has raised up such tyrants to punish his people for their sins—but that the days of such tyrants are numbered. It did not take much imagination to apply this comment to the English situation under both James I and his successor, Charles I. God's people—the Puritans—were suffering; yet this was to be seen as a punishment for their sins, which would not last forever. Notice also how the Genevan notes regularly use the word "tyrant" to refer to kings; the King James Bible *never* uses this word—a fact noted with approval as much as relief by many royalists at this point.

James I held that kings had been ordained by God to rule the nations of the world, to promote justice, and to dispense wisdom. It was, therefore, imperative that kings should be respected and obeyed unconditionally and in all circumstances. The ample notes provided by the Geneva Bible taught otherwise. Tyrannical kings should not be obeyed; indeed, there were excellent reasons for suggesting that they should be overthrown.

This can be seen from the Geneva Bible's comments on the story of Moses, who rose from his humble origins as the son of a Hebrew slave in Egypt to become the deliverer of Israel from its captivity. The Geneva Bible introduces this story as follows, taking care to point out its implications for oppressive tyrants:

*After Jacob by God's commandment in Genesis 46:3 had brought his family into Egypt, where they remained for four hundred years, and from seventy people grew to an infinite number so that the king and the country endeavoured both by tyranny and cruel slavery to suppress them: the Lord according to his promise in Genesis 15:14 had compassion on his Church, and delivered them, but plagued their enemies in most strange and varied ways. The more the tyranny of the wicked raged against his Church, the more his heavy judgments increased against them, till Pharaoh and his army were drowned in the sea, which gave an entry and passage to the children of God.*

According to Exodus 1, Pharaoh was anxious concerning the growing strength of the Hebrews in Egypt, and ordered that measures should be taken to restrict their growth and influence. One of those restrictive measures was a command that midwives were to ensure that all newborn male Hebrew children were killed. The midwives chose to ignore this, and deceived the Egyptian authorities by suggesting that Hebrew mothers gave birth before they could arrive. The translation of this in the Geneva Bible is here provided, along with its comment on the deception practised by the midwives. On being asked why male children were not killed as they had been ordered, the midwives offered the following explanation (Exodus 1:19):

> *And the midwives said unto Pharaoh, Because the Hebrew {g}*
> *women are not as the Egyptian women; for they are lively, and are*
> *delivered ere the midwives come in unto them.*
>
> *(g) Their disobedience in this was lawful, but their deception*
> *is evil.*

The marginal note is clear; the deception practised was morally unacceptable, but it was entirely legal. To deceive tyrants is entirely within the law. In case its readers failed to appreciate this point, the marginal notes stressed that it was Pharaoh who deceived people (Exodus 1:22):

> *And Pharaoh charged all his people, saying, Every son that is born*
> *ye shall {i} cast into the river, and every daughter ye shall save*
> *alive.*
>
> *(i) When tyrants cannot prevail by deceit, they burst into open*
> *rage.*

The suggestion that it was lawful to disobey or deceive kings would hardly have pleased James I of England. Yet it fitted well into the growing trend within Calvinist circles to argue for the resistance to tyrants, whether by force or deception. As radical Protestant factions, such as the Puritans, began to view James as their oppressor, the suggestion that it was lawful to disobey him became increasingly welcome to Puritans and worrying to James.

It is known that James I was also anxious over the marginal comments on 2 Chronicles 15:15–17, which seemed to bear uncomfortably on his own situation.

> *And all Judah rejoiced at the oath: for they had sworn with all*
> *their heart, and sought him with their whole desire; and he was*

*{h} found of them: and the LORD gave them rest round about. And also concerning Maachah the {i} mother of Asa the king, he removed her from being queen, because she had made an idol in a grove: and Asa cut down her idol, and stamped it, and burnt it at the brook Kidron. But the high places were not {k} taken away out of {l} Israel: nevertheless the heart of Asa was {m} perfect all his days.*

*(h) As long as they served him correctly, so long did he preserve and prosper them.*

*(i) Or grandmother, and in this he showed that he lacked zeal, for she should have died both by the covenant, as 2 Chronicles 15:13 and by the law of God, but he gave place to foolish pity and would also seem after a sort to satisfy the law.*

*(k) Which was partly because of lack of zeal on his part, partly through the negligence of his officers and partly by the superstition of the people that all were not taken away.*

*(l) Because God was called the God of Israel, by reason of his promise to Jacob, therefore Israel is sometimes taken for Judah, because Judah was his chief people.*

*(m) In respect to his predecessors.*

The passage describes measures taken by King Asa to eliminate the Canaanite religious practices which had crept into Israel's national life under his predecessors. The passage might be taken to imply that Asa—and, by implication, modern kings who made some attempt to reform the religion of their nation—was to be praised for his actions. The marginal notes ensured that no reader of this passage came away with that impression. Asa was lazy, his officials incompetent or corrupt, and the people were superstitious. And if Asa was "perfect," this was only in comparison to those who came before him.

Most interesting of all, the marginal comments on the fate of Asa's mother merit close attention. The passage mentions that Asa deposed his mother for her idolatry, and destroyed the idol she had created. The marginal comments are quite indignant on this matter. Asa "lacked zeal." If he had behaved properly, he would have executed his mother. Instead, he was overcome by sentimentality, and failed to do his duty. As James I's mother—Mary, Queen of Scots—had been executed by Elizabeth I, it is not difficult to understand why he found this comment slightly painful to read. Yet the implications of the passage for the monarchy are perhaps more important: the king is not above the law, and is required to discharge his religious duties without regard for "foolish pity." The king, according to the Geneva Bible, was accountable for his actions. It was not a view that James I cared for.

The notion of the divine right of kings was often defended from Psalm 105:15. In the King James Bible, this would read as follows: "Touch not mine anointed, and do my prophets no harm." This was argued by many Anglicans to be a reference to the king. After all, was not the king anointed at his coronation, and thus designated as God's anointed one? Such ideas were developed in detail in the anonymous 1642 treatise *The Sovereignty of Kings*.

The Geneva Bible had little time for such ideas, as it made clear in its comments on this verse:

> *Psalm 105:15 [Saying], Touch not mine {h} anointed, and do my {i} prophets no harm.*
>
> *(h) Those whom I have sanctified to be my people.*
>
> *(i) Meaning, the old fathers, to whom God showed himself plainly, and who set forth his word.*

The Genevan notes argued that the term "anointed" was to be understood to refer to God's people as a whole. This was picked up by a series of critics of the "divine right" theory, such as Edmund Ludlow in his *Voice from the Watch Tower*. The text was thus interpreted in a way that made no reference whatsoever to the "divine right of kings."

According to the Geneva Bible the text was actually, if anything, a *criticism* of kings, in that their right to harm the people of God was being absolutely denied.

In short, the Geneva Bible undermined whatever biblical basis there might have been for the idea of "the divine right of kings." As this notion was highly significant in James's understanding of his role in both church and state, he would have reacted with horror to any challenge to it. As a result, James now had a personal agenda—to rid England of what he regarded as the baleful influence of the Geneva Bible and its detestable marginal notes. It was, in his view, the "worst of all" of the English translations.

Yet when James I came to the throne of England in 1603, the position of the Geneva Bible seemed absolutely secure. It had outsold and outperformed all its rivals. It was the version of the Bible that had been used by Shakespeare in his dramas. How could it conceivably be toppled from its place of eminence? The growing sales and influence of this Bible seemed to be beyond James's control. The future of both the English monarchy and the church could depend upon eliminating this most turbulent of Bible translations. But what could be done to topple it from its place of honour?

# 7

# THE DECISION
# TO TRANSLATE:
# THE HAMPTON COURT
# CONFERENCE

E ven as he travelled to London in preparation for his coronation, James found himself under pressure from the English Puritans. They had long been irritated by what they regarded as the compromises of the Elizabethan Settlement of 1559. Elizabeth had retained both bishops and the distinctive robes of the clergy. These were widely seen as vestiges of the popery Puritans had hoped would be eliminated from England. Under Elizabeth, Puritans had few options at their disposal. Most chose to remain within the Church of England, putting up with what they regarded as its inconsistencies, and waiting for the dawn of a new era, when a truly reformed church could be created. Elizabeth's long reign of more than forty-five years caused them considerable distress. Her death in 1603 seemed to throw open the door to Puritan aspirations.

The Puritans were encouraged in this hope by a number of factors, particularly their belief that James VI's own religious views were similar to their own. Many English Puritans, therefore, looked to James as someone who was favourable to an established Presbyterian Church, along the lines set out by Calvin for Geneva, and believed that he would be sympathetic to their demands for a full reformation of the English church. Might not the vision of the Genevan exiles be fulfilled under James, who had earlier given such public support to the Protestant reformer John Knox? It was decided to strike a blow for the Puritan cause at the earliest possible moment, before James formally assumed power in London.

## THE LOBBYING BEGINS: THE PURITAN PETITION

WHILE JOURNEYING SOUTH from Scotland in 1603, James was met by a Puritan delegation and presented with the "Millenary Petition," so called since it was signed by more than one thousand ministers of the Church of England. The authors were clearly aware that James had at least some misgivings concerning their agenda—James had earlier written of Puritans as "pests"—and went out of their way to stress their loyalty to both king and country. They had, they declared, served their church faithfully, despite their serious misgivings concerning its practices; the time had now come to change things.

> *Now we, to the number of more than a thousand, of your Majesty's subjects and ministers, all groaning as under a common burden of human rites and ceremonies, do with one joint consent humble ourselves at your Majesty's feet to be eased and relieved in this behalf. Our humble suit then unto your Majesty is, that of these offences following, some may be removed, some amended, some qualified.*

They then listed four broad areas in which they demanded reforms, in particular the removal of the "burden of human rites and ceremonies" with which they were laden. These included the practice of making the sign of the cross in baptism, the wearing of clerical dress, using a ring in the marriage service, and bowing at the name of

Jesus. All these were unbiblical, they argued, and, therefore, could not be required of any minister of the church. The signatories insisted that they did not want "disorderly innovation but a due and godly reformation," and requested that James should give them an opportunity to set out their concerns, either in writing or by means of a "conference among the learned." The Millenary Petition had asserted that its signatories believed that they would be able to show that their criticisms of abuses were justified, if they were granted a hearing by the king.

> *These, with such other abuses yet remaining and practised in the Church of England, we are able to shew not to be agreeable to the Scriptures, if it shall please your Highness farther to hear us, or more at large by writing to be informed, or by conference among the learned to be resolved. And yet we doubt not but that without any farther process, your Majesty, of whose Christian judgment we have received so good a taste already, is able of yourself to judge of the equity of this cause.*

The bishops of the Church of England were alarmed at these developments, seeing them as presaging a renewal of what had been a relatively quiescent Puritan faction within England. The Puritans, it seemed, had seized the initiative from them, and were in the process of winning James over to their way of thinking. Unease turned to outright panic when they learned that, while still on his way to London, James had decided to end the practice of "impropriate tithes"—a long-standing traditional means of funding bishoprics from parish incomes—in response to Puritan lobbying. The bishops were aghast at this and, at an early meeting with the king, managed to persuade him to abandon the idea. It was, however, an important straw in the wind, which suggested that the new king might well be more sympathetic to the Puritans than the late Gloriana.

Where some despaired for the future, others plotted to change its course. Despite all the ominous signs of an imminent Puritan triumph, one bishop could see how James could be turned against Puritanism. He would win the day.

## RICHARD BANCROFT: ARCHBISHOP IN WAITING

RICHARD BANCROFT WAS one of the most relentless opponents of Puritanism in England. In a famous sermon, preached at St. Paul's Cross, London, in 1589, he declared that the Puritans were "false prophets" who were threatening to destroy the fabric of church and nation. For Bancroft, the facts of the matter were simple. God meant the Church of England to be governed by a monarch and bishops, and that was the end of the matter. Bancroft became indispensable to Archbishop Whitgift in his campaign against Puritan influence within the church by identifying Puritan activists and providing evidence to incriminate them. He came to the notice of Elizabeth I, who appointed him Bishop of London in 1597. The position gave him new opportunities to pursue his anti-Puritan agenda.

The news that James VI of Scotland would succeed Elizabeth caused Bancroft considerable anguish. He knew James only by reputation, and that reputation was inauspicious. His suspicion was that James would convert England to Presbyterianism, and sweep away the bishops—himself included.

Yet Bancroft was aware of James's very high views on the nature of kingship. James had set these views out in his small book *Basilikon Doron* ("The Kingly Gift"), originally written to instruct his son in the responsibilities of kingship. Although first printed in Scotland, the work was published in London within a few days of Elizabeth's death. Those wishing to discover James's views on the nature of kingship had no difficulty in doing so. They would have found that he believed that kingship was a divinely ordained institution. It was equally clear that the English Puritans did not share any such viewpoint. It was in this tension that Bancroft saw his opportunity—and he promptly seized it.

Bancroft's strategy for coping with James was simple. He would

PORTRAIT OF RICHARD BANCROFT

persuade James that the monarchy was dependent upon the episcopacy. Without bishops, there was no future for the monarchy in
England. He would depict both Puritans and Catholics as opponents
of the English monarchy, and the bishops of the Church of England
as guarantors of its future. Bancroft would encourage James to take a
view of the place of the episcopacy that went far beyond anything
that Elizabeth I had envisaged. Elizabeth had never taken the view
that the survival of the English crown depended on the bishops.
Bancroft hoped to talk up the threat to the English crown posed by
Puritanism, and thus to present the bishops as James's only hope for
the long-term survival of the monarchy.

Bancroft, therefore, encouraged an official rhetoric of scorn directed against the opponents of Anglicanism, whether that opposition
came from Protestant or Catholic sources. It was relatively easy for

Bancroft to encourage James to see himself as a figure on the same level as Constantine, the first Christian Roman emperor, who ruled a Christian empire with wisdom and equity. Bancroft argued that the king's real enemies were "Papists" and "Puritans," each having a vested interest in destroying his authority. Only a close working alliance with the bishops would preserve the status quo, and allow James to exercise his (as he saw it) divinely ordained kingly role in state and church.

This view was reinforced by other bishops of the period. Lancelot Andrewes—who would play a key role in the preparation of the King James Bible—preached a remarkable sermon based on Numbers 10:2–3: "Make thee two trumpets of silver . . . And thou shalt have them to assemble the congregation." Andrewes argued that the clear meaning of this verse was that the two trumpets were symbols of church and state, James having authority over each. John King, who became Bishop of London in 1608, succeeding Bancroft, preached a sermon on Song of Songs 8:11: "Solomon had a vineyard in Ball-Hamon: he gave the vineyard unto keepers." According to King, the meaning of this text was perfectly clear. The "vineyard" was the church, and the "keepers" to whom this vineyard was entrusted were the king and his bishops—not a presbytery. Such rhetoric had its desired goal. James became persuaded that his role as the new Constantine could be exercised only with the support of the bishops. "Papists" and "Puritans" posed different, yet equally dangerous, threats to the royal authority in church and state.

Bancroft's influence over James increased significantly with the illness of John Whitgift. Whitgift had served as Archbishop of Canterbury for the latter part of the reign of Elizabeth I. Although he had personally travelled to meet James on the outskirts of London in 1603, and obtained reassurances that James would maintain the Settlement of Religion effected by Elizabeth, it was obvious to all that his days were numbered. There was little doubt as to whom his successor would be. The mantle of Whitgift was widely expected to fall on Bancroft. Yet the final decision rested with James.

Bancroft thus found himself in a pivotal role at the beginning of the new reign. He was strategically placed to shape James's vision of the future of the English church; if James was pleased with what Bancroft proposed, and the way in which he carried it out, Bancroft would succeed Whitgift as Archbishop of Canterbury on his death.

## THE HAMPTON COURT CONFERENCE

BANCROFT'S FIRST MAJOR success came in the aftermath of James's hasty promise to the Puritans to abolish "impropriate tithes." In the event, after somewhat strained consultations with his bishops, James decided not to implement his somewhat precipitate decision to end the tithing practice. Nevertheless, his concern for religious peace and stability led him to propose a conference at which Anglican and Puritan representatives could set out their concerns, with a view to achieving a resolution of religious tensions—tensions that were far worse than James had previously realized. Prudence seemed to him to dictate a conciliatory attitude toward the Puritans.

On October 24, 1603, James issued a proclamation stating that he had convened a conference to be attended by himself, the Privy Council, and various "bishops and other learned men" to deal with these issues at the palace of Hampton Court in January of the following year. This conference was to prove of decisive importance in bringing the King James Bible into being.

Yet it was unquestionably a tactical blunder, one that alarmed his bishops and created false hopes within the Puritan faction. Nothing ferments rebellion more than frustrated hopes. James's incautious decision must be seen as having created a serious tension between what the Puritans anticipated, and what they actually got. Puritan hopes for the Hampton Court Conference were high. James had agreed to consider their complaints—something that Elizabeth had resolutely refused to do.

The bishops of the Church of England were now seriously alarmed. James I seemed to be both sympathetic to Puritanism and politically naive. There was every possibility that he might give the

Puritans the confidence and sense of direction they had so desperately lacked under Elizabeth. The future of the English national church—not to mention their own rather comfortable and lucrative positions—seemed under threat. The English Parliament was now dominated by Puritans, which gave them a major influence over English public life. What could be done?

On Thursday January 12, 1604, James summoned ten of his senior bishops to explain to them what he proposed. The Hampton Court Conference would be convened "for the reformation of some things amiss in ecclesiastical matters."

The conference was heavily weighted toward the established church. The Archbishop of Canterbury was joined by the bishops of Carlisle, Chichester, Durham, London, Peterborough, St. David's, Winchester, and Worcester. The six cathedral deans presented included the deans of Westminster Abbey and St. Paul's Cathedral. When the king's Privy Council is taken into account, there were nineteen representatives of the establishment; only four Puritans were invited to attend.

It is important to note that the Puritans were not allowed to nominate their own representatives. Perhaps fearing the identity and militancy of the preferred Puritan nominees, James and his advisers carefully selected more compliant members of the Puritan constituency. John Reynolds (or "Rainolds") was President of Corpus Christi College, Oxford; Laurence Chadderton was Master of Emmanuel College, Cambridge, at that time known for its Puritan sympathies. These were joined by John Knewstubs, Fellow of St. John's College, Cambridge, and Thomas Sparke, Minister of Bletchley in Buckinghamshire.

The conference opened on Saturday January 14 with what one observer termed "a very admirable speech of an hour long, at least," in which James made it clear that he saw himself, as king, as having a decisive role in the affairs of the church. He regarded this to be well established by historical precedent.

*It is no novel device, but according to the example of all Christian princes, for Kings to take the first course for the establishing of the Church both in doctrine and policy. To this the very heathen related in their proverb a Jove principium. Particularly in this land, King Henry VIII towards to the end of his reign altered much, King Edward VI more, Queen Mary reversed all, and lastly Queen Elizabeth (of famous memory) settled religion as it now standeth. Herein I am happier than they, because they were fain to alter all things they found established, whereas I see yet no such cause to change as confirm what I find settled already.*

The cautious note sounded in these words indicated James's diplomatic approach to the difficult questions facing the conference—specifically, the concerns expressed in the Millennary Petition. James noted the substantial achievement of Elizabeth in settling the religious profile of England, and hinted that he had no particular concern to change matters unnecessarily. There would be no radical revision of the stability that Elizabeth had achieved; James wished to "confirm" what he felt "settled already."

Yet a reform agenda was clearly called for, and James was perfectly prepared to take on the issues that had engendered such discontent. Signalling his concern to promote peace, James affirmed his intention to make changes where these were appropriate.

*I assure you we have not called this assembly for any innovation, for we acknowledge the government ecclesiastical as it now is, to have been approved by manifold blessings from God himself, both for the increase of the Gospel, and with a most happy and glorious peace. Yet because nothing can be so absolutely ordered, but something may be added thereunto, and corruption in any state (as in the body of man) will insensibly grow, either through time or persons, and because we have received many complaints, since our first entrance into this kingdom, of many disorders, and much disobedience to the laws, with a great falling away to popery; our purpose therefore is, like a good physician, to examine and try the complaints, and fully to remove the occasions thereof, if scandalous; cure them, if dangerous.*

The topics to be discussed were grouped together under three general headings, as follows:

*First, concerning the* Book of Common Prayer, *and divine service used in this church.*
*Second,* excommunication *in the ecclesiastical courts.*
*Third, the* providing of fit and able ministers for Ireland.

It is important to note that no mention is made of any proposal for a new translation of the Bible.

The opening debates focused on sections of the Prayer Book, especially those stipulating practices that the Puritans regarded as little more than popery by another name. James proved to be a winsome and skilful negotiator. One particularly illuminating exchange concerned Puritan objections to a phrase in the Prayer Book marriage service, in which John Reynolds—the acknowledged leader of the Puritan faction—instanced the words spoken by the husband to his wife: "with my body, I thee worship." Only God, he argued, should be worshipped; these words ought, therefore, to be changed.

James responded by agreeing that, at least at first sight, this indeed seemed an unusual, if not improper, practice. However, since his arrival in England, he had discovered that the English were in the habit of using the term in a variety of contexts. For example, he had heard the phrase "a gentleman of worship" used as a term of commendation, without any unacceptable theological implications. He then turned to Reynolds, and added, with a smile: "If you had a good wife yourself, you would think all the honour and worship you would do her were well bestowed." After examining all the Puritan objections to certain passages in the Prayer Book, he declared them to be without adequate foundation, and suggested they move on to other topics.

The Puritans soon found that they were at something of a disadvantage. They had perhaps taken it for granted that, since their religious views were so close to the Scottish Presbyterianism that James had known and endorsed as James VI of Scotland, he would be sympathetic to their concerns. This, however, overlooked the rhetorical strategy of Richard Bancroft, the wily Bishop of London. Although nominally only a bishop, the poor health of the Archbishop of Canterbury had allowed Bancroft virtually to take over many of his functions by this stage. In a series of quite remarkable speeches, Bancroft linked his Puritan opponents with popery on the one hand, and Presbyterianism on the other. Bancroft suggested that, if the Puritans had their way, the king would be constantly harassed by aggressive presbyteries that would fail to respect his royal authority.

Bancroft's barbs clearly found their mark; James had been both offended and wounded by his encounters with some Scottish presbyteries, especially the bruising encounter with Melville in 1596, which had challenged his authority. James was outraged. A Scottish presbytery went with a king as well as God went with the devil, he declared. Yet this outburst seems to have been a temporary moment of anger; James soon recovered his bonhomie, and the conference proceeded. Yet none could fail to note James's subsequent lack of enthusiasm for the religious structures proposed by the Puritan delegates. Bancroft had scored a major debating point.

On the second day of the conference—Monday January 16 (the Sunday being regarded as a day of rest), John Reynolds set out four Puritan demands, as follows:

1. That the doctrine of the church might be preserved in purity, according to God's word.
2. That good pastors might be planted in all churches, to preach the same.

3. That the church government might be sincerely administered according to God's word.
4. That the Book of Common Prayer might be fitted to more increase of piety.

It was clear that the basic Puritan demand was for either the abolition of the Prayer Book, or at least a significant relaxation of what they regarded as its more unbiblical demands. Contemporary religious writings give no reasons to suppose that there was any great demand within Puritanism for a new English translation of the Bible. The Puritan agenda on the matter of English Bibles was limited to a hope that the Geneva Bible might be authorized for use in churches and public worship, thus reversing the prohibitions introduced by Archbishop Whitgift.

James was not inclined to view any of these proposals with much sympathy. The abolition or radical modification of the Prayer Book would lead to a new period of religious infighting within his realm, at a time when he wished to foster a sense of unity. There were only too many lessons to be learned from the events of earlier years, and James had little enthusiasm for the baleful history of religious controversy to replay itself. The Puritan demands would have to be resisted at this point.

Nor was James in the least enthusiastic about authorizing the Geneva Bible. He knew this work from his time in Scotland, in that it had become the mainstay of Scottish Protestant church life. As his comments at the conference make clear, James regarded it as the "worst of all" the English versions. To authorize this version for use in the public worship of the church would have been unthinkable.

This left James in a somewhat unpromising position. Wanting to be seen to be conciliatory and pacific, he was finding himself unable to offer any sops to his Puritan subjects. Everything pointed to his ending up endorsing something remarkably close to the status quo ante, which would please the bishops and alienate the Puritans. A gesture was clearly needed, unless the conference was to be perceived as totally one-sided. The Puritans needed to propose something to which he could readily assent. Given that the bishops seemed to oppose virtually everything the Puritans were requesting, he would find himself in conflict with the Church of England in doing so. Yet being a king was about give and take. He had defended the Prayer Book; he could give way on something else.

## THE DECISION:
## A NEW TRANSLATION BY ROYAL AUTHORITY

THE BREAKTHROUGH CAME when John Reynolds, the leader of the small Puritan delegation, proposed a new Bible translation. It is not clear where this proposal came from, nor what the underlying motivation might have been. In his account of the meeting, Toby Matthew, Bishop of Durham, noted a Puritan demand that "one only translation of the Bible" was to be "declared authentical, and read in the church." Was this a negotiating strategy to secure approval for the Geneva Bible, and establish it as the only Bible authorized to be read aloud in churches?

Perhaps Reynolds might have expected his proposal for the Geneva Bible only to be read in churches to have failed, thus allowing him to make the apparently lesser request that the Geneva Bible should simply be one of a number of translations authorized for use in public worship, either in addition to or instead of the Bishops' Bible. In this way, Puritan preachers would be able to use the Geneva Bible in public without falling foul of existing laws.

Bishop Bancroft—who acted as the leader of the Anglican contingent throughout the conference—had opposed virtually everything Reynolds wanted, and saw no reason to change strategy at this point. A new translation? Surely not! "If every man's humour were followed, there would be no end of translating." Bancroft's strategy was simple: uniform hostility to change.

Yet James saw his opening. Here was a major concession he could make without causing any pressing difficulties to anyone. A translation of this magnitude took time, so he was not committing himself to anything with major short-term implications. The longer the translation took, the better. It would postpone religious controversy to an indeterminate point in the future. He concurred immediately with the suggestion. James declared that he had yet to see "a Bible well translated into English," and offered his opinion that "of all, that of Geneva is the worst."

Assuming that the Puritan faction was of the view that the Geneva Bible was the best translation available, it is unlikely that its members would have been encouraged by this declaration. However, it is possible to see this vigorous statement as a sop thrown to the bishops, in the light of the decision he was about to announce. If the king disliked the Geneva version, his proposal for a new translation was unlikely to lead to a Geneva-type translation, much disliked by the religious establishment, especially in regard to the annotations.

James was aware that the situation had been rendered more complex than before by the publication in 1582 of a new English translation of the New Testament by a group of Roman Catholic scholars based at Douai and Rheims. A translation of the Old Testament was also promised, so that a complete English Bible, translated from a Roman Catholic perspective, was only just over the horizon. (In fact, it appeared in two parts over the years 1609–10, too late to be taken into account to any significant extent in the production of the King James Version.)

The Douai-Rheims translation has remarkable parallels with the Geneva Bible. Both had their origins within a community of English scholars who had been exiled from England on account of their religious views. In the case of the Geneva Bible, the English community in question was Protestant, having been forced to leave England under the repressive religious policies of a Roman Catholic queen, Mary Tudor; the Douai-Rheims translation had its origins within a Roman Catholic community exiled from England on account of the equally hostile religious policies of a Protestant queen, Elizabeth I.

The "English College" at Douai was founded in 1568, and tem-

porarily migrated to Rheims for the period 1578–93. The translation
was undertaken by Gregory Martin. Although Martin translated both
Old and New Testaments, it was the New Testament that was published in 1582. The translation was based on the Vulgate Latin, rather
than on the Greek original (although Martin hinted that he had consulted the Greek in making the translation from the Latin). The reason for this decision was that the Council of Trent—which laid down
the teachings of the "Counter-Reformation," or definitive Roman
Catholic response to the Reformation—had insisted that the Vulgate
was the only biblical text that was authoritative for Roman Catholics.
Martin made it clear that his primary motivation for undertaking his
translation was what he regarded as the blatant dishonesty of
Protestant translators, who made all kinds of improper alterations to
the text in order to make it agree with their Protestant opinions. The
integrity of the translation offered by the Geneva Bible was about to
be challenged from a Catholic source.

The Douai-Rheims Bible therefore would pose a threat to both
the Geneva and Bishops' Bible. If there was one thing that united
both Anglicans and Puritans, it was a shared dislike and fear of Roman
Catholicism. Might not a new English translation deal with the threat
posed by this new book, and the criticisms it directed against existing
English translations in use within the church? The proposal met
both Puritan and establishment anxieties at a point of some importance.

James thus directed that the "best-learned in both universities"—
at this stage, England had only two universities, Oxford and
Cambridge—should begin work on a new translation of the Bible,
which would be "reviewed by the bishops and the chief learned of the
church; from them to be presented to the Privy Council; and lastly to
be ratified by royal authority," so that "the whole church would be
bound to it, and none other." It was resolved that:

*A translation be made of the whole Bible, as consonant as can be
to the original Hebrew and Greek; and this to be set out and*

*printed, without any marginal notes, and only to be used in all churches of England in time of divine service.*

There is no record of any final royal authorization of the completed translation—for example, by an Order in Council. However, a fire at Whitehall in January 1618 led to the destruction of the records of the Council, including its registers, for the period 1600–13. Consequently, the fact that there is no known royal "authorization" for the translation cannot necessarily be taken to imply that such authorization was not forthcoming.

The decision to proceed with a new English translation of the Bible was the most important—and some would say, the only—positive decision taken by the Hampton Court Conference. The explicit royal stipulation that all forms of annotation would be excluded ensured that the difficulties created for the establishment by the Geneva Bible would be avoided—or so, at any rate, it was thought.

Richard Bancroft, having once expressed reservations about the idea of a new translation, now became its vigorous supporter. The Hampton Court Conference had given him more than he could have reasonably expected; he could afford to give way on one matter. Part of his motivation for doing so must rest in his realization that it was ultimately in order to preserve the vested interests of the Church of England against Catholics on the one hand, and Puritans on the other.

A further point that helped win Bancroft over to the new translation was that he was able to secure for himself a leading personal role in selecting the translators, and then in limiting their freedom. Bancroft had realized that it was better to create a new official translation that he could influence than to have to contend with the authorization of the Geneva Bible. It was decidedly the lesser of two evils. He was in a position to exercise considerable influence over the new Bible, by laying down rules of translation that would ensure that it would be sympathetic to the position and sensitivities of the established Church of England. And finally, he would be in a position to review the final text of the translation, in case it needed any judicious changes before publication.

It is impossible to overlook another factor that was significant to his thinking at this point. To support the new translation would be to win the royal favour. Whitgift, the ailing Archbishop of Canterbury, died in February, shortly after the conclusion of the Hampton Court Conference. His successor would be appointed from among the present bench of bishops. Bancroft was the front runner for preferment. Yet promotion lay in the king's gift, precisely because of the royal supremacy that Bancroft so persuasively espoused. From February onwards, Bancroft knew that he had no option if he wanted to secure the see of Canterbury. He would have to make sure the king's new translation project went ahead smoothly—whatever his personal views on the matter.

As Bishop of London, Bancroft was well placed to make sure that the translators were appointed as soon as possible, and that the long and arduous translation process began. He personally wrote to the bishops of the Church of England in July 1604, making sure that the translators would be financially supported during their labours. In October of that year, Bancroft's diligence in supporting the new translation paid off; he became Whitgift's successor as Archbishop of Canterbury.

## In the Meantime:
## James I, 1604–11

HAVING SORTED OUT the religious controversies of England to his own satisfaction in January 1604, James turned his attention to other matters he regarded as being of importance. He produced a vigorous critique of one of the habits of the day that he regarded as distasteful, unhealthy, and malodorous. James's *A Counterblast to Tobacco* drew particular attention to the problems caused by the smell of the demon weed. In a fascinating aside, James suggested that tobacco smoke "would serve for a precious relic, both for the superstitious priests and the insolent Puritans, to cast out devils withal." The comment perhaps allows us to understand something of James's religious policy in England, which can be seen as steering a middle way between the extremes of Catholicism and Puritanism, using tobacco smoke as an illustration.

James brought to his critique of tobacco the same love of detail and rhetoric he had already mastered for his religious and political discourses. The treatise is fascinating for many reasons, not least of which is that it indicates James's willingness to critique a habit that some of his successors—most notably, Edward VII—found beguiling. Yet it also opens a window into the popular culture of the era, when the smoking of tobacco was justified on two medical grounds. James sets these out as follows:

> First, it is thought by you a sure aphorism in the administration of medicine that the brains of all men being naturally cold and wet, all dry and hot things should be good for them of which nature this stinking suffumigation is, and therefore of good use to them. . . .
>
> The second argument grounded on a show of reason is that this filthy smoke, as well through the heat and strength thereof, as by a natural force and quality, is able and fit to purge both the head and stomach of rheums and distillations as experience teaches by the spitting and avoiding phlegm immediately after the taking of it.

James offered a vigorous and forceful rejection of both these arguments, based partly on his own observations. Yet his real objections had to do with taste, rather than personal health. The concluding paragraph of his learned discourse shows James to even have perceived a theological dimension to the matter: smoking offered an anticipation of the delights of hell, for those who so foolishly condemned themselves to its bonds through this vile habit.

*Have you not reason then to be ashamed and to forbear this filthy novelty, so basely grounded, so foolishly received and so grossly mistaken in the right use thereof? In your abuse thereof sinning against God, harming yourselves both in person and goods, and raking also thereby the marks and notes of vanity upon you by the custom thereof making yourselves to be wondered at by all foreign civil nations and by all strangers that come among you to be scorned and held in contempt; a custom loathsome to the eye, hateful to the nose, harmful to the brain, dangerous to the lungs, and in the black stinking fume thereof nearest resembling the horrible stygian smoke of the pit that is bottomless.*

More serious matters, however, lay to hand. The first Parliament of his reign opened in March 1604, and quickly made it clear that there was strong opposition to the exercise of royal authority without full consultation. Elizabeth I had managed to cajole Parliament into granting her wishes; James had yet to master this technique. As a result, from the outset he faced a serious challenge to his authority from a Parliament that clearly believed supreme authority rested with itself. The area in which the tension between king and Parliament was most clearly demonstrated concerned financial matters. While James I was entitled to receive the running costs of his royal household, any additional funds had to be sanctioned by Parliament—and Parliament had no great enthusiasm for funding James's requests for additional funds. It is estimated that the royal estate was six hundred thousand pounds in debt in 1604. The precarious situation of the royal finances helps us understand why James I would make no contribution toward the translation and production costs of the new Bible. It would have to support itself.

James countered his financial difficulties in a variety of ways. The "Great Contract," set in place by Robert Cecil, allowed the royal finances to be restructured by a series of measures, including the granting of patents and monopolies to favoured individuals. For an appropriately large financial consideration, James was prepared to grant monopolies in such things as the manufacturing of gold thread.

These measures caused outrage in Parliament, and increased the growing resentment against James's style of government. The importance of this point cannot be overlooked. Robert Barker's privileged position as royal printer can be attributed to precisely such a favour. The interesting but totally unnecessary illustrations added as part of the front matter to early editions of the King James Version were the direct result of a royal privilege granted by the crown to John Speed in October 1610.

On the diplomatic front, relations with Spain improved considerably. Since the defeat of the Spanish Armada, there had been little enthusiasm in either Spain or England for continuing a state of war, which tied up resources that could be used for more promising ventures—such as colonizing the New World. The peace that James concluded in the summer of 1604 was, however, unpopular. Many favoured continuing war against the Spaniards. Was not Spain a Catholic country? And was it not the duty of a Protestant nation, such as England, to counter Catholic expansion? Although James sought to counter this concern by forging alliances with various Protestant European states, his foreign policy did not go down well with a nation that had come to regard hostility toward the Spanish as part of its national identity. These suspicions were reinforced when James failed to provide any substantial support for beleaguered Protestant nations during the last great religious war to be fought in Europe—the Thirty Years War (1618–48). When James announced that he had arranged for his son and heir to the English throne, Charles, to marry the French Roman Catholic princess Henrietta Maria, there was outrage in both Parliament and nation.

If any proof were needed of the importance of the Bible to English culture at this point in history, the reaction to Charles marrying any foreigner provides it. The later books of the Old Testament were totally opposed to Israelites marrying foreign women. After a long period of exile in Babylon, it was imperative that the distinctive religious beliefs and practices of Israel were recovered and re-established. Marrying foreigners was a sure-fire method of importing all kinds of heretical religious ideas and practices. The post-exilic writings of Ezra and Nehemiah were full of condemnations of the practice. Here, for example, is Ezra 10:2–3 in the Geneva Bible translation:

> And Shechaniah the son of Jehiel, [one] of the sons of Elam, answered and said unto Ezra, We have trespassed against our God, and have taken strange wives of the people of the land: yet now there is hope in Israel concerning this thing. Now therefore let us make a covenant with our God to put away all the wives, and such as are born of them, according to the counsel of my lord, and of those that tremble at the commandment of our God; and let it be done according to the law.

Even the suggestion that Charles might marry the Spanish *Infanta* in 1623 had provoked intense criticism: one court preacher was forcibly interrupted when, speaking about Solomon's marriage to an idolater, he announced his intention to "make an application to the present time." It was all too obvious what the application would be, and silence seemed to all present to be by far the most prudent policy. The actual marriage of Charles to Henrietta Maria provoked outrage in many quarters. Comparing Henrietta Maria unfavourably to Jezebel, the anonymous author of the *Sacrae Heplades* (1625) gave vent to his hope that "some Jehu" might cause her to be thrown out of her window, and trodden underfoot by some passing horse.

Recent studies have stressed the importance of anti-Catholicism as an element of James's religious policies in England. James appears to have come to the conclusion that the best way of defusing religious controversies within England was to talk up the threat posed to the English Protestant heritage by Roman Catholicism, at home or abroad. Hostility toward Roman Catholicism was the glue that prevented, at least for a while, Puritans and Anglicans from pursuing open warfare with each other. The thought of a more potent religious threat to both was enough to make them wary of letting their disputes get out of hand.

Richard Bancroft had been appointed Archbishop of Canterbury in October 1604. He saw himself as a vigorous defender of the Church of England, and identified its two chief enemies as a potentially resurgent Puritanism, and a persistent Catholicism that nearly fifty years of Protestant rule had failed to eradicate. Bancroft took measures to repress both these potential enemies. He issued the *Constitutions and Canons Ecclesiastical* in 1604, designed to enforce the authority of bishops and the use of the Prayer Book. However, Bancroft clearly believed that the Hampton Court Conference had, at least temporarily, checked the influence of Puritanism; he was now increasingly concerned with the threat posed by the remnants of Catholicism in England. In 1605, he wrote to all his bishops, setting out the manner in which Catholic recusants were to be found, tried, and punished.

Anti-Catholic sentiment became inflamed in 1605 through the failure of the Gunpowder Plot of that year. The official account of events was that there was a plot to blow up the House of Lords on November 5, when the king was due to be present to open proceedings. Alerted to the plot in advance, the authorities were able to thwart the conspiracy, and arrest its perpetrators. All were prominent Catholics. Eight conspirators were executed in January 1606. Henry Garnet, a Jesuit, was executed outside St. Paul's Cathedral in March 1606, on the grounds that he had knowledge of the plot. This has more than tangential relevance to our story. He was urged to recant by John Overall, Dean of St. Paul's Cathedral. Having failed to do so, Overall witnessed Garnet being hanged, drawn, and quartered. Overall was, as we shall see, a member of one of the companies of translators appointed to oversee the production of the King James Version.

James, however, found time to devote to matters other than affairs of state. A series of Shakespeare plays was premiered in 1604. In 1605, James laid on a spectacular performance of Ben Jonson's *The Masque of Blackness*, staged by Inigo Jones, which caused consternation and scandal, partly on account of its extravagance. Further concerns were expressed over the king's increasingly obvious homosexual tendencies, which led to certain royal favourites being granted favours that were the subject of much comment and envy. Robert Carr, some twenty years younger than James, was one such favourite: he became the Earl of Somerset in 1613. Although James fondled and kissed his favourites in what was widely regarded as a lecherous manner in public, the court was prepared to believe that his private behaviour was somewhat more restrained.

The commissioning of the new translation of the Bible was one of the first positive acts of the new king of England. By the time of its final appearance in 1611, James's popularity had waned substantially. People began to long for the good old days of Queen Elizabeth, with whom James was regularly compared—unfavourably.

There was no doubt what James wanted to achieve during his reign: a unified Protestant England, united around an agreed translation of the Bible. James had every reason to hope that his new translation of the Bible would be a powerful factor in creating a cohesive English national identity, especially over and against Roman Catholicism, which was enjoying a newfound strength and stability on the European mainland. The new Bible would be a rallying point for a Protestant English nation. The production, at the king's initiative, of a new English translation of the Bible would reinforce the image of the king as the political and spiritual leader of his people. The unity of king, Bible, and church would ensure the unity of the English people, and might even stimulate the rebirth of that elusive sense of national identity and pride that had blossomed under Elizabeth. Much, it seemed, would depend on that translation.

# 8

## TRANSLATION:
## THE ENGLISHING
## OF THE BIBLE

It is clear that King James was delighted with the proposal for a new English translation of the Bible. The bishops of the Church of England, led by Richard Bancroft, Bishop of London, may have been initially opposed to the translation, despite James's enthusiasm. By the summer of 1604, however, the Anglican establishment was fully on board. Richard Bancroft—by now confirmed as the new Archbishop of Canterbury—had become the leading Anglican supporter of the proposed new translation, and was actively engaged in setting in place the measures needed to produce it. Everyone, it seemed, was happy.

While still Bishop of London, Bancroft set in motion the procedures to appoint the panel of translators necessary for the new translation. Lancelot Andrewes (then Dean of Westminster) and the Regius Professors of Greek and Hebrew at Oxford and Cambridge Universities were invited to name suitable persons qualified for this task. There seems little doubt that Bancroft ensured that a satisfactory number of his own protégés found their way on to the translation panel. Yet the translators would not be paid for their work; in a letter of June 30, James indicated that the best that the "certain learned men, to the number of four and fifty" could expect was potential preferment in their careers. There were no royal funds available to support the translation. James's coffers were seriously depleted, and there was no prospect of the English Parliament doing anything to remedy his financial situation. On July 31, 1604, Bancroft wrote to his fellow bishops, asking them to help find positions for the translators, as and when suitable openings became available. A sum of not less than twenty pounds was regarded as a suitable remuneration for their efforts.

Bancroft was determined to ensure that the translation process was judiciously guided, and limit the freedom of the translators. The translators were instructed to follow strict "rules of translation," drawn up by Bancroft and approved by James, designed to minimize the risk of producing a Bible that might give added credibility to Puritanism, Presbyterianism, or Roman Catholicism. The deliberate exclusion of any form of marginal annotations or notes was regarded as a matter of special importance, given James's clear anxieties concerning the content and tone of the Geneva Bible's marginal comments.

### *Richard Bancroft's Translation Rules*

1. The ordinary Bible read in the Church, commonly called the *Bishops' Bible*, to be followed, and as little altered as the Truth of the original will permit.

2. The names of the Prophets, and the Holy Writers, with the other Names of the Text, to be retained, as nigh as may be, accordingly as they were vulgarly used.

3. The Old Ecclesiastical Words to be kept, *viz.* the Word *Church* not to be translated *Congregation* &c.

4. When a Word hath divers Significations, that to be kept which hath been most commonly used by the most of the Ancient Fathers, being agreeable to the Propriety of the Place, and the Analogy of the Faith.

5. The Division of the Chapters to be altered, either not at all, or as little as may be, if Necessity so require.

6. No Marginal Notes at all to be affixed, but only for the explanation of the Hebrew or Greek Words, which cannot without some circumlocution, so briefly and fitly be expressed in the Text.

7. Such Quotations of Places to be marginally set down as shall serve for the fit Reference of one Scripture to another.

8. Every particular Man of each Company, to take the same Chapter or Chapters, and having translated or amended them severally by himself, where he thinketh good, all to meet together, confer what they have done, and agree for their Parts what shall stand.

9. As any one Company hath dispatched any one Book in this Manner they shall send it to the rest, to be considered of seriously and judiciously, for His Majesty is very careful in this Point.

10. If any Company, upon the Review of the Book so sent, doubt or differ upon any Place, to send them Word therof; note the Place, and withal send the Reasons, to which if they consent not, the Difference to be compounded at the general Meeting, which is to be of the chief Persons of each Company, at the end of the Work.

11. When any Place of special Obscurity is doubted of, Letters to be directed by Authority, to send to any Learned Man in the Land, for his Judgement of such a Place.

12. Letters to be sent from every Bishop to the rest of his Clergy, admonishing them of this Translation in hand; and to move and charge as many skilful in the Tongues; and having taken pains in that kind, to send his particular Observations to the Company, either at Westminster, Cambridge, or Oxford.

13. The Directors in each Company, to be the Deans of *Westminster* and *Chester* for that Place; and the King's Professors in the *Hebrew* or *Greek* in either University.

14. These translations to be used when they agree better with the Text than the Bishops' Bible: *Tindoll's, Matthew's, Coverdale's, Whitchurch's, Geneva.*

15. Besides the said Directors before mentioned, three or four of the most Ancient and Grave Divines, in either of the Universities, not employed in Translating, to be assigned by the vice-Chancellor, upon Conference with the rest of the Heads, to be Overseers of the Translations as well *Hebrew* as *Greek*, for the better observation of the 4th Rule above specified.

The "Rules" make it clear that previous English translations were to be given full weight in the new work. This raises a fascinating issue, which deserves to be treated in much greater detail.

## STANDING ON THE SHOULDERS OF GIANTS: THE ROLE OF EARLIER ENGLISH TRANSLATIONS

IT IS IMPOSSIBLE to overlook the fact that the King James translators did not begin to translate with blank sheets of paper in front of them. They stood in a long line of translators, and were conscious that their task would be influenced considerably—perhaps more than they cared to admit—by the English translations already in circulation. The fifteen rules by which their translation would be governed specifically directed them to base themselves on earlier versions, especially the Bishops' Bible, but also taking into account others. Thus the fourteenth rule specified that: "These translations to be used when they agree better with the Text than the Bishops' Bible: *Tindoll's, Matthew's, Coverdale's, Whitchurch's, Geneva.*" As each successive translation drew upon those that preceded it, the earliest of the translations—that of William Tyndale—can thus be seen to have had a considerable effect on its successors. Alterations to translations were generally made only on the basis of increased accuracy—for example, through advances in philology.

Lying behind this is an attitude towards wisdom that has largely been lost in the modern period. Writers of the Renaissance were conscious of standing within a stream of cultural and intellectual achievement, from which they benefited and to which they were called to contribute. The wisdom of the past was to be appropriated in the present. One of the images most frequently used to illustrate this understanding of the human cultural endeavour was that of "standing on the shoulders of giants." The image is set out particularly clearly in the twelfth-century writer John of Salisbury, who once commented:

> *We are like dwarves sitting on the shoulders of giants. We see more, and things that are more distant, than they did, not because our sight is superior or because we are taller than they, but because they raise us up, and by their great stature add to ours.*

As such, the "Englishing" of the Bible was understood to be a corporate effort, in which the achievements of earlier generations could be valued and used by their successors. As the preface "The Translators to the Reader" sets out this point:

> *Truly (good Christian Reader) we never thought from the begin-*
> *ning, that we should need to make a new Translation, nor yet to*
> *make of a bad one a good one, (for then the imputation of Sixtus*
> *had been true in some sort, that our people had been fed with gall*
> *of Dragons instead of wine, with whey instead of milk:) but to*
> *make a good one better, or out of many good ones, one principal*
> *good one, not justly to be excepted against; that hath been our*
> *endeavour, that our mark. To that purpose there were many cho-*
> *sen, that were greater in other men's eyes than in their own, and*
> *that sought the truth rather than their own praise. Again, they*
> *came or were thought to come to the work, not* exercendi causa
> *(as one saith) but* exercitati, *that is, learned, not to learn.*

The King James translators saw themselves as standing on the shoulders of giants, those who had translated before them and blazed a trail that they were proud to follow. Certainly alterations had to be made—but the King James translators believed that their predecessors would have approved of those alterations, as they were based on principles (such as a better understanding of Hebrew) that would have led to the same general outcome had these been available earlier.

The King James Bible is, therefore, not to be dismissed as a mere tinkering with earlier versions—the verdict of our modern era, in which originality and novelty often seem to be prized above all other virtues. The King James Bible is an outstanding example and embodiment of the ideals of its own period, by which it must be judged. It is to be seen in the light of the Renaissance approach to human wisdom, in which one generation is nourished and sustained by the intellectual achievements of its predecessors. Each era draws on the wisdom of the past, and builds upon it, before handing a greater wisdom on to its successors. The King James Bible can be seen as one of the most outstanding representatives of this corporate approach to cultural advance and the enterprise of gaining wisdom.

## THE SIX COMPANIES OF TRANSLATORS

JAMES DIRECTED THAT the entire text of the Bible was to be divided into six sections, with roughly the same number of men allocated to the translation of each section. Two were assigned to meet at Westminster, two at Oxford University, and two at Cambridge University. The first group of three companies were assigned the Old Testament, and a second group of two the New Testament. A sixth group was entrusted with the apocryphal works. When each section had completed its tasks, twelve delegates were to be chosen (two from each company from the entire body of translators). These would meet together to review and revise the entire work.

Finally, the finishing touches would be applied to the work by the bishops of Winchester and Gloucester. Though Bancroft appears to have drawn no attention to the fact, he had reserved for himself the privilege of making revisions to what all had hitherto thought of as the final draft.

Careful study of the various lists of translators shows that the maximum number of fifty-four translators specified by James was not achieved. In his magisterial study *The History of the Reformation of the Church of England*, Gilbert Burnet (1643–1715) identifies only forty-seven names. Other lists allow up to fifty-one to be identified. The traditional explanation for the inconsistency may well be correct: it is suggested that early deaths led to the number of translators being reduced from the original intention of the king. Another explanation is offered by the fifteenth of Bancroft's translation rules, which allows for "three or four" additional persons to be allocated as required to the translation teams; this suggests that a translation team of fifty or fifty-one was appointed, on the assumption that three or four others would be called upon as required.

The details of the six companies of translators, along with brief biographical details, are set out below. This list has been drawn up on the basis of the best records of the seventeenth century, but uncertainties remain at several points concerning the precise identity of some figures. It is clear that the translators were all highly educated, and were virtually entirely supporters of the religious and political establishment. The translators were drawn almost entirely from the southeast of England, with important implications for the type of English used in the translation.

## THE FIRST WESTMINSTER COMPANY

ASSIGNATION: Old Testament: Genesis to 2 Kings

HEAD: Lancelot Andrewes, Dean of Westminster Abbey, subsequently Bishop of Chichester (1605), Bishop of Ely (1609) and Bishop of Winchester (1619)

MEMBERS:

William Bedwell, Rector of St. Ethelburgh's, London; a noted Arabic scholar of his day

Richard Clark, Vicar of Minster, Isle of Thanet, Kent

Geoffrey King, Regius Professor of Hebrew, Cambridge University (1607)

John Layfield, Rector of St. Clement Danes, London

John Overall, Dean of St. Paul's Cathedral, London

Hadrian à Saravia, Prebendary of Westminster Abbey

Richard Thompson, Fellow of Clare Hall, Cambridge

Robert Tighe, Archdeacon of Middlesex

## THE FIRST CAMBRIDGE COMPANY

ASSIGNATION: I Chronicles to the Song of Songs
HEAD: Edward Lively, Regius Professor of Hebrew, Cambridge
University
MEMBERS:

Roger Andrews, Rector of St. Martin's, Ongar, Essex
Andrew Bing, Fellow of Peterhouse
Laurence Chadderton, Master of Emmanuel College, Cambridge
(and one of the Puritan representatives at the Hampton Court
Conference)
Thomas Harrison, Fellow of Trinity College, Cambridge
John Richardson, Regius Professor of Divinity, Cambridge
University
Robert Spalding, Fellow of St. John's College, Cambridge

## THE FIRST OXFORD COMPANY

ASSIGNATION: Isaiah to Malachi
HEAD: John Harding, President of Magdalen College, Oxford
(1607)
MEMBERS:

Richard Brett, Rector of Quainton, Buckinghamshire
Richard Fairclough, Rector of Bucknell, Oxfordshire
Thomas Holland, Rector of Exeter College, Oxford
Richard Kilby, Rector of Lincoln College, Oxford
John Reynolds, President of Corpus Christi College, Oxford,
from 1598–1607 (and one of the Puritan representatives at
the Hampton Court Conference)
Miles Smith, Prebendary of Hereford Cathedral

## THE SECOND OXFORD COMPANY

ASSIGNATION: the Four Gospels, Acts, and Revelation

HEAD: Thomas Ravid, Dean of Christ Church, Oxford, Bishop of Gloucester (1605); Bishop of London (1607)

MEMBERS:

George Abbot, Dean of Winchester

John Aglionby, Principal of St. Edmund Hall

Richard Eedes, Dean of Worcester

John Harmer, Warden of St. Mary's College, Winchester

James Montague, Bishop of Bath and Wells (1608)

John Perin, Regius Professor of Greek, Oxford University

Ralph Ravens, Rector of Great Easton, Essex

Sir Henry Savile, Warden of Merton College, Oxford

Giles Thomson, Fellow of All Souls' College, Oxford

## THE SECOND WESTMINSTER COMPANY

ASSIGNATION: the New Testament letters

HEAD: William Barlow, Dean of Chester, Bishop of Rochester (1605)

MEMBERS:

William Dakins, Regius Professor of Divinity, Gresham College, London

Roger Fenton, Prebendary of St. Paul's Cathedral

Ralph Hutchinson, President, St. John's College, Oxford

Michael Rabbet, Vicar of St. Vedast, Foster Lane, London

Thomas Sanderson, Rector of All Hallows the Great, London

John Spencer, President of Corpus Christi College, Oxford, from 1607

## THE SECOND CAMBRIDGE COMPANY

ASSIGNATION: the Apocryphal books
HEAD: John Duport, Master of Jesus College, Cambridge
MEMBERS:

John Boys, Rector of Boxworth, Cambridgeshire
William Branthwaite, Master of Gonville and Gaius College (1607)
Andrew Downes, Regius Professor of Greek, Cambridge University
Jeremiah Radcliffe, Vicar of Orwell, Cambridgeshire
Robert Ward, Prebendary of Chichester Cathedral (1606)
Samuel Ward, Master of Sidney Sussex College, Cambridge

It is important to note that, with virtually no exceptions, the scholars assembled for the purpose of translating the Bible were based in the south of England. It is true that William Barlow, who headed the Second Westminster Company, was Dean of Chester. Yet Barlow was born in London, educated at Cambridge, and was Prebendary of St. Paul's Cathedral from 1597–1601, when he exchanged his stall at St. Paul's for one at Westminster Abbey. He was appointed Dean of Chester in 1602, but did not stay long in this northern city; he became Bishop of Rochester in 1605. The implications of this point for the form of English used in the translation will be discussed later in this work.

It seems that the work began immediately, although the documentary evidence is not as clear as might be hoped. The Dean of Westminster Abbey, Lancelot Andrewes, excused himself from a meeting of the Society of Antiquaries in November 1604; that afternoon, he explained, was "translation time." It is clear that initial progress was slow—so slow, in fact, that some accused the translators of laziness. In fact, the initial stages of the work were bound to be somewhat ponderous, as James had made it clear that he wanted existing English translations to be reviewed and, where possible, to be the basis of the new version.

## THE TRANSLATION PROCESS

RELATIVELY LITTLE DOCUMENTARY evidence has survived to allow us to form a picture of the typical working life of these companies of translators. A biographical sketch of John Boys—also "Bois," a member of the Second Cambridge Company—has survived, which offers some illuminating details concerning his lifestyle over the period of the translation. The biography was written in a rather trenchant style by his contemporary Anthony Walker, who took a certain delicious pleasure in pointing out how Boys needed little encouragement to neglect his parish duties at Boxworth for the academic delights of Cambridge.

> [Boys] went not from the university when he left Cambridge, only he made his way a little longer to the schools. For he used constantly to come and hear Mr Downes and Mr Lively (those two worthy professors of the Greek and Hebrew tongues) . . . When it pleased God to move King James to that excellent work, the translation of the Bible; when the translators were to be chosen for Cambridge, he was sent for thither by those therein employed, and was chosen one; some university men thereat repining . . . All the time he was about his own part, his commons were given him at St John's; where he abode all the week until Saturday night; then went home to discharge his cure, returning thence on Monday morning . . . Four years were spent in this first service; at the end whereof the whole work being finished, and three copies of the whole Bible sent from Cambridge, Oxford and Westminster, to London; a new choice was to be made of six in all, two out of every company, to review the whole work . . . For the dispatch of which business Mr Downes and Mr Boys were sent for up to London. Where meeting (though Mr Downes would not go till he was either

ST. JOHN'S COLLEGE, CAMBRIDGE,
AS SEEN FROM FISHER'S LANE, 1815

*fetched or threatened with a pursuivant) their fellow-labourers,
they went daily to Stationers' Hall, and in three quarters of a year,
finished their task. All which time they had from the Company of
Stationers 30 s. per week duly paid them . . . Whilst they were
employed in this last business he, and he only, took notes of their
proceedings, which notes he kept till his dying day.*

Walker's comments suggest that the selection of translators
involved the choice of a limited number of individuals from a larger
group established by consultation. Walker implies that selection took
place by interview at the places at which the companies were to meet
regularly. This point is of no small interest, as it is well known that
some who might have expected to be appointed to the companies of
translators were, in fact, passed over. Two notable omissions from the

final list of translators have attracted special attention: Hugh Broughton (1549–1612) and Andrew Willett (1567–1621) were both able Hebraists, and might have been expected to have been included among the king's translators. While the reasons for excluding Willett remain unclear, there is little difficulty in working out why Broughton was passed over. Noted for his violent temper and aggressive behaviour toward his opponents, Broughton would have caused considerable difficulties within the committee structures envisaged for the translation process. Broughton took his exclusion badly. He had seven years to nurse his grudges before wreaking a savage revenge on his colleagues.

Walker's account of Boys's activities also casts light on the process of translation itself. Walker's account indicates that Boys spent only Sundays in his parish, devoting the remainder of the week to attending to translation issues. The process, according to Walker, took four years in the case of the Second Cambridge Company, which was assigned the Apocrypha. Others took longer. The best way of making sense of the existing documentary evidence—which is disappointingly sparse—is to suggest that the companies, who began their work in 1604, finished their translation assignments at different points: some in 1608, some in 1609, and some at the last moment, in 1610. At this point, all the translations were assembled centrally at Stationers' Hall in London, when a further review took place. Each company contributed two representatives to this meeting; in the case of the Second Cambridge Company, as Walker's account makes clear, these were Boys and Downes.

In his narrative, Walker refers to six representatives gathering together at Stationers' Hall; another, apparently more reliable account of the same process makes reference to twelve delegates, two appointed by each company. This account is written by Samuel Ward, who was also a member of the Second Cambridge Company. Ward presented his account of the translation of the King James Bible at the Synod of Dort on November 20, 1618, a few years after its publication. In his version of the complex translation process, Ward stated that the general meeting of the editors at Stationers' Hall involved

1890 WATERCOLOUR OF STATIONERS' HALL
BY JOHN CROWTHER (1876-1903)

twelve individuals, two being drawn from each group of translators. It
is difficult to know which account to accept. We know that Boys and
Downes were present at the editorial meeting at Stationers' Hall, as
well as John Harmer of the Second Oxford Company. It is far from
clear how many others were present.

Walker's narrative of Boys's life makes reference to his keeping
notes of the proceedings at Stationers' Hall, which he kept until his
dying day. What appears to be a corrected copy of those notes was discovered in the library of Corpus Christi College, Oxford, and published in 1966. The Boys manuscript provides a hint that six may be
the correct number for those present at the final editorial meeting.
Boys apparently decided to record the views of individual contribu-
tors at certain points, and identified them by abbreviations or initials.
The following initials or abbreviations are found: A.D.; B.; C.; H.; D.H;

Hutch.; D.Hutch. The last two may well be abbreviations for Dr. Ralph Hutchinson, who had died four years earlier, leaving some notes for the benefit of his cotranslators. The manuscript appears to suggest that the Stationers' Hall meeting interacted with these notes. This being the case, the number of initials points to six persons being present.

This neat conclusion must be treated with suspicion because a copy of only part of Boys's manuscript, dealing with some New Testament writings, has been found. The Hebraists would have been more concerned with the Old Testament translations, which are not covered in the material at our disposal. Suggestive though the evidence from Boys's manuscript may well be, it is not sufficient to adjudicate finally in this matter.

An important contemporary witness to the events at Stationers' Hall is to be found in the *Table Talk* of John Selden.

> *The translation in King James' time took an excellent way. That part of the Bible was given to him who was most excellent in such a tongue (as the Apocrypha to Andrew Downes), and then they met together, and one read the translation, the rest holding in their hands some Bible, either of the learned tongues, or French, Spanish, Italian, etc. If they found any fault, they spoke up; if not, he read on.*

There is an important point to be made here relating to the often-praised literary quality of the translation. Selden's account explicitly states that the draft translation *was read out aloud* to the assembled delegates, who were then free to suggest alterations. The King James Bible was designed to be read publicly in church, and there is no doubt that the translators gave careful consideration to ensuring that the translation could be understood by those *to whom it was read*, rather than just those who read it.

Yet a comparison of Boys's notes with the final published text of the King James Bible suggests that few of the changes proposed at the

Stationers' Hall meeting may actually have been incorporated into the final text. The notes reveal a lively and learned debate over the best way of representing Greek nouns and verbs. Boys himself suggested that Paul's command not to steal (Titus 2:10) should be rendered in terms of "not filchering"—an earthy piece of Elizabethan slang that did not find its way into the final version.

Having completed their recommendations for revision, the text was passed on to Miles Smith and Thomas Bilson, who were charged with adding the finishing touches. It is not clear whether their role was to review the overall text of the translation, or simply to comment on the specific changes proposed by the editorial committee that had met at Stationers' Hall. Then, in an apparently unscripted development, Richard Bancroft reviewed what had been hitherto regarded as the final version of the text. It would be one of his final acts; Bancroft died on November 2, 1610, and never lived to see the translation over which he had held so much sway. Smith complained loudly to anyone who would listen that Bancroft had introduced fourteen changes in the final text without any consultation. Yet we remain unclear as to what those alleged changes might have been.

Finally, Smith and Bilson composed the front matter to the work. This consisted of two items: the "Epistle Dedicatory" to James I (which is thought to have been written by Bilson) and the lengthy "Translators to the Reader"—an extended preface, setting out the basic principles used by the translators—penned by Smith. In view of the importance of this lengthy document, it is worth exploring the basic points it makes.

## THE TRANSLATORS TO THE READER: THE PREFACE

WHILE MODERN VERSIONS of the King James Bible continue to print the dedication "to the most high and mighty King James," the lengthy preface is generally omitted. While this is understandable, given both the length and the verbosity of the piece, this omission deprives readers of a fascinating defence of the principle of translation of the Bible into the vernacular, and the specific features of the King James Bible.

> *Truly (good Christian Reader) we never thought from the beginning, that we should need to make a new Translation, nor yet to make of a bad one a good one, . . . but to make a good one better, or out of many good ones, one principal good one, not justly to be excepted against; that hath been our endeavor, that our mark.*

The point being made is that the translation now being set before the public can be thought of as representing the best possible distillation of the wisdom, grace, and beauty of existing translations, corrected where necessary against the original biblical documents in their original languages.

The preface comments briefly on the circumstances that led to the decision to prepare a fresh translation. For Smith, the origins of the King James Bible are not to be seen in Puritan concerns over the accuracy of existing translations, or the need to ensure that the biblical translations included in the Prayer Book were reliable. The credit for the decision to translate is firmly given to James himself.

> *The very Historical truth is, that upon the importunate petitions of the Puritans, at his Majesty's coming to this Crown, the Conference at Hampton Court having been appointed for hearing their complaints: when by force of reason they were put from other grounds, they had recourse at the last, to this shift, that they could not with good conscience subscribe to the Communion book, since it maintained the Bible as it was there translated, which was as they said, a most corrupted translation. And although this was judged to be but a very poor and empty shift; yet even hereupon did his Majesty begin to bethink himself of the good that might ensue by a new translation, and presently after gave order for this Translation which is now presented unto thee.*

So why translate in the first place? In answering this question, Miles Smith began by stressing the immense spiritual richness of the Bible, and its central place in Christian life and thought.[1]

*[The Bible] is not only an armour, but also a whole armoury of weapons, both offensive and defensive; whereby we may save ourselves and put the enemy to flight. It is not an herb, but a tree, or rather a whole paradise of trees of life, which bring forth fruit every month, and the fruit thereof is for meat, and the leaves for medicine. It is not a pot of Manna, or a cruse[2] of oil, which were for memory only, or for a meal's meat or two, but as it were a shower of heavenly bread sufficient for a whole host, be it never so great; and as it were a whole cellar full of oil vessels; whereby all our necessities may be provided for, and our debts discharged. In a word, it is a Panary[3] of wholesome food, against fenowed traditions; a Physician's shop (Saint Basil called it) of preservatives against poisoned heresies; a Pandect[4] of profitable laws, against rebellious spirits; a treasury of most costly jewels, against beggarly rudiments; finally a fountain of most pure water springing up unto everlasting life. And what marvel? The original thereof being from heaven, not from earth; the author being God, not man; the inditer, the holy spirit, not the wit of the Apostles or Prophets; the Penmen such as were sanctified from the womb, and endued with a principal portion of God's spirit; the matter, verity, piety, purity, uprightness; the form, God's word, God's testimony, God's oracles, the word of truth, the word of salvation, etc.; the effects, light of understanding, stableness of persuasion, repentance from dead works, newness of life, holiness, peace, joy in the holy Ghost; lastly, the end and reward of the study thereof, fellowship with the Saints,*

---

1. As some of the English terms used by Miles Smith have now fallen out of use, these are explained in accompanying footnotes.
2. A small bottle.
3. A breadbasket.
4. A collection of texts.

*participation of the heavenly nature, fruition of an inheritance immortal, undefiled, and that never shall fade away: Happy is the man that delighted in the Scripture, and thrice happy that meditateth in it day and night.*

*But how shall men meditate in that, which they cannot understand?*

The strategy developed by Smith is to stress the importance of direct access to the Bible for Christian spiritual growth, personal integrity, and doctrinal correctness. Without these, the Church cannot hope to prosper. But if ordinary Christians cannot cope with the biblical languages, they will be denied access to these treasures.

The Roman Catholic Church had argued that the Latin Vulgate translation was the bedrock of Western Christian life and thought. Smith contests this position hotly. The Bible was translated into Latin precisely because it was the language of the Roman Empire. In order for the riches of Scripture to be brought to the Latin-speaking world, the Bible was translated into its everyday speech. By virtue of precisely the same argument, the time had now come for the Bible to be translated into English. The same principles applied—the need to translate the Bible into the everyday language of the world. If salvation depended on knowledge of the gospel, it was imperative that the Bible should be made accessible to all in a language they understood. As Smith concluded his argument on this point:

*Now what can be more available thereto, than to deliver God's book unto God's people in a tongue which they understand?*

Smith is highly critical of those who deny God's people direct access to the text of the Bible.

Smith and his colleagues saw translation as the essential means by which the people of God could gain access to the spiritual nourishment found in the Bible. In an elegant section, the preface sets out a series of images to illustrate the importance of translation.

*Translation it is that openeth the window, to let in the light; that breaketh the shell, that we may eat the kernel; that putteth aside the curtain, that we may look into the most Holy place; that removeth the cover of the well, that we may come by the water, even as Jacob rolled away the stone from the mouth of the well, by which means the flocks of Laban were watered [Genesis 29:10]. Indeed without translation into the vulgar tongue, the unlearned are but like children at Jacob's well (which is deep) [John 4:11] without a bucket or something to draw with; or as that person mentioned by Isaiah, to whom when a sealed book was delivered, with this motion, "Read this, I pray thee," he was fain to make this answer, "I cannot, for it is sealed" [Isaiah 29:11].*

This passage clearly points to the high degree of motivation experienced by the companies of translators. To translate the Bible was an act of service to the people of God as a whole.

The King James Bible was not the first English translation; as we have seen, it build upon a substantial foundation laid by others, such as William Tyndale. Smith is explicit on this point; King James's translators were aware that they were building on honourable foundations laid by others.

*And to the same effect say we, that we are so far off from condemning any of their labours that travailed before us in this kind, either in this land or beyond sea, either in King Henry's time, or King Edward's (if there were any translation, or correction of a translation in his time) or Queen Elizabeth's of ever renowned memory, that we acknowledge them to have been raised up of God, for the building and furnishing of his Church, and that they deserve to be had of us and of posterity in everlasting remembrance . . . Yet for all that, as nothing is begun and perfected at the same time, and the later thoughts are thought to be the wiser: so, if we, building upon their foundation that went before us, and being holpen by their labours, do endeavour to make that better*

*which they left so good; no man, we are sure, hath cause to mis-
like us; they, we persuade ourselves, if they were alive, would
thank us.*

The preface is commendably honest; the science of biblical translation is not as precise as many would like, not least because of continuing difficulties in understanding what certain rare Hebrew words
meant. For this reason, the translators inserted marginal notes in
which alternative translations were suggested. Some, the preface
notes, might see this as challenging the reliability and trustworthiness
of the Bible itself, let alone this specific translation. Yet the preface
affirms that this is the only honest policy that could be adopted.
Readers have the right to know where there are difficulties or uncertainties.

*There be many words in the Scriptures, which be never found there
but once, (having neither brother or neighbor, as the Hebrews
speak) so that we cannot be holpen by conference of places. Again,
there be many rare names of certain birds, beasts and precious
stones, etc. concerning the Hebrews themselves are so divided
among themselves for judgment, that they may seem to have
defined this or that, rather because they would say something,
than because they were sure of that which they said, as S. Jerome
somewhere saith of the Septuagint. Now in such a case, doth not
a margin do well to admonish the Reader to seek further, and not
to conclude or dogmatize upon this or that peremptorily? For as it
is a fault of incredulity, to doubt of those things that are evident:
so to determine of such things as the Spirit of God hath left (even
in the judgment of the judicious) questionable, can be no less than
presumption.*

The translators also avoided what—at least, to them—seemed a
wooden and dogmatic approach to translation, which dictated that
precisely the same English words should regularly be used to translate

Greek or Hebrew words. The preface sets out clearly the view that the translators saw themselves as free to use a variety of English terms.

> *Another things we think good to admonish thee of (gentle Reader) that we have not tied ourselves to an uniformity of phrasing, or to an identity of words, as some peradventure⁵ would wish that we had done, because they observe, that some learned men some-where, have been as exact as they could that way. Truly, that we might not vary from the sense of that which we had translated before, if the word signified that same in both places (for there be some words that be not the same sense everywhere) we were espe-cially careful, and made a conscience, according to our duty. But, that we should express the same notion in the same particular word; as for example, if we translate the Hebrew or Greek word once by PURPOSE, never to call it INTENT; if one where JOUR-NEYING, never TRAVELING; if one where THINK, never SUP-POSE; if one where PAIN, never ACHE; if one where JOY, never GLADNESS, etc. Thus to mince the matter, we thought to savour more of curiosity than wisdom, and that rather it would breed scorn in the Atheist, than bring profit to the godly Reader. For is the kingdom of God to become words or syllables? why should we be in bondage to them if we may be free, use one precisely when we may use another no less fit, as commodiously?*

This principle suggests that the translators saw variety as a means of enhancing the beauty of the text, by avoiding crude verbal repeti-tions. Yet it must be pointed out that this principle led to some quite puzzling consequences.

The translation of Romans 5:2–11 reveals this concern to ensure variety. According to the King James Bible, Paul and his colleagues "*rejoice* in hope of the glory of God . . . we *glory* in tribulations . . . we

5. Perhaps.

also *joy* in God." The same Greek verb—which would normally be translated as "rejoice"—is, in fact, being translated using different words (here italicized) in each of the three cases. There can be no doubt that this flexibility allowed the translators to achieve a judicious verbal balance that enhanced the attractiveness of the resulting work. Yet inevitably, a price was paid for this in terms of the accuracy that some had hoped for.

The translation, of course, used the standard orthography of the period, which seems strange to modern readers. The following extract sets out the original spelling of Luke 1:57–65, to allow this point to be appreciated. The passage describes the birth of John the Baptist:

> *Now Elizabeths full time came, that shee should be deliuered, and shee brought foorth a sonne. And her neighbours and her cousins heard how the Lorde had shewed great mercy upon her, and they rejoyced with her. And it came to passe that on the eight day they came to circumcise the childe, and they called him Zacharias, after the name of his father. And his mother answered, and said. Not so, but he shalbe called John. And they said unto her, There is none of thy kinred that is called by this name. And they made figures to his father, how he would have him called. And he asked for a writing table, and wrote, saying, His name is John: and they marueiled all. And his mouth was opened immediately, and his tongue loosed, and hee spake, and praised God. And feare came on all that dwelt round about them, and all thse saying were noised abroad thorowout all the hill countrey of Judea.*

While many differences with modern orthography are obvious, the similarities are perhaps even more impressive.

So the final text was delivered to the king's printer, Robert Barker. But precisely what form did this text take? However it was presented, the text has not survived.

Two main hypotheses have been developed, each with their

respective merits. One school of thought holds that an annotated manuscript text, incorporating all the changes, was delivered to the printers. This is supported by some comments found in a 1660 pamphlet, which complained of printers who had obtained "the manuscript copy of the Holy Bible in English, attested with the hands of the remarkable and learned translators in King James, his time." If such a manuscript existed, it is possible that it was destroyed in the Great Fire of London (1666), which laid waste to most of the central area of the city.

Another possibility, however, must be noted. The first rule laid down for the translators by Richard Bancroft reads as follows:

*The ordinary Bible read in the Church, commonly called the Bishops' Bible, to be followed, and as little altered as the Truth of the original will permit.*

This indicates that the text of the Bishops' Bible was to be the base of the revision.

It is known that Robert Barker, the king's printer, furnished the translators with forty large-format editions of this text to assist them in their work. A number of scholars have suggested that what was actually delivered to the printer was a copy of the Bishops' Bible, with alterations entered directly into the text of the work. In 1956, Edwin Willoughby discovered a heavily annotated 1602 edition of the Bishops' Bible in the Bodleian Library, Oxford. There is at least some degree of correspondence between the annotated text and the final version of the King James Bible. Attractive though this theory may be, the correspondence is not as great as one might expect. The simple truth is that we shall probably never know precisely what was delivered to Robert Barker in 1611, enabling him to begin the process of production.

# 9

## PRODUCTION:
## THE EARLY PRINTINGS OF
## THE KING JAMES BIBLE

The production of the King James Bible was a massive undertaking, both on account of the length of the work itself, and the considerable number of copies that were demanded of the first printing. While some have suggested that the full resources of the state were put at the disposal of the translators and printers, in order to ensure the quality of the resulting Bible, the reality is somewhat different. The new Bible would be a work of private enterprise throughout. The king might well have authorized a new translation of the Bible. He had, however, no intention of paying for its translation or production costs. The new translation would have to be funded by venture capitalists. To understand how the production of the work was financed, we must consider the nature of the "royal privilege" granted to Robert Barker, the king's printer.

### THE KING'S PRINTER: THE ROYAL PRIVILEGE

THE ENGLISH BOOK trade was regulated by the Stationers' Company. As printing was permitted only at four centres—London,

York, Oxford, and Cambridge—until 1695, regulation of the trade was not especially difficult. The printing of Bibles, however, was seen as a matter of particular importance, and was subject to additional regulations. Since the time of Henry VIII, Bibles printed within England by official sanction—such as Matthew's Bible, the Great Bible, and the Bishops' Bible—were subject to a trade monopoly. The monarch granted a "privilege" to favoured subjects allowing them a monopoly on the production of certain types of Bible—an honour or favour usually indicated with the words *cum privilegio* on the title page of the Bible in question. The crown, in turn, received a proportion of the "royalty" paid to the holder of the privilege.

Richard Jugge had secured a "privilege" for the production of theological books in general under Elizabeth I. While Jugge held the office of "Queen's Printer," this was not seen as automatically conferring any special privileges in relation to the printing of Bibles. However, this association was not long in developing. The office of Queen's Printer passed, in part, to Christopher Barker in 1577, the year of Jugge's death. Through the influence of friends at court, Barker was able to secure a complete monopoly in England for the printing of "all and singular books, pamphlets, acts of Parliament, injunctions, and Bible and New Testaments in the English tongue of whatever translation with notes or without notes." While Barker was at liberty to assign these privileges to other printers, he retained absolute control of the printing of English translations of the Bible throughout his lifetime.

These monopolies did not, of course, extend to English translations produced outside England, perhaps the most important of which were various editions of the Geneva Bible. However, printings of the Geneva Bible within England fell within the scope of the patent, and Barker had no hesitation in exploiting this privilege. Interestingly, Barker appears to have done relatively little to encourage the printing of the various "official" translations, such as the Bishops' Bible, but was enthusiastic in his support for the popular and profitable Geneva Bible. Barker's support for biblical translations appears to have been directly proportional to their profitability.

In 1589, Barker managed to achieved something of a business *coup de force*. He persuaded Elizabeth to extend his patent as Queen's Printer for the remainder of his own life, and that of his son, Robert. Barker had originally had to share the privilege with Sir Thomas Wilkes under the deal negotiated in 1577. Wilkes fell out of favour in 1589, opening the way to a renegotiation of the royal printing privilege in Barker's favour. Barker Senior died in 1599, and his son assumed the role of Queen's Printer immediately. With the accession of James I, Robert Barker became the King's Printer. Under the 1589 privilege, it was inevitable that the responsibility of printing the new Bible would fall to him.

It will thus be clear that the use of the King's Printer for this important new translation did not rest upon any perception that this would ensure a more accurate or reliable printing, but upon the belief that this was potentially a profitable project that would bring financial advantage to Barker and his partners. If any printings showed scrupulosity in ensuring textual accuracy, these were the editions that subsequently came from the university printing houses at Oxford and Cambridge.

It was a responsibility that Barker viewed with some hesitation, not least on account of the very substantial financial investment it demanded. Barker is estimated to have had to set aside £3,500 to cover the production costs of the massive work. He yielded to the inevitable, and sought partners in the venture. John Bill, Bonham Norton, and John Norton duly signed up, and the capital required was made available. The partnership fell into disarray within five years, with a furious dispute between the partners threatening to disrupt the later printing of the work. Barker was obliged to hand over the copyright to Bonham Norton in 1617 as financial security. Norton promptly took over the printing process, and moved the entire operation to Hunsdon House in Blackfriars. It was not until 1629 that Barker managed to regain control of the patent. Norton went on to be imprisoned for bribery, and Barker for debt. Barker spent the last ten years of his life in the King's Bench Prison in Borough High Street, Southwark. Under the terms of the patent granted to his father, he remained the King's Printer until his dying day. All this, however, lay in the future.

## THE TECHNOLOGY OF THE FIRST PRINTING

THE FIRST PRINTING of the King James Bible in 1611 was carried out at Barker's printing house, located at Northumberland House in Aldersgate Street, close to the centre of London, using newly cast type on high-quality linen and rag paper. The volume consisted of 123 signatures—that is, gatherings of paper—with 366 sheets of paper, each folded to yield two "leaves" of paper, consisting of four printed pages, measuring 16 by 10$^{1}/_{2}$ inches. Most of the signatures consisted of three sheets of paper, folded over and sewn together to yield six leaves (that is, twelve printed pages). It is clear that the Bible was printed section by section, with binding taking place at the end of the printing process. Barker does not appear to have possessed the resources needed to allow simultaneous printing of each section of the work.

Printing methods had not changed substantially since the time of Gutenberg or Caxton, a century and a half earlier. Although the cost of producing printed books was still substantially less than handwritten manuscripts, the process was still immensely time-consuming and labour-intensive. Although the precise production methods used in Barker's printing house are not known, it is likely that the first printing of the King James Bible would have taken place along the following lines.

First, the type would have to be cast. The type used in the first printing gave a very clear impression, which strongly suggests that it was cast especially for this project. The first printing used black letter type, despite the fact that this was beginning to fall out of favour, being increasingly seen as archaic. It is possible that the selection of this type was intended to add to the gravity of the final text. A small amount of roman type was used to set words inserted by the translators (to distinguish this from the remainder of the text). Roman characters were also used for the summaries that appeared at the head of each chapter, cross-references in the margins, and the subject headlines at the top of each page. The basic intention was that the authentic words of Scripture itself should be set in black letter, with additional material in roman. A small amount of italic type was also required to indicate alternative translations of difficult or obscure words.

The production of sufficient type would have required a substantial financial investment, and would need to have begun well in advance of the printing process itself. The technology for this had been set in place by Gutenberg, and had advanced relatively little in the intervening period. Gutenberg's type mould allowed type to be produced of uniform height yet with varying widths, to accommodate the different horizontal sizes of letters. For example, the letters *l* and *m* take up a significantly different horizontal space; Gutenberg's type mould was sufficiently flexible to allow for this variation in width.

A relief pattern for each letter was then cut into a copper matrix, often using a punch. This created a matrix in which each letter was imprinted as an indented mirror image of its normal form. The matrix was then fitted to the bottom of the type mould, which generally took the form of a metal box, enclosed in wood to insulate the typecaster's hands from the heat of the molten metal that was used in the type-casting process. Once the mould had been adjusted for width, the process of typecasting could begin.

The typecaster would typically hold the mould in his right hand, pouring liquid type metal into the mould from a ladle. The mould was immediately jerked upward, to ensure that that molten metal was forced into the indentation on the copper matrix. Contemporary records indicate that the technique of jerking the mould at just the right moment was not easily mastered, and made considerable demands of the typesetter. In particular, it demanded extensive use of the wrist muscles, as an experienced typecaster is reckoned to have been capable of producing up to four thousand pieces of type a day. Once the typecaster had produced sufficient stock of one letter or character, he would insert a different matrix, and repeat the process. It is assumed that Barker would have ensured that this process was completed in advance of receiving the text of the King James Bible from Bancroft, so that his printers could proceed directly to the process of composition.

Composition is the process by which a page is constructed, including the layout of the type itself, along with any illustrations or ornaments. A typical page of the King James Bible was laid out as follows. The text is laid out in two columns, each of which is enclosed within ruled margins, containing fifty-nine lines of text per column. Each verse began on a new line, with its number clearly indicated at the beginning of the line, in the same size of type as the remainder of the verse itself. At the top, the title of the biblical book is displayed as a central headline, with the subject matter of the pages being displayed on either side. No page numbers were provided.

With this basic pattern in mind, the compositor would set up the type for each page. The type was stored in cases adjacent to the composing table. Since the time of the famous Venetian printer Manutius Aldus, type had been stored in two cases: capital letters in the upper case, and minuscule letters in the lower case. The compositor would assemble the type using a "composing stick," which is best thought of as a small tray, equal to the width of the printed line. As each line was assembled, it was transferred to the galley tray. Once the two columns of text were completely assembled, headlines and other marginal material were added. Two pages would be printed at a time. During the stage of "imposition," two completely set pages would be placed together on what was often known as the "imposing stone." After ensuring that the pages were aligned correctly, they were enclosed within a metal or wooden frame known as a "chase." Padding would be inserted to ensure that the type did not move during the printing process. The result of this process was known as a "forme." A draft sheet was then printed from the forme, and checked against the original copy for errors. There is substantial evidence to suggest that many late Renaissance printers checked their text by having the original copy read aloud to them while they checked the proof text against what they heard being read.

In the meantime, paper would have been prepared for the printing process. Limitations in ink technology meant that it was difficult to apply ink evenly to dry paper. The solution to this particular difficulty was to dampen the paper in advance. Typically 250 sheets of paper were dampened on the day before printing was due, and allowed to stand overnight to ensure even distribution of the moisture.

The forme would then be placed on the bed of the printing press. A series of devices (including the "tympan" and "frisket") had been developed over the years to ensure that ink smudges were avoided, and that the paper was correctly aligned—a matter of no small importance, if both sides of the paper were to be printed. In the early days of printing, up to ten small pricked holes in the margins of the paper had to be aligned with corresponding pinpoints on the press itself. By the early seventeenth century, things had improved considerably; only two points were now generally used, located in the middle of the forme. These would subsequently become invisible as a result of the binding process.

Two men were required to operate a typical printing press of the period. One applied ink to the type using an "inkball"; the other operated the lever that forced the platen on top of the paper, and thus ensured its smooth contact with the inked type. The "inkballs" were leather pads, mounted in wooden cups with handles attached, which were stuffed with wool or horsehair. These were dipped in ink, then rolled over the type to ensure even distribution of the ink. Once this was done, paper was inserted into the press and aligned correctly. The pressman then pulled the lever of the press toward him, which operated the screw that brought the platen into contact with the paper, forcing it against the inked forme. The platen ensured that pressure was evenly distributed across the paper, thus avoiding uneven impressions. However, difficulties in technology meant that a platen could not be constructed wide enough to print both pages in the forme simultaneously. The first pressman thus made two pulls to print each forme, allowing his colleague to realign the forme between the pulls. Pulling required considerable physical effort, and was very tiring. As a result, the two pressmen would swap tasks halfway through the process.

Once the first side of a sheet of paper was printed, it was important to print the second as quickly as possible. The paper was still wet at this stage; if it was allowed to dry out, any changes in shape would make realignment very difficult. A second forme would, therefore, be inserted, and the entire process repeated until four pages had been printed. Once this was done, the paper was hung up to dry, while the ink was removed from the forme and the type broken down, ready to be used again in a new forme.

In order to ensure that the Bible was assembled in the correct order, the pages were then assembled into "gatherings" or "signatures." With occasional exceptions, the King James Bible was printed in gatherings of three sheets of paper, to yield twelve pages of text. (As explained earlier, each sheet of paper was printed with two pages on each side.) These were then gathered and sewn together. To ensure that the many gatherings that went to make up the King James Bible were assembled in the correct order, the first page of each was given a "signature." Traditionally, this took the form of a letter of the alphabet. Thus a short book consisting of five "gatherings" or "signatures" would be arranged in "gatherings" signed as follows: A; B; C; D; E. Where there were more gatherings than letters of the alphabet, later "gatherings" would be signed Aa; Bb; Cc; and so forth. The first printing of the King James Bible of 1611 was arranged as follows:

Front matter: A–D
Old Testament and Apocrypha:
A–Z; Aa–Zz; Aaa–Zzz; Aaaa–Zzzz; Aaaaa–Ccccc.
New Testament: A–Z; Aa.

Finally, the work was bound. It had long been customary to offer printed Bibles in two forms: bound, or as sheets. The latter were cheaper, and allowed purchasers to make their own arrangements for the precise form of binding they wanted. In 1541, the Great Bible could be purchased for ten shillings in sheet form, or twelve shillings bound.

Barker produced additional versions of the work from 1612, with the needs of private readers in mind. The smaller quarto and octavo editions appeared in 1612; an even smaller duodecimo version in 1617. Two important differences should be noted between these later versions and the original version of 1611. First, they were smaller than the original folio edition. The octavo version was one quarter of the size of the original. Whereas these later editions were designed to be laid on a table or desk, or even held in the hand, the original folio edition was meant to be placed on a substantial church lectern, capable of bearing its weight and supporting its large pages. The trend toward smaller editions continued unabated throughout the remainder of the seventeenth century. In 1620, Norton and Bill published a vicesimoquarto edition— that is, with forty-eight printed pages per sheet of paper—which was a mere 4 by 2 inches, capable of being carried in the pocket.

The second development of interest relates to the type used to set these smaller Bibles. As noted above, the folio edition of 1611— designed to be read in churches—used the archaic black letter type, modelled on German Gothic types of the fifteenth century. The smaller editions followed the practice of the Geneva Bible, and used the more modern and legible roman type.

## THE PRESENTATION OF THE TEXT IN THE FIRST PRINTING

ONE OF THE most important developments in sixteenth-century book production was the gradual rise to prominence of the title page. The origins of this can be traced back to the formation of the firm Fust & Schoeffer in 1462, following the failure of Johannes Gutenberg's original printing firm. As a means of identifying their products, Fust & Schoeffer began to print a simple woodblock design as a trademark at the end of their books. The idea was that the reader of the work would realize who had produced the book. Although a tradition had developed of leaving the first page of the book blank— perhaps to protect the text from wear—it gradually became increasingly common to find the author and title of the work printed on this otherwise blank opening page.

In the early sixteenth century, Parisian printers began to experiment with larger trademarks, which often would not fit into the lim-

ited space available at the end of a book. As a result, the first page of
the text was seized upon as a means of identifying the author, title,
and publisher of the work. This trend, which led to increasingly decorative title pages, can be observed clearly in the *editio princeps* of the
King James Bible (1611), which includes an impressive and ornate
engraved title page. As the page is of such importance in relation to
the presentation of the work, it is worth considering it in a little detail.
The title reads as follows:

*THE HOLY BIBLE, containing the Old Testament and the New.*
*Newly translated out of the original tongues: and with the former*
*translations diligently compared and revised by his Majesty's spe-*
*cial commandment. Appointed to be read in Churches. Imprinted*
*at London by Robert Barker, Printer to the King's most excellent*
*majesty. Anno Domini 1611.*

The use of the phrase "appointed to be read in churches" has
attracted much interest. It is sometimes assumed that the words
"appointed to be read in churches" imply that the work has been
authorized for this purpose. In fact, this is not the case. Although a
twenty-first-century reader would naturally interpret the word
"appointed" to mean "authorized," this is not the seventeenth-century
meaning of the English term. The words—which were in any case
omitted from many later editions—simply mean that the work was
laid out in a way suitable for public reading in churches.

As noted earlier, the Hampton Court Conference had set out a
proposal for the translation of the Bible, in which translation would
be undertaken by "the best-learned men in both Universities, then
reviewed by the Bishops, presented to the Privy Council, lastly ratified by Royal authority." Yet there is actually no documentary evidence that the 1611 Bible ever received final written authorization
from the bishops, Privy Council, or the king. While it is possible that
such authorization—which would have taken the form of an Order in
Council—may have been lost in the Whitehall fire of January 12,

1618 (which destroyed the Privy Council registers for the years 1600–13), it is more likely that no such order ever existed.

Yet, as matters turned out, the new Bible did not really need the royal authority to command respect. As the noted English New Testament scholar B. F. Westcott commented in 1868:

> *From the middle of the seventeenth century, the King's Bible has been the acknowledged Bible of the English-speaking nations throughout the world simply because it is the best. A revision which embodied the ripe fruits of nearly a century of labour, and appealed to the religious instinct of a great Christian people, gained by its own internal character a vital authority which could never have been secured by an edict of sovereign rulers.*

But such acceptance actually lay some distance in the future. The new translation's first decades were marked by violent criticism from both Protestant and Catholic opponents, and a failure to gain widespread support. We shall consider the troubled reception of the new work in a later chapter; for now, the presentation of the text of the new translation is worth studying.

The title itself is surrounded by a decorative frame, designed by Cornelius Boel, an artist originally based in Antwerp who had settled in Richmond, and who had painted portraits of members of the royal family. The upper panel depicts the Trinity in a conventional style. God the Father is represented by the four Hebrew letters "YHWH," a combination of letters that is often referred to as the "tetragrammaton." This word is the Hebrew name for the God of Israel, and is used extensively in the Old Testament to distinguish the God of Israel from all other deities of the Ancient Near East. The King James Bible occasionally translates this special name as "Jehovah"; more often, it is translated as "the LORD." Immediately below this is an image of a dove, often used as a representation of the Holy Spirit. This imagery is based partly on the account of the baptism of Jesus, as related in Matthew 3:16–17:

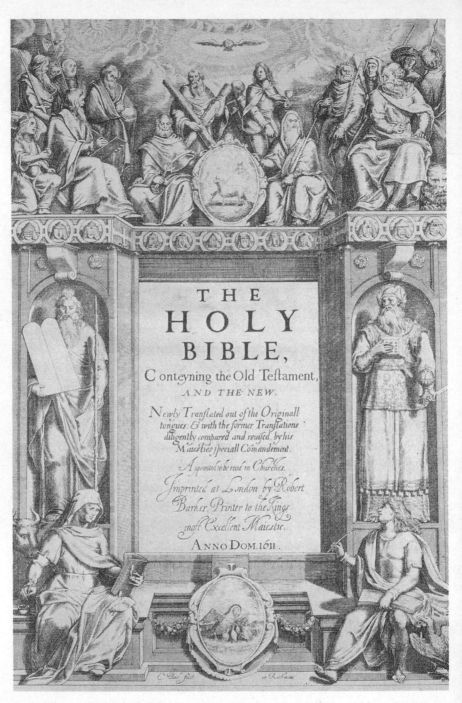

# THE HOLY BIBLE,

Conteyning the Old Testament,

AND THE NEW.

Newly Translated out of the Originall tongues: & with the former Translations diligently compared and reuised, by his Maiesties speciall Comandement.

Appointed to be read in Churches.

Imprinted at London by Robert Barker, Printer to the Kings most Excellent Maiestie.

ANNO DOM. 1611.

**THE TITLE PAGE OF THE 1611 EDITION OF THE KING JAMES BIBLE**

*And Jesus, when he was baptized, went up straightway out of the water: and, lo, the heavens were opened unto him, and he saw the Spirit of God descending like a dove, and lighting upon him: And lo a voice from heaven, saying, This is my beloved Son, in whom I am well pleased.*

Jesus Christ himself is depicted within an oval frame, toward the base of the panel, using the image of a lamb and flag. This image is based partly on the book of Revelation, especially the reference to "the Lamb that was slain to receive power, and riches, and wisdom, and strength, and honour, and glory, and blessing" (Revelation 5:12). The "lamb and flag" is generally interpreted as a symbol of the resurrection of the crucified Christ. To make sure that the reference to the crucifixion is not overlooked, Boel places a cross slightly to the left of the image of the lamb and flag. The figures of Peter and James are directly to the left and right of the oval, with figures of the apostles—including Paul—dispersed in the background.

Four figures are placed in the corners of the rectangular frame, each holding a pen. These figures are the evangelists—the gospel writers. Matthew is placed in the top left; Mark in the top right; Luke at bottom left, and John at bottom right. To the sides of the frame, at the same level as the title itself, stand the figures of Moses and Aaron. Boel has placed them in niches, similar to those familiar with the church architecture of the period. The six figures just mentioned—Moses, Aaron, and the four gospel writers—are seen as representing the Old and New Covenants, which are contained in the translation. Although this edition of the King James Bible includes the Apocrypha, attention is not drawn to this fact on the title panel.

Finally, an oval panel is placed on the bottom of the frame, depicting a pelican feeding her young. This symbol is of particular interest, and merits close attention. The image of the pelican is widely used in Christian iconography to depict Christ's work of salvation. It was once thought that the pelican fed her young with blood pecked from her own breast, and this was interpreted as an image of Christ's blood sustaining the faithful. The image of the pelican "vulning" herself seemed ideally suited to expressing the basic Christian idea that Christ saved and sustained his people through his shedding of blood on the cross. The image is thus intended to supplement that of the lamb and flag, already noted, to stress the centrality of Jesus Christ to the message of the Bible.

There is a curious irony to this symbol. In the Middle Ages, the image of a pelican came to be linked with the Lord's Supper or Mass, especially with the medieval ecclesiastical feast of Corpus Christi (literally, "the body of Christ"). Oxford and Cambridge colleges were often named after the religious festival nearest to the day of their founding. One Oxford and one Cambridge college derived their names from this medieval religious feast. And who was the president of Corpus Christi College, Oxford, at the time of commissioning of the new Bible? None other than the same John Reynolds, who had been the original inspiration for the new translation.

The title page is followed by the "Dedication to the Most High and Mighty Prince James, by the grace of God, King of Great Britain, France and Ireland, Defender of the Faith, etc." Note that English monarchs had ceased to have any authority in France with the loss of the final English possession—Calais—under Mary Tudor fifty years earlier. However, the title was retained as a minor conceit for some time. This dedication was written by Thomas Bilson. It was followed by the extended literary preface entitled "The Translators to the Reader," written by Miles Smith, which explained some of the thinking that lay behind the new translation.

After this, we find a substantial amount of material relating to the ordering of the church year, reflecting the primary purpose of the volume—to be read aloud in the churches of England. First, a "calendar" identified the main holy days for the church year. This was followed by "An Almanack for 39 years," which set out the main religious festivals for the period 1603–1641. This was followed by a series of directions intended to allow readers to work out the precise date of Easter in perpetuity. A lectionary then followed, setting out the order of Psalms and other readings from the Bible set for Morning and Evening

Prayer throughout the year. Finally, the names and order of the books of the Old and New Testaments were set out, along with the numbers of chapters they contained.

This section of material is of considerable interest, as it indicates that the primary envisaged function of the King James Bible was ecclesiastical. This was not intended to be a Bible for personal study. In addition to being far too large for personal use—its folio size demanded that it rested on some kind of lectern—the Bible included material that showed its users how it was to be used in church services. It is this material which was "appointed"—that is, laid out—to enable the Bible to be read in churches, as the title page makes clear. Later editions dropped this material altogether, as it was provided in the 1662 edition of the Book of Common Prayer.

This section was followed by another section consisting of thirty-four pages of highly decorative biblical genealogies, followed by a map of Canaan, with a list of its main place names printed on the reverse. This material, which was of little use to anyone, was added on account of an arrangement negotiated with James I by the noted entrepreneur John Speed in October 1610. On the basis of this "privilege," every edition of the Bible printed for the next ten years had to include this largely useless material. Speed gained something in the region of sixpence to two shillings per copy for this material, a proportion of which had to be paid to the crown. This increased the cost of the Bible considerably. There are good reasons for thinking that these thirty-six pages were printed by Speed, and bound into the Bible at a late stage; the material is occasionally found inserted at different locations, suggesting that it was originally distinct from the material produced by Robert Barker.

Finally, the reader passes to the body of the translation itself. The text is laid out in two columns, using black letter type. This contrasted sharply with the much more legible and attractive roman type used by the Geneva Bible. The two columns of text were enclosed within rules, with each verse beginning on a new line. Words that were added to the text to allow English readers to make sense of the original Greek or Hebrew were indicated, not by the use of italic type—as in later versions of the text—but by the use of small roman type. This unsatisfactory solution gave rise to an inelegant presentation, particularly on pages where many such words had been added. The first printing used fifty-nine lines of type per column; later printings increased this. For example, the folio edition of 1613 used seventy-two lines per column, allowing the work to be reduced from 732 leaves to 508.

The ruled margins allowed space for the insertion of marginal notes. These, however, did not take the form of the Geneva Bible's annotations—which were basically a theological commentary on the text—but explained the literal meaning of Hebrew translations, or identifying variant readings of the text. The Old Testament alone contained 6,637 marginal notes of this kind, of which roughly a thousand dealt directly with the literal meaning of Hebrew words.

The New Testament is prefaced by its own title page. Whereas the title page to the volume as a whole was engraved on metal, that for the New Testament was a cheaper woodcut, reproducing some features of the earlier page. The title page reads as follows:

*THE NEW TESTAMENT of our Lord and Saviour Jesus Christ. Newly translated out of the original Greek; and with the former translations diligently compared and revised by his Majesty's special command. Imprinted in London by Robert Barker, Printer to the King's most excellent majesty. Anno Domini 1611. Cum privilego.*

Demand for the work was such that a reprint was inevitable. This came in 1613, when a new folio edition was printed, which corrected some of the errors noted in the first printing of the work. Sadly, the magnificent title page engraving of 1611 was replaced by a less satisfactory woodcut, based on the 1611 title page for the New Testament. Some of the copies of the 1613 edition appear to have included a number of printed sheets left over from the 1611 printing—presumably an economy measure, reflecting the weak financial base of the operation.

ST. LUKE'S BIRTH OF CHRIST FROM
THE KING JAMES BIBLE

# ERRORS IN EARLY PRINTINGS OF THE
# KING JAMES BIBLE

THE EARLY PRINTINGS of the King James Bible included many errors. Many of these arose from weaknesses in the book production processes of the period. Proofing was often a haphazard business. From what we know of the book production methods of this period, it seems that the greatest effort was put into the process of typesetting. The compositor would take considerable care in setting the text, presumably on the assumption that accuracy was of the greatest importance at this critical stage. Most printers had only one or two presses at their disposal, and were reluctant to waste too much time by checking for typographical errors. It seems that the first printed sheet to be "pulled" from the press was checked for such errors, while printing continued.

Contemporary sources suggest that a "reading-boy" would then read the proof copy aloud to the compositor, who would check it against the original copy. Errors could arise in all kinds of ways—such as homophones (words that are pronounced identically, yet have different meanings and are spelled differently—such as "there" and "their"). It is thus little cause for surprise that Bibles should contain at least some errors, despite the best standards of the day being employed in an attempt to eliminate them.

A further factor contributing to the large number of errors in English Bibles was the constant pressure to reduce their production costs. The annual "privilege" enjoyed by the King's Printer was bought at a considerable price, and had to be recouped somehow. Cost savings introduced in the later phase of Barker's career included the reduction of the number of proofreaders used to check the text for errors. It is known that the four proofreaders employed by Barker in the 1630s were so fed up with the constant pressure to reduce their wages—or get rid of them altogether—that they appealed to the then-Archbishop of Canterbury, William Laud, to intervene on their behalf.

Many around this time preferred Dutch-printed Bibles, which were much more accurate, and generally printed on better quality paper. A number of late-seventeenth-century anecdotes pillory the textual inaccuracies of the English Bibles of this period. The story is told of a bishop who, having been invited to preach around 1675 on a certain biblical text in St. Paul's Cathedral—then being rebuilt following the great fire of London—went into a nearby London stationer's to buy a London-printed Bible so that he could study the text. On turning to the appropriate page, he found that the verse had been left out altogether.

The first printing of the King James Bible in 1611 included a number of printing errors. For example, a small slip in the typesetting of the description of the interior of the tabernacle led to the following reading (Exodus 28:11):

*And for the north side the hangings were an hundred cubits, their
pillars were twenty, and their sockets of brass twenty; the hoops of
the pillars and their fillets of silver.*

But there were probably few who noticed, let alone cared, that the
pillars really bore hooks, not hoops. This error was corrected in the
1613 reprint.

A further difference between the 1611 printing of the work and
the 1613 reprint is of interest. Their variant translations of Ruth 3:15
led to the earlier printing being known as the "Great He Bible" (1611)
and the later one as the "Great She Bible" (1613) respectively. The
passage in question describes how Boaz measured out "six measures
of barley," and gave it to Ruth. The "Great He Bible" then has Boaz
going off to a nearby city, whereas the "Great She Bible" reports that
it is Ruth who made this journey. The "Great She Bible" also caused
bewilderment to some of its readers by confusing Jesus and Judas at
one point (Matthew 26:36).

Some errors in the early printings of the King James Bible caused
considerable distress and concern at the time. Part of the problem was
that the production of the King James Bible was privately financed.
Pressure to cut production costs meant that the "formes" were not left
intact after they had been printed, so that printing errors could be
corrected easily for future printings. A huge amount of type would be
necessary if every forme was to be retained in this way. As far as can
be ascertained, each forme was broken up after it had served its purpose, and the type was then used to set another forme. If an error was
not spotted on the first printed sheet, it was impossible to correct at
a later stage in production.

Yet these printing errors were regarded as scandalous by some.
William Kilburne issued a vigorous denunciation of these in 1659,
when he published his *Dangerous Errors in Several Late Printed Bibles
to the Great Scandal and Corruption of Sound and True Religion.*
Kilburne claimed to have identified as many as twenty thousand
errors in various recent printings. Some of these errors were bizarre.

For example, a warning to the Israelites about the devious ways of the Midianites took an unusual turn, thanks to an amusing misprint in one edition (Numbers 25:17–18): "Vex the Midianites, and smite them: For they vex you with their wives." The possibilities suggested by this passage are immense and intriguing, to say the least. Yet "wives" was merely a misprint for "wiles."

More serious was the misprint in an edition of 1631, which rendered Exodus 20:14 as follows: "Thou shalt commit adultery." The omission of the word "not" was speedily corrected, but not before this had caused some consternation among the Bible's readers. Robert Barker and Martin Lucas, the printers of this "Wicked Bible"—as it came to be known—were fined severely for this unfortunate lapse.

The first edition of the King James Bible to be published by Oxford University Press appeared in 1675; this was followed in 1682 by a sumptuous edition prepared by the Oxford printer John Baskett. The value of the edition was greatly reduced by its many printing errors. For example, it made reference to the "Parable of the Vinegar" instead of the "Parable of the Vineyard"—an error which led it to being nicknamed the "Vinegar Bible." Its amused critics panned it as "a Bastkett-full of Printer's Errors." Such printing errors were perhaps inevitable, given both the complexity of the text being produced, and the generally poor quality of English printing and proofing methods during the seventeenth century.

Other corrections to the text were introduced later to avoid possible misunderstandings. For example, the original printing of Acts 24:24 in 1611 referred to Drusilla, the wife of the Roman governor Felix, as a Jew; in 1629, this was altered to "Jewess." The original translation of Mark 10:18 read thus: "there is no man good, but one, that is, God." This could be misunderstood as implying that God was a human being. A small alteration was introduced in 1638, avoiding this implication: the text now read "there is none good but one, that is, God."

We have considered some of the problems that the King's Printer faced in producing the work. But what of the issues faced by those charged with making the translation in the first place?

# 10

## TRANSLATORS
## AND TRAITORS:
## THE PROBLEMS OF
## BIBLE TRANSLATION

The translators of the King James Bible faced issues that have confronted translators down the centuries. How can the complexities of a text originally written in one language be expressed in another? The difficulty is traditionally expressed in an Italian saying: "the translator is a traitor." How can one combine faithfulness to the text with elegance of translation? It is a perennial issue that torments those who are called to translate. A French writer made the startling and rather crude suggestion that translations are like women: if they are beautiful, they are not faithful; if they are faithful, they are not beautiful. Perhaps a nugget of truth lies hidden in that outrageous statement.

Yet some would argue that the quality of the text under consideration in this specific case raises particular challenges, as well as conferring some distinct advantages. Before considering some of those challenges, it is worth noting the view of Matthew Arnold on the unique nature of the Bible as an object of translation. In his 1861 lectures *On Translating Homer*, Arnold suggested that the Bible had an inherent dignity, which would still be evident in its English translation:

> He [the translator] will find one English book and one only, where, as in the Iliad itself, perfect plainness of speech is allied with perfect nobleness; and that book is the Bible.

Arnold clearly took the view that simplicity and nobility went hand in hand, inseparably, in the Bible, both in its original and its translation. The translators, in effect, could not but be guided and directed by the quality of the original.

Something like this understanding of translation lay behind the King James translation. In his Seventy-Fifth Sermon, the great English preacher and poet John Donne (1572–1631) declared his judgment that "the Holy Ghost is an eloquent author, a vehement and an abundant author, but yet not luxuriant." The passage in Donne's sermon gives no indication of irony or sarcasm; Donne's belief is clearly that the biblical text itself is possessed of an eloquent style, and that a translation that aims at accuracy will allow this stylistic excellence to be carried over into the resulting English. Elegance results from a faithful translation, and does not require to be imposed upon the text. There was thus no sense of the translators imposing a style or "voice" upon the Bible; they believed such a voice to be present already, and that the process of translation, if accurately and carefully executed, would allow it to be retained and projected in the English language.

In this chapter, we shall begin to explore the issues and challenges that faced the six companies of translators assembled by King James. We begin by examining the nature of the text that was to be translated—the Bible itself.

## THE COMPONENTS OF THE BIBLE

THE TRANSLATORS WERE divided into six companies, with the following assignments:

The First Westminster Company, responsible for the "Pentateuch" [that is, the first five books of the Bible] and "the Story from Joshua to the first Book of Chronicles, exclusive."

The First Cambridge Company, responsible for "the First of the Chronicles, with the rest of the Story, and the *Hagiographi*, viz. Job, Psalms, Proverbs, Canticles, Ecclesiastes."

The First Oxford Company, assigned to "the four, or greater, Prophets, with the Lamentations, and the twelve lesser prophets."

The Second Oxford Company, assigned to "the four Gospels, Acts of the Apostles, Apocalypse."

The Second Westminster Company, responsible for "the Epistles of St. Paul, the Canonical Epistles."

The Second Cambridge Company, responsible for "the Prayer of Manasses and the rest of the Apocrypha."

These six companies were thus responsible for three sections of the Bible: The Old Testament; the Apocrypha; and the New Testament. Both this division and some of the issues that it raises need exploring.

First, the term "Bible" is itself worth examining. The term "Bible" is used to refer to the collection of writings regarded as authoritative and foundational by Christians. Like many words in modern English, it derives from a Greek phrase: *ta biblia*, which literally means "the books." Other terms are also used, such as "Sacred Scripture" or "Holy Scripture."

James I himself had a firm understanding of the importance of the Bible both for personal faith and communal behaviour and values. He set out something of his understanding of the role of the Bible in the opening section of the *Basilikon Doron*, intended to provide instruction to his son for godly princely living.

*The whole Scripture is dited by God's Spirit, thereby (as by his lively word) to instruct and rule the whole Church militant, till the end of the world. It is composed of two parts, the Old and New Testament. The ground of the former is the Law, which sheweth our sin and conteyneth justice. The ground of the other is Christ, who pardoning sin contayneth Grace. The sum of the Law is the ten Commands, more largely dilated in the Law, interpreted by the Prophets: and by the histories are the examples shown of obedience or disobedience thereto, and what praemium or poena was accordingly given by God. But because no man was able to keepe the Lawe, nor any parte thereof, it pleased God of his infinite wisdom and goodness, to incarnate his only Son in our nature, for satisfaction of his justice in his suffering for us: that since we could not be saved by doing, we might (at least) be saved by beleiving. The ground therefore of the Law of Grace, is contayned in the foure histories of the birth, life, death, and resurrection of Christ.*

## THE OLD TESTAMENT

The Old Testament consists of thirty-nine books, beginning with Genesis and ending with Malachi. It is almost entirely written in Hebrew, the language of Israel; however, some short sections are written in Aramaic, an international language widely used in the diplomacy of the Ancient Near East. We shall consider these languages shortly.

The Old Testament includes a number of different kinds of writings, of which the most important are the following:

1. The *Five Books of the Law* are sometimes also referred to as *The Five Books of Moses*, reflecting a traditional belief that they were largely written by Moses. In more scholarly works, they are sometimes referred to as *The Pentateuch*, from the Greek words for "five" and "books." They are: Genesis, Exodus, Leviticus, Numbers, and Deuteronomy. These deal with the creation of

the world, the calling of Israel as a people, and its early history, including the Exodus from Egypt. The story they tell ends with the people of Israel being about to cross over the Jordan, and enter the promised land. One of the most important themes of these books is the giving of the Law to Moses, and its implications for the life of Israel.

2. The *Historical Books*: Joshua, Judges, Ruth, 1 and 2 Samuel, 1 and 2 Kings, 1 and 2 Chronicles, Ezra, Nehemiah, and Esther. These books deal with various aspects of the history of the people of God from their entry into the promised land of Canaan to the return of the people of Jerusalem from exile in the city of Babylon. It includes detailed accounts of the conquest of Canaan, the establishment of a monarchy in Israel, the great reigns of kings David and Solomon, the breakup of the single nation of Israel into two parts (the northern kingdom of Israel and the southern kingdom of Judah), the destruction of Israel by the Assyrians, the defeat of Judah and the exile of her people by the Babylonians, and the final return from exile and the rebuilding of the Temple. The books are arranged in historical order.

3. The *Wisdom Writings*: Job, Psalms; Proverbs, Ecclesiastes; Song of Solomon. These works deal with the question of how true wisdom may be found, and often provide some practical examples of wisdom.

4. The *Prophets*. This major section of the Old Testament contains the writings of a group of individuals, inspired by the Holy Spirit, who sought to make the will of God known to their people over a period of time. There are sixteen prophetic writings in the Old Testament, which are usually divided into two categories. First, there are the four *major (or "greater") prophets*: Isaiah, Jeremiah, Ezekiel, and Daniel. These are followed by the twelve *minor (or "lesser") prophets*: Hosea, Joel, Amos, Obadiah,

Jonah, Micah, Nahum, Habakkuk, Zephaniah, Haggai, Zechariah, and Malachi. The use of the words "major" and "minor" does not imply any judgment about the relative importance of the prophets. It refers simply to the length of the books in question. The prophetic writings are arranged roughly in historical order.

An additional group of writings has, since the sixteenth century, come to be known as the "Apocrypha."

## THE APOCRYPHA

It must be remembered that the Reformation saw major debates within Western Christianity over many aspects of the Christian faith. One of those, which had a significant impact in England, concerned the authority and religious value of a group of writings traditionally considered as part of the Old Testament. As we have seen the collection of Latin translations known as the Vulgate had considerable importance within medieval Christianity. Translation errors discovered in this Latin translation constituted one major contributing factor to the pressure for reform. For medieval Christian writers, the word "Scripture" or "the Bible" meant something like "those works that are included in the Vulgate."

The Protestant reformers, however, felt able to call this judgment into question. While all the New Testament works were accepted as canonical (that is, belonging to the Bible), doubts were raised by Protestant biblical scholars concerning the canonicity of a group of works traditionally treated as part of the Old Testament. A comparison of the contents of the Old Testament in the Hebrew Bible on the one hand, and the Greek and Latin versions (such as the Vulgate) on the other, shows that the latter contain a number of works not found in the former.

Following the lead of the great patristic writer and scholar Jerome, the reformers argued that the only Old Testament writings that could be regarded as belonging to the canon of Scripture were those originally included in the Hebrew Bible. A distinction was thus drawn between the "Old Testament" and "Apocrypha": the former consisted of works found in the Bible that were originally written in Hebrew (or Hebrew and Aramaic), while the latter consisted of works found in the Greek and Latin Bibles (such as the Vulgate), but not in the Hebrew Bible. While some reformers allowed that the apocryphal works were edifying reading, there was general agreement that these works could not be used as the basis of doctrine. Medieval theologians, however, to be followed by the Council of Trent in 1546, defined the "Old Testament" as "those Old Testament works contained in the Greek and Latin Bibles," thus eliminating any distinction between "Old Testament" and "Apocrypha."

As a result, a fundamental distinction developed between Roman Catholic and Protestant understandings of what the term "Scripture" actually meant. This distinction persists to the present day. One outcome of this debate was the production and circulation of authorized lists of books that were to be regarded as "scriptural." The fourth session of the Council of Trent (1546) produced a detailed list, which included some of the works of the Apocrypha as authentically scriptural, while the Protestant congregations in Switzerland, France, and elsewhere produced lists that deliberately omitted reference to these works, or else indicated that they were of no importance in matters of doctrine.

In England, this debate was regarded as of importance. An integral element of the Elizabethan Settlement of Religion was the compilation of the "Thirty-Nine Articles of Religion," a set of short statements that defined the distinctive position of the Church of England. These articles were agreed on in 1562, and were of considerable importance in shaping English attitudes to the translation of the Bible throughout the reigns of Elizabeth I and James I. The sixth of those articles, which is reproduced in full below, sets out the Anglican position on the canonical books of the Old Testament:

## *Article VI*

### OF THE SUFFICIENCY OF THE HOLY SCRIPTURE FOR SALVATION

Holy Scripture containeth all things necessary to salvation: so that whatsoever is not read therein, nor may be proved thereby, is not to be required of any man, that it should be believed as an article of the faith, or be thought requisite or necessary to salvation.

In the name of Holy Scripture, we do understand those Canonical books of the Old and New Testament, of whose authority was never any doubt in the Church.

*Of the names and number of the Canonical Books.*
  Genesis.
  Exodus.
  Leviticus.
  Numbers.
  Deuteronomy.
  Joshua.
  Judges.
  Ruth.
  The First Book of Samuel.
  The Second Book of Samuel.
  The First Book of Kings.
  The Second Book of Kings.
  The First Book of Chronicles.
  The Second Book of Chronicles.
  The First Book of Esdras.
  The Second Book of Esdras.
  The Book of Esther.
  The Book of Job.
  The Psalms.
  The Proverbs.

Ecclesiastes, or the Preacher.
Cantica, or Songs of Solomon.
Four Prophets the Greater.
Twelve Prophets the Less.

All the books of the New Testament, as they are commonly received, we do receive, and account them canonical.

And the other books (as Hierome saith) the Church doth read for example of life and instruction of manners; but yet doth it not apply them to establish any doctrine. Such are these following:

The Third Book of Esdras.
The Fourth Book of Esdras.
The Book of Tobias.
The Book of Judith.
The rest of the Book of Esther.
The Book of Wisdom.
Jesus the Son of Sirach.
Baruch the Prophet.
The Song of the Three Children.
The Story of Susanna.
Of Bel and the Dragon.
The Prayer of Manasses.
The First Book of Maccabees.
The Second Book of Maccabees.

This article clearly sets out a distinction between the canonical works of the Old Testament and the Apocrypha. Although the latter is declared to be of use for "example of life and instruction of manners"—in other words, it is edifying—it does not contain material that can be said to "establish any doctrine."

The issue that had to be addressed was whether the King James

Bible would include the Apocrypha, or omit it altogether. The decision to include it was taken by Richard Bancroft—yet another example of his influence over the King James Bible. The task of translating the apocryphal books was entrusted to the Second Cambridge Company, who are generally thought to have discharged their duties well. The decision to include the Apocrypha was not particularly controversial at the time; the Geneva Bible had also included it. Yet it was a decision that would *become* controversial in later years. The Westminster Confession of Faith (1646), which set out the core beliefs and values of English Puritanism at the time of the Commonwealth, was quite explicit on the purpose and place of the Apocrypha. The third article of that Confession reads as follows:

> *The books commonly called Apocrypha, not being of divine inspiration, are no part of the Canon of Scripture; and therefore are of no authority in the Church of God, nor to be any otherwise approved, or made use of, than other human writings.*

As the Puritans regarded the Apocrypha as being on the same level of value as human publications, they believed that it should have no place in printed Bibles. James I himself appears to have held to this view, as can be seen from an early passage in the *Basilikon Doron*:

> *As to the Apocriphe bookes, I omit them because I am no Papist (as I said before) & indeed some of them are as like the dietement of the Spirit of God, as an Egg is to an Oyster.*

Sadly, the full force of James's analogy here is lost to modern readers, and it can only be assumed that the point being made is that the Apocrypha is poor fare indeed compared with the richness and delicacy of the Old and New Testaments. However, it is possible that James's early views on the role of the Apocrypha were tempered by the religious situation in Scotland, where attitudes similar to those set out in the Westminster Confession were well established by the close of the sixteenth century. Perhaps James felt that, while in Scotland, one believed what the Church of Scotland taught, but while in England, one subtly shifted to attitudes associated with the Church of England. Or perhaps he took the view that this was precisely the kind of decision that Richard Bancroft ought to take, and was content to leave it to him.

Puritan critics of the King James Bible during the time of the Commonwealth therefore lobbied for the removal of the Apocrypha from its contents, seeing this as a further cause for complaint against the religious establishment of the day. With the restoration of the monarchy under Charles II, the Apocrypha regained its former status. It continued to be included in printed versions of the King James Bible.

Yet it became clear that there was a commercial market for versions of the King James translation that omitted the Apocrypha. Part of the market pressure came from the Puritans and their nonconformist successors in the eighteenth century, who wished these works to be excluded on theological grounds. The first English-language Bible to be printed in North America (1782–83), in which the Puritan heritage exercised a major influence, did not include the Apocrypha. Yet there was another pressure of importance—the production of English-language Bibles for the mission field. These needed to be produced as cheaply as possible.

Major British missionary societies that were active during the late eighteenth or early nineteenth century include the Baptist Missionary Society (founded in 1792, and initally known as the Particular Baptist Society for the Propagation of the Gospel); the London Missionary Society (founded in 1795, and initially known as the Missionary Society); and the Church Missionary Society (founded in 1799, and originally known as the Church Missionary Society for Africa and the East). There was now a commercial reason for removing the Apocrypha—Bibles without it were both cheaper to produce, and smaller (and hence cheaper to transport overseas). Sensitive to the importance of both production and transportation costs, the missionary societies gradually came to the view that the Apocrypha would be omitted—primarily for financial, rather than theological reasons.

As far as is known, the first missionary society to take this decision was the British and Foreign Bible Society. Its decision of 1826 to cease including the Apocrypha in their Bibles is known to have given a major stimulus to the growing trend to publish Bibles without the Apocrypha. In very general terms, Bibles produced for a predominantly Protestant readership now tend to exclude the Apocrypha, and those intended for a Roman Catholic readership include it.

## THE NEW TESTAMENT

The New Testament, which consists of twenty-seven books, is entirely written in Greek. The main components of the New Testament are the following.

1. The four Gospels. The word "gospel" basically means "good news." Each of the four gospel writers—or "evangelists," as they are sometimes known—sets out the basic events lying behind the good news. The term *Synoptic Gospels* is often used to refer to the first three Gospels (Matthew, Mark, and Luke). This term refers to their similar literary structure, which has important implications for the way in which they are translated.

2. The Acts of the Apostles. This is basically an account of the expansion of Christianity in the decades after the crucifixion and resurrection of Christ. How were events described in the Gospels received at the time? How did the gospel spread from Palestine to Europe? These questions are addressed in the fifth work to be found in the New Testament, the full title of which is "the Acts of the Apostles," but which is more usually referred

to simply as "Acts." The Gospel of Luke and Acts are widely agreed to have been written by the same person—Luke.

3. The next major section of material in the New Testament are the *letters*, referred to by the older English word *epistles* in documents dealing with the King James Bible. These letters provide teaching concerning both Christian beliefs and behavior, as important today as they were when they were first written. Some of the false teachings that arose in the early period of the Church's history are in circulation once more, and these letters provide important resources for defending the integrity of the Christian faith today. Most of the letters were written by Paul, whose conversion to the Christian faith led him to undertake a major programme of evangelism and church planting. Many of his letters were written to churches he had planted, giving them advice. Other letter-writers include the apostles Peter and John.

4. The Book of Revelation. The New Testament ends with the book of Revelation, which stands in a class of its own. It represents a vision of the end of history, in which the writer is allowed to see into heaven, and gain a glimpse of the new Jerusalem that is prepared for believers. This complex and difficult work is sometimes referred to as "the Apocalypse."

There were some interesting translation problems that awaited the translators, to which I shall return presently. First, it is essential to examine the languages in which the Bible was originally written, and the issues that they raised.

## HEBREW AND ARAMAIC:
## SOME ISSUES OF TRANSLATION

THE PRIMARY LANGUAGE of the Old Testament is Hebrew, a complex language that presents a number of difficulties to translators. In order to appreciate the most important of these, it is necessary to understand the way in which Hebrew is written. Classic Hebrew consists of twenty-two letters, each representing a consonant. Vowel sounds were not represented in writing; it was left to the reader to work out what the right vowels were. Most Hebrew words consist of a root with three consonants. These basic principles can be illustrated with some English words.

Suppose that English were to be written without vowels. The reader would use the context to work out what the appropriate vowel sounds might be. Thus the three-letter root *btr* could be read as "batter," "better," or "butter," depending on the context (the duplication of the central letter being characteristic of English orthography, even though only one of the central letters is pronounced).

As noted above, the Old Testament is written predominantly in Hebrew, with some short sections in Aramaic, the international language of diplomacy of the Ancient Near East. These sections often take the form of proclamations by Persian monarchs of relevance to the Jews. The book of Ezra, for example, describes the gradual return of the Jews to Jerusalem after their forcible deportation to the great city of Babylon a generation earlier. Examples of these documents include:

A letter to Artaxerxes from some Samaritan officials (Ezra 4:11–16)

A letter from Artaxerxes to some Samaritan officials (Ezra 4:17–22)

A letter from Darius to the governor of Syria (Ezra 5:7–17)

Aramaic presents no particular translation difficulties, and the evidence available concerning the competence of the companies of translators assigned to the Old Testament is impressive.

Hebrew possesses some characteristics that can cause difficulties for translators, and appear to have done so for the King James translators. It must be remembered that our understanding of the Hebrew language has developed considerably since 1600 for a number of reasons. A wealth of knowledge has been accumulated on other languages of the Ancient Near East, such as Akkadian and Ugaritic, which often casts light on the meaning of a Hebrew root. This means that modern translators often have a better understanding of the distinctives of Hebrew, and are able to see that the King James translators have, at times, made errors.

## IDIOMS

One of the most important features of the Hebrew language is its idioms—that is, distinctive ways of speaking which do not mean what they literally suggest. To take two English idioms as examples, "To be hot under the collar," if taken literally, would imply a sudden rise in temperature at the base of the neck. In fact, it is an idiomatic way of speaking, which means something like "to get angry." The French express something like the same idea in the idiomatic expression "to have mustard up the nose." Likewise, "To be in the soup" is not to be taken literally, but is an idiomatic way of saying "to be in trouble." German expresses a similar idea with the idiom "to sit in the ink." The King James translators had to wrestle with the question of which Hebrew expressions were to be taken literally, and which were to be seen as idiomatic. Some illustrations will make this point clearer.

The First Oxford Company was assigned to translate the major prophets, including the prophet Jeremiah. At eleven points during this work, Jeremiah uses the Hebrew idiom "to rise up early to do something." The Oxford Company of translators chose to translate this literally, giving the following translations:

> *Jeremiah 7:13: "And now, because ye have done all these works, saith the LORD, and I spake unto you, rising up early and speaking, but ye heard not; and I called you, but ye answered not."*

The difficulty is that this does not really make sense. The same difficulty can be seen in each of the remaining instances, such as the following:

> *Jeremiah 29:19: Because they have not hearkened to my words, saith the LORD, which I sent unto them by my servants the prophets, rising up early and sending them; but ye would not hear, saith the LORD.*

What has the idea of "rising up early" got to do with the point at issue? Here we have an example of a Hebrew idiom that the translators interpreted literally, and so failed to appreciate the general drift of the text. The idiom "to rise up early to do something" actually means "to do something *continually*." Hence the second of the quotations just noted has the following meaning: "They did not listen to my words which I sent unto them by my servants the prophets; even though I sent them continually, they still would not listen to them."

Yet at other points, the King James translators correctly interpreted Hebrew idioms. For example, the Hebrew idiom "bone of" is often used to mean something like "the essence of" or "very." The King James Bible generally gets this right—for example, translating the literal Hebrew expression "bone of the day" (Genesis 7:13; Ezekiel 2:3) as "this selfsame day" or "this very day."

## RARE WORDS

The King James translators were occasionally faced with rare Hebrew words whose meaning was obscure, including some that were used only once or twice throughout the entire Bible. Working out what these words meant placed considerable strain on the translators. This point is explicitly noted in the preface, in which the translators own up to the difficulties they encountered.

> *There be many words in the Scriptures, which be never found there but once, (having neither brother or neighbour, as the Hebrews speak) so that we cannot be holpen by conference of places. Again, there be many rare names of certain birds, beasts and precious stones, etc. concerning the Hebrews themselves are so divided among themselves for judgment, that they may seem to have defined this or that, rather because they would say something, than because they were sure of that which they said.*

Some examples will illustrate the severe difficulties that the translators faced.

In the Old Testament, 2 Kings 2:42 tells us of an episode in which Elisha was brought some food by a visitor.

> *And there came a man from Baalshalisha, and brought the man of God bread of the firstfruits, twenty loaves of barley, and full ears of corn in the husk thereof. And he said, Give unto the people, that they may eat.*

Our interest concerns the final item that was brought to Elisha— the "full ears of corn in the husk thereof." The Hebrew phrase translated in this way occurs only once in the entire Old Testament, and it is far from clear what it means. The context is suggestive, but not decisive. Here, the King James translators had little option; they had to allow the context to determine the meaning, in the knowledge that the matter was ultimately not of decisive importance. Not being sure about what was brought to Elisha was not going to disqualify anyone from being saved, in their view. Modern scholarship has seen an affinity between this phrase and a Ugaritic counterpart. In the light of this evidence concerning the meaning of the root in other languages of the Ancient Near East, this word would now be translated as something like "heads of new grain."

A similar issue can be seen arising in Isaiah 2:16. Again, a word is found that occurs in this passage, and at no other point in the Bible. The King James Bible translates this passage as a declaration of coming divine judgment against "all the ships of Tarshish, and upon all pleasant pictures." At first sight, this does not make much sense. Looking at the full passage (Isaiah 2:12–16), it is clear that the Hebrew poetic device of parallelism is in operation—that is, the repetition of ideas within or across lines:

> For the day of the LORD of hosts shall be upon every one that is proud and lofty, and upon every one that is lifted up; and he shall be brought low: And upon all the cedars of Lebanon, that are high and lifted up, and upon all the oaks of Bashan, And upon all the high mountains, and upon all the hills that are lifted up, And upon every high tower, and upon every fenced wall, And upon all the ships of Tarshish, and upon all pleasant pictures.

The parallels between "cedars of Lebanon" and "oaks of Bashan," or between "high mountains" and "hills that are lifted up," suggests that the final line of the passage ought to end with a word or phrase that somehow parallels "ships of Tarshish." Again, access to additional ancient Near Eastern texts, not available to the King James translators, suggests that the Hebrew word means a specific kind of ship, presumably noted for its grandeur or speed. While we still do not know exactly what kind of ship the passage had in mind, it is clear that it refers to some special type of ship that would have been known to its readers on account of some outstanding quality.

## THE DIVINE NAME

The Old Testament is rich in special names, titles and designations for God, which place translators under considerable pressure. The mere use of the word "God" to translate all of these terms has two immediate effects. First, it impoverishes the richness of the biblical language, reducing a galaxy of words to one single term. More seriously, the practice fails to make distinctions that are often important to understanding the meaning of the original Old Testament text.

Among the Old Testament titles for God, one stands out as being of special importance. This is the combination of four Hebrew letters, often written YHWH, and referred to by scholars as the "tetragrammaton." This combination of four letters—remember that Hebrew does not indicate vowels, which have to be supplied by the reader—was used to designate God. It is now thought that this word would have been pronounced "Yahweh," although many Jewish writers felt that the term was too sacred even to be pronounced, and substituted "Adonai" in deference to this.

The word is often found linked to others, including the Hebrew word *sabaoth*, which literally means "armies" or "hosts." The translation of the phrase "*YHWH sabaoth*" thus posed considerable challenges to translators. The King James Bible can be said to have had a considerable influence on English ways of referring to God, by translating "YHWH" as "LORD"—note the deliberate and systematic use of uppercase letters—and the phrase "*YHWH sabaoth*" as "the LORD of hosts." At four points (Exodus 6:3; Psalm 83:18; Isaiah 12:2, and Isaiah 26:4), however, a new name is introduced, which has entered into the English language. This is the word JEHOVAH, perhaps now most associated with a sectarian group known as the "Jehovah's Witnesses." This term is used to translate YHWH in contexts in which the simple use of LORD causes various difficulties. The unusual word is constructed by taking each of the four consonants of the Hebrew word YHWH—here represented as JHVH—and inserting vowel sounds.

## NEW TESTAMENT GREEK:
## SOME ISSUES OF TRANSLATION

THE NEW TESTAMENT is entirely written in Greek, with the exception of a few words here and there drawn from Aramaic. Yet to the Oxford and Cambridge educated classicists of the King James translation companies, it must have seemed a very strange form of Greek. It appeared to bear little relation to the classic Greek of Plato, Aristotle, or Homer. Certainly, the Greek of some New Testament documents—such as the Letter to the Hebrews, and the First Letter of Peter—can be thought of as truly literary, using a form of the language that is clearly classical in origin and influence. But many passages in the Gospels—especially those relating the conversation of ordinary people—seemed to belong to a different linguistic world, one that is now lost to us.

Even as late as 1853, the form of Greek found in the New Testament continued to puzzle scholars. Lecturing at the University of Cambridge in 1853, the great New Testament scholar J. B. Lightfoot remarked:

> *If we could only recover letters that ordinary people wrote to each other without any thought of being literary, we should have the greatest possible help for the understanding of the language of the New Testament generally.*

It was an interesting—and in some ways, prophetic—comment. But what hope was there of ever gaining access to the everyday Greek of the New Testament world? Surely it was doomed to remain inaccessible?

In the late nineteenth century, however, significant advances were made in understanding the everyday Greek of the eastern Mediterranean world into which Christianity was born. The German scholar Adolf Deissmann noticed remarkable similarities between the Greek of the New Testament and a series of vernacular papyri and other documents of the period. The type of Greek in question is often referred to as *koine*—an everyday Greek of the first century, which has developed considerably from the more formal classical Greek of writers such as Thucydides or Plato.

From the many papyri, that is, fragments of paper made from papyrus, on which small portions of text are written, as well as fragments of pottery, and other items recovered from ancient rubbish dumps—especially in Egypt, where the dry air aided conservation—it has become clear that the Greek spoken at the time of the New Testament has moved on considerably from that of the classical period, four or five hundred years earlier—in much the same way as English has moved on considerably since 1611. Today's reader of the King James Bible is able to read the text without too much difficulty, but is aware that it is written in the English of a much earlier period.

This raises an important point concerning the companies of translators assembled by King James. There is no doubt that these included some of the finest classical scholars of the period, well used to dealing with questions of translation of classical Greek. Yet the Greek they were being asked to translate dates from much later, and seems to follow more fluid grammatical rules. To translate it on the basis of an earlier form of Greek would cause difficulties. Words change their meaning over time, alongside other shifts in use. Again, the problem can be illustrated for modern readers of the King James Bible, who will find themselves puzzled by words that now bear significantly different meanings than in 1611. At that time, the word "let" often had the sense of "hinder" or "prevent," whereas its modern sense is "permit" or "allow." The word "prevent" then meant something like "go before" or "precede." Shifts in meaning can easily lead to misunderstandings of what an older translation meant. Consider the King James translation of Psalm 59:10, which reads "The God of my mercy shall prevent me." The meaning of this verse might seem singularly unclear, until it is realized that the English really has the following sense: "The God of my mercy shall go before me."

The same issue arose with the King James translation of the Greek of the New Testament. Changes in Greek usage over the centuries can easily lead to confusion. There is little doubt that the King James translators worked on the assumption that the same vocabulary rules of grammar that applied to the classical period also applied to the New Testament. Yet this is not always the case, and can lead to some serious misjudgments.

An example may help illuminate the point being made. In classical Greek, the word *apantesis* bears the general meaning of "meeting." The King James translators used this translation without any particular hesitations, as it made sense in every case—for example, as in Luke's account of the Roman Christians coming out to meet Paul as he travelled along the Appian way (Acts 28:15):

> *And from thence, when the brethren heard of us, they came to meet*
> *us as far as Appii forum, and the three taverns:*

Although this translation is not misleading, it fails to appreciate the developed use of the word *apantesis* at the time. The word now bore the sense of "an official welcome for a distinguished visitor who has just arrived." The word continues to refer to a meeting—but it is a special kind of meeting, indicating the esteem in which a newly arrived visitor is held. Luke's narrative, therefore, indicates that the Roman Christians travelled to meet Paul along the Appian way in order to give him the kind of distinguished welcome reserved for persons of great importance—a point that the King James Bible fails to bring out, through an apparent lack of awareness of the shift in meaning of the term since classical times. Although the King James Bible rarely leads its readers astray through its lack of familiarity with *koine* Greek, it occasionally fails to bring out the full depth of meaning in passages for this reason.

Yet there is a final issue that needs to be noted here. The *koine* Greek of the New Testament is the "everyday" Greek language of working people rather than of self-conscious literary scholars and poets. The King James translators were not aware of this fact. Their location in history denied them access to this knowledge. The result has important implications for the tone and style of those passages in the King James Bible that translate this form of Greek. The language of the workplace and the market is thus subtly changed into the high cadences of the palaces of Westminster and the high tables of Oxford and Cambridge. Many readers of the King James Bible often comment on its elegance and excellent style—yet the considerations just set out mean that, on occasion, the style and elegance will be those of the translators, rather than those of the passages they translated.

## THE GOSPELS:
## THE SYNOPTIC ISSUE

THE FIRST THREE Gospels—Matthew, Mark, and Luke—are often known as the "Synoptic Gospels," as they present summary accounts of the life and teachings of Jesus. The Synoptic Gospels include a significant amount of common material, which is sometimes presented in one setting in Mark, another in Matthew, and perhaps even a third in Luke. The same story may be told from different perspectives in different Gospels. Sometimes a story is told at greater length in one Gospel than in another. This is widely believed to be due to the fact that all three draw on several common sources, such as collections of the sayings of Jesus, which were committed to memory at a very early stage.

Some of this material is common to all three Gospels; some is common to Matthew and Luke (which are much longer than Mark); and some is found only in Matthew or Luke. In each case, the evangelist (as the gospel writers are known) has drawn on his own set of historical sources to allow his readers access to the details of the central figure of the Christian faith.

So what relevance does this have for the problems facing the King James translators? The answer is this: at many points, Matthew, Mark, and Luke present passages which, in the original Greek, are virtually identical to each other. It is precisely this observation which gives rise to the exploration of how the Synoptic Gospels were put together. It would therefore seem to be a matter of some importance to ensure that, where identical Greek passages are encountered across two or three Gospels, that the English translations of those passages should be the same in each case. After all, it is the same passage that is being translated in each case.

The evidence, however, suggests that the Second Oxford Company of translators, who were responsible for translating the Gospels, did not see things in quite this light. Identical Greek passages in two or three Gospels were regularly translated in quite different manners in the King James Bible. Two reasons may be given for this. First, as the preface "The Translators to the Reader" makes clear, the translators did not see themselves as being under an obligation to use precisely the same English translation in each and every case; they allowed themselves a flexible creativity in rendering the text which did not bind them absolutely to a fixed convention of rendering words and phrases. Second, the observations which led scholars to reflect on the nature of the Synoptic Gospels had not been fully co-ordinated in the seventeenth century; indeed, it could be argued that two more centuries would pass before the matter was given proper attention. The translators were therefore not alerted to the issues which are taken for granted in biblical translation circles today.

The difficulty in translating what are usually referred to as "gospel parallels" can be seen by comparing the following, bearing in mind that exactly the same Greek words are being translated in each case.

> *Watch and pray, that ye enter not into temptation: the spirit indeed is willing, but the flesh is weak (Matthew 26:41).*
> *Watch ye and pray, lest ye enter into temptation. The spirit truly is ready, but the flesh is weak (Mark 14:38).*

The casual reader might gain the impression that quite different Greek words were being translated in each passage; in fact, the Greek text is identical in each case. As will be clear from what has just been said, the simplest explanation of this puzzling phenomenon is that the King James translators were simply not aware of the parallelism between the texts, and hence did not realize the inconsistencies which might arise.

## THE TEXT TO BE TRANSLATED

AT FIRST SIGHT, the question of the identity of the text to be translated might seem to be so simple that it need not require comment.
The translators, in the best traditions of biblical interpretation, set out
to translate the original Hebrew and Greek texts into English. In what
follows, I shall confine my discussion to the Greek text of the New
Testament, as it is here that the issues we shall be considering are of
special importance.

The sixteenth century saw important new developments in biblical translation. As we saw earlier (page 57), Erasmus of Rotterdam
produced a printed Greek text of the New Testament in 1516, which
called into question some of the Latin translations found in the
Vulgate. Erasmus was obliged to compile his Greek text on the basis
of various manuscripts he was able to consult. None of these was
especially ancient; Erasmus had to work on the basis of the criterion
of accessibility. As far as can be ascertained, none of the half dozen
manuscripts was earlier than the tenth century.

Erasmus's edition of the Greek text of the New Testament was
revised over the next century. The Parisian printer Robert Estienne
produced a number of editions based on Erasmus's text, as did the
Genevan theological and biblical scholar Theodore Beza later. It is
known that the King James translators made use of Beza's edition of
the Greek text of the New Testament; it was, after all, the best edition
of the text then available.

This particular version of the text has come to be known as the
*textus receptus* ("the received text"), not because of any "official"
church judgment or decision, but simply because New Testament
scholars based their work upon it.[1] Yet biblical scholarship has

---

1. It must also be pointed out—although this is a somewhat technical matter—
that the *textus receptus* is not to be directly identified with the Byzantine text, the
form of text that established itself during the period of ecclesiastical and
theological consolidation in the eastern Roman Empire from the fourth century
onwards.

advanced considerably over the years. Much older manuscripts of the New Testament, or parts of it, have come to light. The richness of the New Testament manuscript tradition can be appreciated by considering another work dating from around the same time—Julius Caesar's *Gallic War*, a famous account of the Roman wars in France, written around 50 B.C. The oldest known manuscript of this text dates from nine hundred years after Caesar's time. Similarly, the oldest known manuscript of Thucydides' *History*—which was written sometime in the fifth century before Christ—was written down about fourteen hundred years later.

In the sixteenth century, the best editions of the Greek New Testament were based on manuscripts dating from no earlier than the tenth century. Since then, many new manuscripts have been discovered, of which the most famous is the *Codex Sinaiticus*, probably written in the fourth century. This was found in the monastery of St. Catherine on Mount Sinai in 1844, and is now held in the British Museum. The *Codex Alexandrinus*, probably written in the fifth century, was presented to King Charles I in 1627 by the patriarch of Alexandria. Theodore Beza himself presented an early Greek New Testament to the University of Cambridge in 1581; this contains the four Gospels and the Acts of the Apostles in both Greek and Latin, and is thought to date from the fifth and sixth centuries. A vast range of papyri have also been found. As a result, a much more accurate edition of the text of the New Testament is accessible now than the King James translators knew.

It must be made clear immediately that this does not call into question the general reliability of the King James Bible. The issue concerns minor textual variations. Not a single teaching of the Christian faith is affected by these variations, nor is any major historical aspect of the gospel narratives or early Christianity affected. The important point is that, in general, the King James Bible was based on the *textus receptus*. Scholarly fashions have changed, and the Alexandrine text— named after the *Codex Alexandrinus*—is now preferred within the scholarly community to the Byzantine text, which the *textus receptus* reflects. Before going on to explore the kind of variations involved,

and their possible significance, it is worth noting a remarkable exception to the statement, made above, that the King James Bible followed
Erasmus's text (see page 241).

The point is best understood by comparing the translation of
1 John 5:7–8 offered by the King James Bible and the Revised
Standard Version:

### King James Bible

*For there are three that bear record in heaven, the Father, the
Word, and the Holy Ghost: and these three are one. And there are
three that bear witness in earth, the Spirit, and the water, and the
blood: and these three agree in one.*

### Revised Standard Version

*And the Spirit is the witness, because the Spirit is the truth. There
are three witnesses, the Spirit, the water, and the blood; and these
three agree.*

There is more than a translation difference here; the translations
seem to be based on different texts. The issue identified by Erasmus
in 1516 was that the words "the Father, the Word, and the Holy
Ghost: and these three are one. And there are three that bear witness
in earth" are not found in any Greek manuscript. They were added
later to the Latin Vulgate, probably after 800, despite not being
known in any ancient Greek version. The most likely explanation is
that these words were initially added as a "gloss" (that is, a brief comment set beside or above the text), which a later scribe misunderstood
to be something that should be added to the text itself. Subsequent
scribes, basing themselves on this faulty copy, then included the words
in later Latin texts. They are not part of the original Greek text of the
New Testament.

For Erasmus, the solution was simple: the words should be deleted,
as they were not part of the text of the New Testament. They were a late
addition to the Latin Vulgate text, and had no right to be there. Their

removal would cause nobody to lose sleep at night. Yet the translators of the King James Bible appear to have felt that tradition demanded that the additional words be retained. Subsequent revisions of English translations have, of course, removed the words as manifestly inauthentic.

This, however, is an exceptional case. In general, the variations between the *textus receptus* and *Codex Alexandrinus* are interesting, but slight, as the following two examples show. These are drawn from the translation work of the Second Oxford Company, responsible for the translation of the Gospels.

The first is the text widely known as the Lord's Prayer (Matthew 6:9–13), which reads as follows in the King James Bible:

> *Our Father which art in heaven, Hallowed be thy name. Thy kingdom come. Thy will be done in earth, as it is in heaven. Give us this day our daily bread. And forgive us our debts, as we forgive our debtors. And lead us not into temptation, but deliver us from evil: For thine is the kingdom, and the power, and the glory, for ever. Amen.*

The *textus receptus* here includes what is known as a "doxology"— that is, a closing section of praise: "For thine is the kingdom, and the power, and the glory, for ever. Amen." This is not found in earlier Greek manuscripts, and is, therefore, not included in later English translations such as the Revised Standard Version. However, the influence of the King James Bible was such that this closing section is still included in the traditional form of the Lord's Prayer, and has largely successfully resisted attempts to eliminate it.

A second is Matthew 5:43–44, which is part of the Sermon on the Mount. The King James Bible, again following the *textus receptus*, offers the following translation:

> *Ye have heard that it hath been said, Thou shalt love thy neighbour, and hate thine enemy. But I say unto you, Love your enemies, bless them that curse you, do good to them that hate you, and pray for them which despitefully use you, and persecute you.*

The phrase "bless them that curse you, do good to them that hate you" is not found in most Greek manuscripts, and is therefore omitted from modern English translations.

None of these alterations are earth-shattering. It is not, for example, as if every reference to the resurrection of Jesus turns out to date from the fourth century, not the apostolic period itself! Yet they are interesting in their own right, and cast important light both on the strengths and weaknesses of the King James Bible, and also the motivations for revision in later years. One such motivation may be set out very simply: as New Testament scholarship now regards the Alexandrian text of the New Testament as the most authentic, and the King James Bible is based on what is now seen as a slightly less reliable text, is not this a sufficient reason for requesting a revised translation?

## POETRY IN THE BIBLE

THE BIBLE CONTAINS a wide range of literary types. Its many pages include historical narratives, personal letters, official documents, proverbs, and poems. The question of how poetry was to be represented in biblical translations became a matter of some debate in the sixteenth century. It was clear, for example, that the Psalms were examples of religious poetry. Should they not be identified as such typographically, by laying them out in the same manner as normal poetry?

An example of the point at issue can be seen from Paul's first letter to Timothy, in which Paul quotes from what is clearly an early Christian hymn, which he expects Timothy to know. Modern versions of the Bible mark the transition from prose to poetry and back again by displaying the material in a manner appropriate to its literary character. Thus the Revised Standard Version presents 1 Timothy 3:14–4:3 as follows:

*I hope to come to you soon, but I am writing these instructions to you so that, if I am delayed, you may know how one ought to behave in the household of God, which is the church of the living*

*God, the pillar and bulwark of the truth. Great indeed, we con-
fess, is the mystery of our religion:*

> *He was manifested in the flesh,*
> *vindicated in the Spirit,*
> *seen by angels,*
> *preached among the nations,*
> *believed on in the world,*
> *taken up in glory.*

*Now the Spirit expressly says that in later times some will
depart from the faith by giving heed to deceitful spirits and doctrines of demons, through the pretensions of liars whose consciences
are seared, who forbid marriage and enjoin abstinence from foods
which God created to be received with thanksgiving by those who
believe and know the truth.*

Poetry and prose are displayed in a conventional manner, with the
transition from one to the other being clearly indicated by the layout
of the text.

Similar issues arise in relation to many sections of the Bible, especially the Old Testament. The Psalter consists entirely of verse; many
other works include both prose and poetry. As a result, the issue of
how the poetic sections of the Bible should be presented was a live
issue for the King James translators. The sixteenth century had seen a
number of attempts to preserve the poetic character of the Psalms in
English translations, both in terms of the typographical display and
the metre of the verse. In his *Apology for Poetry* (1580), the great
Elizabethan man of letters Sir Philip Sidney argued that the presence
of poetry in the Bible itself was a more than adequate reason for
encouraging this form of literature:

*May I not presume a little farther . . . and say that the holy
David's Psalms are a divine poem? If I do, I shall not do it with-*

*out the testimony of great learned men, both ancient and modern. But even the name Psalms will speak for me which, being interpreted, is nothing but songs; then, that it is fully written in metre, as all learned Hebricians agree, although the rules be not yet fully found.*

Sidney, emboldened by such thoughts, offered a metrical translation of the Psalms, which remained unpublished until 1828. Sidney's verse translation of Psalm 8:4—"what is man that thou art mindful of him, and the son of man that thou dost care for him?"—runs as follows:

*Then think I: Ah, what is this man*
*Whom that great God remember can?*
*And what the race, of him descended,*
*It should be of God attended?*

Other versifications were perhaps more successful, most notably the famous Sternhold and Hopkins Psalter, the first edition of which appeared in 1549.

Of significance to us, however, is the awareness of the poetic nature of parts of the biblical text, and the debate over how best to translate and present such verse. Tyndale's New Testament often presented the text with considerable sensitivity to the literary issues involved. Thus in the printing of his translation of Luke 1, Tyndale lays his text out as prose in paragraphs where appropriate, then as lines of poetry when presenting the Magnificat—the Song of Mary.

This was an issue that the King James translators could not overlook. In the event, the translators used an identical textual presentation for all literary genres within the Bible, irrespective of whether it was poetry or prose. Every biblical verse was printed out as an individual paragraph, with the verse number in a type identical in size to the text itself. This completely obliterated the poetic nature of a text. For example, Psalm 23 is laid out in the King James Bible as:

1 *A Psalm of David. The LORD is my shepherd; I shall not want.*

2 *He maketh me to lie down in green pastures: he leadeth me beside the still waters.*

3 *He restoreth my soul: he leadeth me in the paths of righteousness for his name's sake.*

4 *Yea, though I walk through the valley of the shadow of death, I will fear no evil; for thou art with me; thy rod and thy staff they comfort me.*

5 *Thou preparest a table before me in the presence of mine enemies; thou anointest my head with oil, my cup runneth over.*

6 *Surely goodness and mercy shall follow me all the days of my life; and I will dwell in the house of the LORD for ever.*

This may be compared with a purely prose section—the opening of Paul's letter to the Romans—which is not distinguished typographically from the very different literary style of Psalm 23:

7 *To all that be in Rome, beloved of God who are called to be saints: Grace to you and peace from God our Father, and the Lord Jesus Christ.*

8 *First, I thank my God through Jesus Christ for you all, that your faith is spoken of through out the whole world.*

9 *For God is my witness, whom I serve with my spirit in the gospel of his Son, that without ceasing I make mention of you always in my prayers;*

10 *Making request, if by any means now at length, I might have a prosperous journey by the will of God to come unto you.*

11 *For I long to see you, that I may impart unto you some spiritual gift to the end ye may be established;*

12 *That is, that I may be comforted together with you by the mutual faith both of you and me.*

As a result, it was impossible for the reader of the King James Bible to determine whether he or she was reading prose or poetry. It is clear that the decision was taken to follow the Geneva Bible's practice of imposing verse divisions—which, it must be stressed, often failed to take into account literary issues—and thus destroying any visual or presentational distinction between verse and prose. Consequently, the typographical convention forced upon the translators gave them little freedom in this matter, and they cannot be censured for this action. Nevertheless, it remains a serious difficulty, which has been intensified since the eighteenth century, when the poetic nature of large parts of the Old Testament began to be appreciated and praised. One of the pressures for revision of the King James Bible in the nineteenth century was precisely this recognition of the need to treat poetry as poetry.

## WHAT IS TRANSLATION ANYWAY?

IN CONSIDERING THE work of the King James translators, it is important to discern what they understood the task of translation to involve. These issues are addressed by Miles Smith, writing on behalf of the whole body of translators in the important preface entitled "The Translators to the Reader," and need to be given careful weight.

Some of the issues that are of importance here have ben noted already—for example, the decision not to translate each Hebrew or Greek word with exactly the same English word or phrase in every case. While this unquestionably led to a more elegant English translation, issues of accuracy inevitably arose. For example, the same Hebrew word—*khiydah*—is translated in a number of different ways, including "riddle" (Judges 14:12–17; Ezekiel 17:2), "hard question" (1 Kings 10:1), "dark saying" (Psalm 49:5; Proverbs 1:6), and "dark sentence" (Daniel 8:23).

However, it must be pointed out here that the Hebrew word *khiydah* is relatively uncommon. Even though the King James translators stated from the outset that they intended to reserve the right to offer more than one English rendering of cognate words where they believed this was appropriate, it is significant that the King James

Bible remains the most cautious and conservative of the Renaissance translations in this matter. Tyndale and the Geneva Bible, for example, showed little attention to the issue of what might be termed "verbal equivalence"; the King James translators moved much closer to the notion of providing set formulas for translating the more common original terms and phrases, as determined by their context.

It is clear that the translators of the King James Bible used a formal approach to translation, which required each word of the original to be translated into its closest English equivalent. Approaches to translation can be broadly broken down into two groups—those that place emphasis on the *donor language* (that is, the language in which the work is originally written) and those that give priority to issues concerning the *receptor language* (the language into which the translation is taking place).

A careful study of the way in which the King James Bible translates the Greek and Hebrew originals suggests that the translators felt obliged to:

1. Ensure that every word in the original was rendered by an English equivalent;
2. Make it clear when they added any words to make the sense clearer, or to lead to better English syntax. These words were originally indicated in roman type, the remainder of the biblical text being typeset in black letter type. In more recent times, they are indicated by italics, following a precedent set by the Geneva Bible in 1560.
3. Follow the basic word order of the original wherever possible.

This general approach to translation was widespread in the late Middle Ages. The Wycliffite translations of the Latin Bible are exceedingly literal, perhaps reflecting a belief that the sacred quality of the text could be reproduced only in a word-for-word translation. For example, Hebrews 1:1–2 read as follows in the Latin version of the Bible, known by Wycliffe:

Multifariam multisque modis olim Deus loquens patribus in prophetis, novissime diebus istis locutus est nobis in filio; quem constituit heredem universorum, per quem fecit et secula.

The Wycliffite version of this follows the Latin word for word, leading to a translation that is literally accurate, but not particularly good English:

*Manyfold and many manners sometime God speaking to fathers and prophets, at the last in these days spake to us in the son; whom he ordained heir of all things, by whom he made and the worlds.*

This can be seen especially in the way the Latin phrase *et secula* is translated literally as "and the worlds," where the Latin is actually idiomatic, and should be rendered as "also the worlds."

In his 1598 translation *Seven Books of the Iliad*, George Chapman set out what he regarded as being the ideal approach to be adopted by a translator.

*The worth of a skilful and worthy translator is to observe the sentences, figures and forms of speech proposed in his author, his true sense and height, and to adorn them with figures and forms of oration fitted to the original in the same tongue to which they are translated: and these things I would gladly have made the questions of whatsoever my labours have deserved.*

These comments date from only a few years before the companies of translators began their work, and there is little doubt that Chapman's comments reflect the scholarly consensus of his day on this important matter. As such, the hallmarks of a translation were fidelity to the original, both in terms of content and style, mingling technical precision with an awareness of the challenges and opportunities afforded by the language into which translation was to take place. The translator of the English Renaissance was thus not merely a verbal mechanic, but one who was concerned to achieve and retain elegance in the resulting translation.

Some such understanding is found in the King James Bible, which retains the word order of the original to a remarkable extent, while still making allowances for the need for the resulting text to be, in the first place, recognizably English, and in the second, intelligible. The King James translators seem to have taken the view—which corresponds with the consensus of the day—that an accurate translation is, by and large, a literal and formal translation.

One of the results of this important decision is that a significant number of essentially Hebrew ways of speaking became incorporated into the English language (see page 231). This approach to translation has resulted in the receptor language being enriched by idioms drawn from the donor language. For this reason, the King James Bible has had a highly significant impact on the development of the English language—a matter that deserves to be considered in much greater detail.

# 11

## THE BIBLE
## AND THE SHAPING
## OF MODERN ENGLISH

"No other book has so penetrated and permeated the hearts and speech of the English race as has the Bible. What Homer was to the Greeks, and the Koran to the Arabs, that—or something not unlike it—the Bible has become to the English," wrote Albert Stanburrough Cook, Professor of English Language and Literature at Yale University in the 1920s. Few would quarrel with his judgment over the historical influence of the English Bible on the shaping of the English language. Yet one of the greatest paradoxes linked to the King James Bible is that it achieved literary excellence precisely by choosing to avoid it. Literary elegance was not even mentioned in the translation criteria set before its seventeenth-century team of translators.

The King James Bible, along with the works of William Shakespeare, is regularly singled out as one of the most foundational influences on the development of the modern English language. It is no accident that both date from the late English Renaissance, when English was coming into its own as a language. Samuel Johnson liked to speak of this as the period of "Revival of Learning in Europe," and dates what he terms "the golden age of our language" from "the accession of Elizabeth" in 1558. In the preface to his *Dictionary of the English Language* (1755), Johnson asserts that "every language has a time of rudeness antecedent to perfection, as well as of false refinement and declension." For Johnson, there was no doubt that the Renaissance marked the beginning of the linguistic perfection of English, and that this period was of critical importance in shaping the contours of the new language.

## ELOQUENCE BY ACCIDENT: ACCURACY OF TRANSLATION AS THE PRIMARY GOAL OF THE KING JAMES BIBLE

THERE WAS VIRTUALLY universal agreement in the nineteenth and early twentieth centuries that the King James Bible had made a massive contribution to the development of the English language in general, and English prose in particular. The "noblest monument of English prose" was recognized as being of decisive importance in the moulding of English.

Yet there is no evidence that the translators of the King James Bible had any great interest in matters of literature or linguistic development. Their concern was primarily to provide an accurate translation of the Bible, on the assumption that accuracy was itself the most aesthetic of qualities to be desired. Paradoxically, the king's translators achieved literary distinction precisely because they were not deliberately pursuing it. Aiming at truth, they achieved what later generations recognized as beauty and elegance. Where later translations deliberately and self-consciously sought after literary merit, the king's translators achieved it unintentionally, by focusing on what, to them, was a greater goal. Elegance was achieved by accident, rather than design.

The central objective of the king's translators was scholarly accuracy—the finding of proper English words and phrases to render the original Hebrew, Greek, and Aramaic. Sense and meaning took priority over elegance. The achievement of prosaic and poetic elegance that resulted was, so to speak, a most happy accident of history. Nevertheless, the idea of "the Bible as literature" was unknown to the sixteenth and seventeenth centuries, which saw accuracy as the supreme goal in translation.

One possible contributing factor to the elegance of the King James Bible is its refusal to adopt a purely mechanical approach to translation, in which a Hebrew or Greek word is woodenly rendered by exactly the same English term throughout. The translators clearly felt themselves free to use a range of English words and phrases, as they judged appropriate—a clear sign of a growing sense of confidence in English as a living language. This principle was set out in the preface to the work:

> *We have not tied ourselves to an uniformity of phrasing or an identity of words, as some peradventure would wish that we have done . . . But that we should express the same notion in the same particular word, as for example, if we translate the Hebrew or Greek word once by "purpose," never to call it "intent" . . . we thought to savour more of curiosity than wisdom.*

This decision allowed the translators to achieve a wider lexical range than would otherwise have been possible. On the one hand, this led to a lack of strict accuracy where it might have been expected; on the other, it allowed for a greater richness of the text than a more mechanical approach to the issue might have engendered.

To note with approval the grace and refinement of the translation is not to say that there is a total absence of inelegancies in the King James Bible. It is a relatively easy matter to identify passages in which a certain lack of elegance is all too obvious. The following will serve as examples:

> *The noise thereof sheweth concerning it, the cattle also concerning the vapour (Job 36:33).*

*For the Pharisees, and all the Jews, except they wash their hands oft, eat not, holding the tradition of the elders. And when they come from the market, except they wash, they eat not. And many other things there be, which they have received to hold, as the washing of cups, and pots, brasen vessels, and of tables (Mark 7:3–4).*

*O ye Corinthians, our mouth is open unto you, our heart is enlarged. Ye are not straitened in us, but ye are straitened in your own bowels. Now for a recompence in the same, (I speak as unto my children,) be ye also enlarged (2 Corinthians 6:11–13).*

Yet these clumsy lines (the apparent inelegance of which is often enhanced by the use of words that are now archaic) may be seen as relatively rare exceptions. More generally, the King James Bible achieves a degree of elegance that has been the envy of its successors.

However, the shaping of a language has to do with more than the modelling of written eloquence. A living language develops a vocabulary and turns of phrase that both enrich and illuminate its forms of expression. So what contribution did the King James Bible make to the shaping of the English language?

## FACTORS IN THE SHAPING OF MODERN ENGLISH

THE MOVEMENT TOWARD the standardization of vernacular languages proceeded apace throughout Western Europe in the late sixteenth century. The abandoning of Latin as the language of government and diplomacy led to an increased interest in the standardization, refinement, and fixing of national languages. The question of who should be allowed to determine the shape of "standard" English, French, or Italian was immensely contentious, in that highly subjective matters of taste were involved. It Italy, the Accademia della Crusca, founded in 1582, set as its stated aim the refinement of the Italian language, and published works designed to encourage this process. Cardinal Richelieu founded the Académie Française in 1634, again with the aim of rendering the French language "pure, eloquent, and capable of treating both arts and sciences."

James I had little interest in such matters. Indeed, the one national society that might have acted as a catalyst to the development of English—the Society of Antiquaries, founded in 1572—languished and eventually folded during his reign. It was not until the reign of Charles II that serious discussion began in England over the establishment of an English equivalent to the much-admired (at least, in private) Académie Française.

In the absence of any official body willing to take a lead in such matters, the development of English was shaped by a number of influential factors. One factor of growing importance was the ready availability of printed material. As George Puttenham pointed out in 1589, speakers of English "were already ruled by the English dictionaries and other books written by learned men, and therefore need none other direction in that behalf." Even in the time of William Caxton, the potential of the printing press for shaping living languages had been recognized. The English of Caxton's translations was largely based on London English, as used by civil servants and lawyers. The more published English was read, the more its English would be accepted as "normative."

One of the unintended functions of the King James Bible was to establish norms in written and spoken English. Should not the language of the Bible shape the language of the people? The growing acceptance of the King James Bible in shaping public and private religious discourse inevitably had its impact on the language as a whole. Yet the English used in the King James Bible was not a "universal" English, accepted by all throughout King James's realm. Northern forms of English made little, if any, impact on the translation. As was stressed when considering the identity and origins of the companies of translators, virtually all were drawn from the southeast of England. The King James Bible is written in a standard literary language, free from the confusing variations of local dialects.

Initially, the language of the King James Bible might seem unnatural, artificial, and stilted to some. Yet continuity of usage, private and public, soon diminished the apparent "strangeness" of the translation. Hebraic phrases—initially regarded with some amusement—became accepted parts of the English language. The growing acceptance of the King James Bible must be seen as a major force in the shaping of standard English. The production of editions of the King James Bible suitable for personal use—such as the quarto and octavo editions—increased the influence of the work on the growing reading public.

By the first decade of the seventeenth century, it was clear that the English language was in a state of flux. The Elizabethan and Jacobean periods can now be seen to have been the periods in which modern English received its distinctive cast. The influence of printed books had been of critical importance: fixed forms of spelling were now beginning to emerge, and certain lexical patterns were becoming accepted as normative. The King James Bible was published within a window of opportunity, which allowed it to exercise a substantial and decisive influence over the shaping of the English language. It is no accident that the two literary sources most widely identified as defining influences over English—the King James Bible and the works of William Shakespeare—both date from this critical period.

## The Acceptance of Foreign Terms and Phrases

ONE OF THE most interesting features of the English language is its willingness to absorb words and phrases that have their origins elsewhere. The use of loanwords can be seen as early as the late fifteenth century, as a growing interest in classical learning led to pressure to "borrow" classical terms to enrich the English language. The Jacobean period was particularly important in this respect. Robert Cawdry's *The Table Alphabetical of Hard Words* (1604) listed 2,500 unusual or borrowed words, on the assumption that many of his readers—

assumed, incidentally, to be primarily female—would not yet be familiar with them. John Bullokar's *An English Expositor* (1616) listed words that had now become archaic on account of the "loanwords" that had gradually displaced them.

This capacity for assimilation has led to modern English being an exceptionally rich medium of expression. In part, this willingness to naturalize foreign words rests on England's rise to global status as a trading nation in the late sixteenth century, its economic and cultural relationships with other European nations, and its complex and chequered history as a colonial power. The large number of Hindi words and phrases that can be identified in late Victorian English reflect the intimate British involvement with the Indian subcontinent over many generations.

One of the most fundamental contributing factors to this willingness to accept and use verbal immigrants at this formative period was the influence of the King James Bible. Many phrases having their origins in a Hebraic, Hellenistic, or Latin context have been naturalized in English through the simple yet inexorable force of their regular use in biblical contexts. The public and private reading of the Bible in English created an atmosphere that encouraged and ensured their ready acceptance. This process of naturalization of verbal immigrants was accelerated by the subtle yet significant failure of many users of the King James Bible to realize that the Bible was originally written in any language other than English. "Biblical English" came to possess a cultural authority on the same level as that of Shakespeare. As a result of centuries of use, many Hebraic phrases and idioms have become so common in normal English use that most modern English speakers are unaware of their biblical origins. They have become assimilated into English, perhaps the global language that has been most welcoming to words whose origins lie elsewhere.

In part, the success of the King James Bible lies in the way in which a robustly Anglo-Saxon vocabulary is enriched by a judicious—and never intrusive—vocabulary deriving from Latin terms. Achieving the right balance between Anglo-Saxon and Latinate words was always a matter of debate in the sixteenth century, not least as English began to establish itself as a language in its own right. As the scope of the language developed, a debate emerged over how new words should be coined. Should they be formed from existing English roots—or should the classical languages be used as a source for new words?

This lexical anxiety can be seen in the biblical translations of the early modern period. Sir Thomas Elyot (c. 1490–1546) produced an important treatise on what would now be termed "neologisms" (from the Greek for "new words") in a deliberate attempt to develop and improve the English language. This was fiercely resisted by a group of writers. In 1587, Arthur Golding set out to develop a new English technical vocabulary, capable of meeting the growing needs of the arts and sciences, which drew on Anglo-Saxon rather than classical roots. Some examples of his recommendations are: "threlike" (for "equilateral triangle"); "likejamme" (for "parallelogram"); "endsay" (for "conclusion"); and "saywhat" (for "definition"). In every case, the classical alternative would pass into general use, despite Golding's vigorous rearguard action. His new words failed to catch on within the increasingly classically minded academic community.

Much the same concerns were expressed earlier in the writings of Sir John Cheke (1514–57), the first Regius Professor of Greek at the University of Cambridge, who was strongly opposed to what his colleague Roger Ascham (1515–68) dismissively referred to as "inkhorn" terms—that is, words coined from Latin or Greek to make the resulting English words sound more sophisticated and dignified. Cheke set out his approach in a letter written to his friend Sir Thomas Hoby:

> *I am of this opinion that our own tongue should be written clean and pure, unmixt and unmangeled with borrowing of other tongues; wherein if we take not heed by time, ever borrowing and never paying, she shall be fain to keep her house as bankrupt. For then doth our tongue naturally and praisably utter her meaning when she borroweth no counterfeitness of other tongues to attire herself withall, but useth plainly her own.*

Cheke had no doubts that his principles could and should be applied to biblical translation. He produced translations of Matthew and Mark in which he attempted to avoid as many classical terms as possible, and replace them with Anglo-Saxon equivalents. This was far from easy; the Roman imperial context in which the gospel narratives are set led to a significant number of technical Roman terms appearing in the New Testament. Examples of Cheke's attempts to eliminate "inkhorn" religious terms include the following: "frosent" (for "apostle"); "hundreder" (for "centurion"); "crossed" (for "crucified"); "mooned" (for "lunatic"); "byword" (for "parable"); "uprising" (for "resurrection"); and "wizards" (for "wise men"). Cheke's translation languished, totally overlooked, until it was published in 1843 as a quaint intellectual curiosity.

Yet if one error in biblical translation was the systematic elimination of all Latin-based words, the other extreme was equally unsatisfactory. The Douai-Rheims translation aimed, as a matter of policy, to retain as much as possible of the traditional Latin vocabulary of the medieval Church. The result was as unsatisfactory as it was inevitable; the ensuing translation did not read as natural English. For example, the Douai New Testament's translation of a phrase in Philippians 2:8 reads as follows: "He exinanited himself." This unintelligible Latinate phrase may be contrasted with the perfectly clear English of the King James Bible: "He humbled himself." This point can be illustrated further by setting side by side the Douai-Rheims and King James Bible translation of Ephesians 3:8–11, in which Paul sets out his understanding of his role as an apostle. Latinate terms in the Douai-Rheims version are underlined.

### DOUAI-RHEIMS

*To me the least of all saints is given this grace, among the Gentiles to _evangelize_ the unsearchable riches of Christ, and to _illuminate_ all men what is the _dispensation_ of the _sacrament_ hidden from worlds in God, who created all things, that the manifold wisdom of God may be _notified_ to the princes and _potestates_ in the _celes-*

_tials_ by the church, according to the _prefinition_ of worlds, which he
made in Christ Jesus our Lord.

### KING JAMES BIBLE

_Unto me, who am less than the least of all saints, is this grace given,
that I should preach among the Gentiles the unsearchable riches of
Christ; And to make all_ men _see what is the fellowship of the mystery, which from the beginning of the world hath been hid in God,
who created all things by Jesus Christ: To the intent that now unto
the principalities and powers in heavenly_ places _might be known
by the church the manifold wisdom of God, according to the eternal purpose which he purposed in Christ Jesus our Lord._

It has been estimated that about 93 per cent of the words used in
the King James Bible (including repetitions of the same word) are
native English, rather than Latinisms or other linguistic imports.
While some of the terms used in the King James Bible translation of
this passage from Ephesians clearly owe their origins to Latin or
Greek, none of them stand out as crude neologisms or awkward terms
sitting ill at ease with their neighbours. Quite simply, they have all
been absorbed into the complex and shifting linguistic amalgam
known as the English language.

## HEBREW IDIOMS IN THE KING JAMES BIBLE

MANY OF THE Semitic turns of phrase that have gained an accepted
place in modern English can be traced directly to the King James
Bible of the Old Testament. In his careful study of the way in which
the King James Bible translated Hebrew idioms, William Rosenau
concluded that:

> The [King James Bible] is an almost literal translation of the
> Masoretic text, and is thus on every page replete with Hebrew

idioms. *The fact that Bible English has to a marvellous extent shaped our speech, giving peculiar connotations to many words and sanctioning strange constructions, is not any less patent. The [King James Bible] has been—it can be said without any fear of being charged with exaggeration—the most powerful factor in the history of English literature. Though the constructions encountered in the [King James Bible] are oftentimes so harsh that they seem almost barbarous, we should certainly have been the poorer without it.*

Rosenau argued that the King James Bible possessed a penetrative force that could best be demonstrated by observing how its turns of phrase came to be absorbed, often unconsciously, within everyday English. Hebraic idioms that have crept into regular English usage include the following:

"to lick the dust" (Psalm 72:9; Isaiah 49:23; Micah 7:17)

"to fall flat on his face" (Numbers 22:31)

"a man after his own heart" (1 Samuel 13:14)

"to pour out one's heart" (Psalm 62:8; Lamentations 2:19)

"the land of the living" (Job 28:13; Psalm 27:13; Psalm 52:5; Isaiah 38:11; Jeremiah 11:19; Ezekiel 32:23–27)

"under the sun" (Ecclesiastes 1:4 and at least twenty other occurrences in this biblical book)

"sour grapes" (Ezekiel 18:2)

"from time to time" (Ezekiel 4:10)

"pride goes before a fall" (Proverbs 16:18)

"the skin of my teeth" (Job 19:20)

"to stand in awe" (Psalm 4:4; Psalm 33:8)

"to put words in his mouth" (Exodus 4:15; Deuteronomy 18:18: 2 Samuel 14:3; 2 Samuel 14:19; Jeremiah 1:9)

"to go from strength to strength" (Psalm 84:7)

"like a lamb to the slaughter" (Isaiah 53:7)

Other standard English phrases represent minor modifications or developments of Hebraic originals in the King James Bible, including:

"rise and shine" (a minor variant on "arise, shine": Isaiah 60:1)
"to see the writing on the wall" (from Daniel 5:5)
"a fly in the ointment" (from Ecclesiastes 10:1)
"a drop in a bucket" (a slight variant on Isaiah 40:15)

It may, of course, be pointed out that some set phrases in English derive from the King James translation of the New Testament, often of passages in which the original Greek has been influenced by Semitic turns of phrase. Examples of such phrases that owe their origins to the King James New Testament include:

"the salt of the earth" (Matthew 5:13)
"a thorn in the flesh" (2 Corinthians 12:7)
"to give up the ghost" (meaning "to die": Mark 15:37; John 19:30)
"the powers that be" (Romans 13:1)
"and it came to pass" (Mark 1:9 and more than four hundred other passages)
"the scales fell from his eyes" (based on Acts 9:18)

A comparison of the King James Bible with the Geneva Bible suggests that the king's translators were much more likely to retain the Hebrew word order or structure, even when this resulted in a reading that did not sound quite right to English ears at the time. The passage of time, and increased exposure to their translation, has eliminated any awareness of its initial "strangeness," and led to its phrases being accepted as "normal" or "standard" English. William Tyndale had argued that there was a natural affinity between English and Hebrew, so that the ploughboy would not have any great difficulties with Semitic turns of phrase. Others were not so sure, perhaps feeling that Tyndale was somewhat optimistic about the linguistic abilities of ploughboys—at least, the ones that they knew. John Selden (1584–1654), noted as a Hebrew scholar of considerable distinction, was the cause of considerable irritation for the Puritans assembled at the Westminster Assembly. The latter were in the habit of citing proof-texts from the Bible to make theological points. Selden dismissed the translations found in their "little pocket Bibles with gilt-leaves," and suggested that they would do better to learn Greek or Hebrew and study the original texts. Selden was very doubtful whether the widespread use of Hebrew idioms would make sense to the unlearned. Translation required conversion of Hebrew idioms into real English, not Hebraized English. He expressed his concerns as follows in his *Table Talk*, published posthumously in 1689.

> *If I translate a French book into English, I turn it into English phrase and not into French English. "Il fait froid": I say "it is cold," not "it makes cold." But the Bible is translated into English words rather than English phrases. The Hebraisms are kept and the phrase of that language is kept. As for example, "he uncovered her shame," which is well enough so long as scholars have to do with it, but when it comes among the common people, Lord what gear do they make of it.*

It is interesting to note that Selden's English makes perfect sense to modern readers until he lapses into the slang of the period. For the record, "gear" is here best translated as "nonsense."

## Archaic English Forms in the King James Bible

ONE OF THE most interesting aspects of the King James Bible is its use of ways of speaking that were already becoming archaic in the standard English of the first decade of the seventeenth century. By adopting these older forms, the King James Bible had the unintended effect of perpetuating ways of speaking that, strictly speaking, were dying out in everyday English speech. In what follows, I shall focus on the three broad areas in which archaic forms are used, and consider their significance.

## 1. 'THOU' AND 'YOU'

One of the most distinctive features of the King James Bible is its use of "Thee," "Thou," "Thy," and "Thine," where modern English would simply use "you," "your" and "yours." In early Middle English, the situation was quite simple: "thou" was the singular form of "ye," and was, therefore, used to address one other person. It may be helpful to set out the situation in tabular form.

|  | Singular | Plural |
|---|---|---|
| Nominative | Thou | Ye |
| Accusative | Thee | You |
| Genitive | Thy | Your |

However, the widespread use of French in England during the Middle Ages led to what was originally a simple situation becoming more complex. The English word "you" came to have the same associations as the French "vous." Following normal French practice, the singular forms (thou; thee; thy) were used within a family, or to address children or people of inferior social class. The plural forms (ye; you; your) were adopted as a mark of respect when addressing a social superior. By the sixteenth century, the use of the singular form to address a single individual had virtually ceased in English, except in the specific case of family and inferiors. To address another as "thou" was thus to claim social superiority over him or her. There is considerable evidence that, at least in certain circles, it was used as a form of studied insult.

A careful study of the court records of the northern English city of Durham suggests that "you" had replaced "thou" as the normal form of address in spoken English by about 1575. The decision to use "thou" was a departure from the norm, intended to make a point—for example, in the following exchange between a social inferior and his superior:

> Roger Donn:   For although ye be a gent, and I a poor man, my
> honesty shall be as good as yours.
> Mr. Ratcliff:   What saith thou? Likens thou thy honesty to
> mine?

A further complexity concerned the distinction between "ye" (nominative) and "you" (accusative). Although the terms were spelled differently, there is substantial evidence to suggest that they were pronounced virtually identically. The King James Bible occasionally retains this distinction, even though it had passed out of general use by 1600. For example, consider the following construction found in Job 12:2–3:

> No doubt but ye are the people, and wisdom shall die with you.
> But I have understanding as well as you; I am not inferior to you.

The interplay of "ye" and "you" in this passage—and elsewhere—rests on a series of nice distinctions that had become somewhat blurred and vague by 1611.

As is well known, the King James Bible retains the use of "thou" to refer to God, a human being, or even the devil. The following passages indicate the general lines of this usage:

## GENESIS 40:12–14

*And Joseph said unto him, This is the interpretation of it: The three branches are three days: Yet within three days shall Pharaoh lift up thine head, and restore thee unto the place: and thou shalt deliver Pharaoh's cup into his hand, after the former manner when thou wast his butler. But think on me when it shall be well*

*with thee, and shew kindness, I pray thee, unto me, and make*
*mention of me unto Pharaoh, and bring me out of this house:*

### LUKE 4:5–8

*And the devil, taking him up into an high mountain, shewed unto*
*him all the kingdoms of the world in a moment of time. And the*
*devil said unto him, All this power will I give thee, and the glory*
*of them: for that is delivered unto me; and to whomsoever I will I*
*give it. If thou therefore wilt worship me, all shall be thine. And*
*Jesus answered and said unto him, Get thee behind me, Satan: for*
*it is written, Thou shalt worship the Lord thy God, and him only*
*shalt thou serve.*

### ACTS 24:1–4

*And after five days Ananias the high priest descended with the*
*elders, and with a certain orator named Tertullus, who informed*
*the governor against Paul. And when he was called forth, Tertullus*
*began to accuse him, saying, Seeing that by thee we enjoy great*
*quietness, and that very worthy deeds are done unto this nation by*
*thy providence, We accept it always, and in all places, most noble*
*Felix, with all thankfulness. Notwithstanding, that I be not further*
*tedious unto thee, I pray thee that thou wouldest hear us of thy*
*clemency a few words.*

Some have suggested that the King James Bible's use of "Thee,"
"Thou," and "Thy" to refer specifically to God is a title of respect, and
argued that modern Christianity should retain this practice. This is
clearly indefensible, at least for the following two reasons:

1. These same forms of address are used indiscriminately for God,
   Satan, and human beings, reflecting the usage of the early
   sixteenth century;
2. The use of these forms of address was, if anything, derogatory,
   implying superiority on the part of the user over the one being

addressed. It is one thing for God to address a human being as "thou"; for this hint of superiority to be returned is quite another.

Yet this raises a fascinating question: why does the King James Bible retain this mode of speaking, when it was already falling out of use? The answer is not difficult to discern, and lies in the first of the very specific directions given to the translators:

*The ordinary Bible read in the Church, commonly called the Bishops' Bible, to be followed, and as little altered as the Truth of the original will permit.*

The King's translators were forbidden to depart to any significant extent from the text of the Bishops' Bible of 1568. Yet what were the instructions given to those who prepared the Bishops' Bible? To use the Great Bible of 1539 except where it did not accurately represent the original texts. The directions given to the translators over the years 1539–1604 were thus virtually guaranteed to ensure continuity of language over a period in which the English language itself underwent considerable change and development. The inbuilt conservatism of the translation process, reflecting the concerns of those who sponsored and directed the three "official" English Bibles, therefore led directly—yet unintentionally—to the retention of older English ways of speaking in religious contexts, creating the impression that religious language was somehow *necessarily* archaic.

But the Great Bible of 1539 is in reality little more than Miles Coverdale's revision of Matthew's Bible, which is turn was a revision of Tyndale's translation—at least, those parts of the Bible that Tyndale managed to translate. As study after study has shown, the vast bulk of Tyndale's translation has consequently been incorporated indirectly into the King James Bible, on account of the instructions provided to official translators of the Bible.

This point can be illustrated by setting out, side by side, Tyndale's 1525 New Testament translation of a well-known passage and the translation provided by the Second Oxford Company, who were entrusted with the four Gospels, the Acts of the Apostles, and the Book of Revelation. The passage in question is Matthew 7:1–7.

### WILLIAM TYNDALE (1525)

*Judge not, that ye be not judged. For as ye judge so shall ye be judged. And with what measure ye mete, with the same it shall be measured to you again. Why seest thou a mote in thy brother's eye, and perceivest not the beam that is in thine own eye. Or why sayest thou to thy brother: suffer me to pluck out the mote out of thine eye, and behold a beam is in thine own eye. Hypocrite, first cast out the beam out of thine own eye, and then shalt thou see clearly to pluck out the mote out of thy brother's eye. Give not that which is holy to dogs, neither cast ye your pearls before swine, lest they tread them under their feet, and the other turn again and all to rent you. Ask, and it shall be given you. Seek and ye shall find. Knock and it shall be opened unto you.*

### KING JAMES BIBLE (1611)

*Judge not, that ye be not judged. For with what judgment ye judge, ye shall be judged: and with what measure ye mete, it shall be measured to you again. And why beholdest thou the mote that is in thy brother's eye, but considerest not the beam that is in thine own eye? Or how wilt thou say to thy brother, Let me pull out the mote out of thine eye; and, behold, a beam is in thine own eye? Thou hypocrite, first cast out the beam out of thine own eye; and then shalt thou see clearly to cast out the mote out of thy brother's eye. Give not that which is holy unto the dogs, neither cast ye your pearls before swine, lest they trample them under their feet, and turn again and rend you. Ask, and it shall be given you; seek, and ye shall find; knock, and it shall be opened unto you.*

Although nearly a century separates these translations—a century in which English underwent immense changes—the use of "ye," "thou," and so forth remains unchanged. The King James translators simply did not believe that they had the authority to make changes reflecting developments in the English language, and so continued to reproduce the English of nearly three generations earlier.

This can also be seen in a second archaic feature—the use of the old verbal endings.

## 2. 'SAYETH' OR 'SAYS'? THE VERBAL ENDINGS

A casual reading of the writing of Geoffrey Chaucer shows that the English verb has undergone considerable development. The Middle English verb endings remained in use during the sixteenth century, even though they were beginning to be changed. The most important of these, as far as our story is concerned, are the second and third person singular forms of the present tense, of which some examples are:

| | | |
|---|---|---|
| Thou sayest | Thou givest | Thou hast |
| He sayeth | She giveth | He hath |

Yet during the sixteenth century, things began to change. As we have already seen, the widespread use of "you" meant that the second person singular form of the verb ceased to be used extensively. The tendency to use the plural form led to a trend toward regularization. In three of the cases noted above, this led to the following shifts in conversational English:

| | | |
|---|---|---|
| You say | You give | You have |

Changes were also under way with the third person. In general, the ending "-eth" was replaced with "-s." It is not clear how this development came about. However, a close reading of Shakespeare shows that the older and newer verbal forms were both used in written

English at this time. For example, look at the following famous extract from *The Merchant of Venice*, written over the period 1596–98, in which Portia declares:

> *The quality of mercy is not strained,*
> *It droppeth as the gentle rain from heaven*
> *Upon the place beneath: it is twice blessed;*
> *It blesseth him that gives and him that takes:*

Here the older forms dominate. Yet elsewhere in the drama, the newer forms of the verb are seen to be well established.

> *How sweet the moonlight sleeps upon this bank!*
> *Here will we sit, and let the sounds of music*
> *Creep in our ears; soft stillness and the night*
> *Become the touches of sweet harmony.*
> *Sit, Jessica: look, how the floor of heaven*
> *Is thick inlaid with patines of bright gold:*
> *There's not the smallest orb which thou behold'st*
> *But in this motion like an angel sings*
> *Still quiring to the young-eyed cherubims;*
> *Such harmony is in immortal souls;*
> *But, whilst this muddy vesture of decay*
> *Doth grossly close it in, we cannot hear it.*

Interestingly, Shakespeare appears to retain the older forms "doth" and "hath" as a matter of principle.

What is particularly interesting is that there is strong evidence that, while the older "eth" ending continued to be *written*, it was *pronounced* as if it were "-s." In his *Special Help to Orthography*, published in 1643, Richard Hodges comments that although it was customary to write such words as "*leadeth* it, *noteth* it, *raketh* it, per-*fumeth* it," and so forth, in everyday speech it was customary to say "*leads* it, *notes* it, *rakes* it, per-*fumes* it," and so on. As English is not a phonetic language, words can undergo significant changes in pronunciation without any need for changes in their spelling. The implications of this are, to say the least, remarkable. Would those who read the King James Bible aloud in church have pronounced "knoweth" as "knows"? For example, consider John 2:9–11:

> He that saith he is in the light, and hateth his brother, is in darkness even until now. He that loveth his brother abideth in the light, and there is none occasion of stumbling in him. But he that hateth his brother is in darkness, and walketh in darkness, and knoweth not whither he goeth, because that darkness hath blinded his eyes.

Notice how many "-eth" verbs occur in this brief section. Richard Hodges's comments might lead us to think that this passage could have been *read aloud* using the modern "-s" endings in many cases.

This is an extremely important issue when dealing with the question of how works that make extensive use of the language of the King James Bible should be *sung*. An excellent example, of course, is provided by Handel's *Messiah*. The opening words of this oratorio are taken from Isaiah 40:1–4.

> Comfort ye, my people, saith your God; speak ye comfortably to Jerusalem, and cry unto her, that her warfare is accomplished, that her iniquity is pardoned. The voice of him that crieth in the wilderness: Prepare ye the way of the Lord, make straight in the desert a highway for our God.

The quest for authenticity of performance has led to this major work being performed using period instruments, in an attempt to re-create the actual sound of the period. But what about the words that are sung? Might "crieth" actually have been sung as "cries"? The issues raised are fascinating!

So why did the King James translators use an archaic verbal form in what was meant to be a modern translation? Again, the answer seems to lie with the rules provided for the translators, which more or less bound them to use the language of 1525 in their translations. A comparison of Tyndale's translation of Matthew 7:1–7 (see above) with the King James Bible shows that precisely the same older Middle English verbal endings are found in both translations. In Tyndale's time, they were in general use; by 1611, they were virtually obsolete.

### 3. 'HIS' AND 'ITS'

Middle English did not know the word "its," meaning "belonging to it." In its place, Middle English used the word "his." This word could mean one of two things: "belonging to him," and "belonging to it." By 1600, however, the word "his" was increasingly being used solely as the masculine possessive pronoun. Yet the same word was still used, even if increasingly rarely, to act as the *neuter* possessive pronoun. Even though "its" was unquestionably gaining the upper hand, it had yet to achieve dominance. This is reflected in the King James Bible, which uses the term "its" only *once*, at Leviticus 25:5:

> *That which groweth of its own accord of thy harvest thou shalt not reap, neither gather the grapes of thy vine undressed: for it is a year of rest unto the land.*

This leads to a number of features of the King James Bible that seem a little puzzling to modern readers. Take the translation of Matthew 5:13, one of the more familiar sayings of the Sermon on the Mount:

> *Ye are the salt of the earth: but if the salt have lost his savour, wherewith shall it be salted?*

This needs to be read twice before the issue becomes clear. To modern English readers, "salt" appears to be treated as a masculine noun in the second phrase, and a neuter noun in the third. This apparent absurdity needs to be appreciated in light of the discussion above. At this point, the translators have retained the increasingly rare usage of "his" as the *neuter* possessive pronoun. While this was normal in Middle English, it was dropping out of general use.

So how could the King James translators respond to this? They were standing at a linguistic junction, in which the word "its" was gradually gaining acceptance—but had yet to be universally recognized. To use the word "its" would cause confusion or bewilderment to at least some of their readers. On the other hand, they were aware that the use of the word "his" to mean "belonging to it" was passing out of use, and to make extensive use of this word would therefore cause confusion to later readers once this development had reached its inevitable conclusion. So what could be done? In the end, the only viable solution was to use a clumsy paraphrase, based on the word "thereof." Instead of writing—as we would today—"its width was five feet"—the King James translators rendered this as "the width thereof was five feet." It was clumsy, and arguably led to some of the least elegant passages in the entire King James Bible. But the use of this device avoided the problem caused by the change in English usage around this time.

The difficulties raised by the continuing use of "his" as the equivalent of the modern word "its" was felt especially by the First Westminster Company of translators, responsible for the "Pentateuch"; and "the Story from Joshua to the first Book of Chronicles, exclusive." It is clear that this company wanted to avoid the use of "his" as the neuter possessive pronoun wherever possible. This section of the Old Testament, however, included an unusually high number of passages that virtually demanded its usage—especially eleven passages giving details of measurements of buildings. Consider Exodus 30:2–3, which describes the measurements and structure of an altar.

*A cubit shall be the length thereof, and a cubit the breadth thereof; foursquare shall it be: and two cubits shall be the height thereof: the horns thereof shall be of the same. And thou shalt overlay it with pure gold, the top thereof, and the sides thereof round about, and the horns thereof; and thou shalt make unto it a crown of gold round about.*

The extensive and highly cumbersome use of "thereof" reflects a deliberate decision to avoid the use of the possessive pronoun. Note how the altar is clearly regarded as neuter, forcing the use of the neuter possessive. A modern translation, the Revised Standard Version, makes this point clear:

*A cubit shall be <u>its</u> length, and a cubit <u>its</u> breadth; it shall be square, and two cubits shall be <u>its</u> height; <u>its</u> horns shall be of one piece with it. And you shall overlay it with pure gold, <u>its</u> top and <u>its</u> sides round about and <u>its</u> horns; and you shall make for it a molding of gold round about.*

The natural use of "its" at seven points—here underlined for clarity—contrasts sharply with the clumsy construction used by the First Westminster Company to avoid the use of "his" as a neuter possessive pronoun.

The general points raised in this section are of considerable interest, in that they suggest that the King James Bible would actually have been perceived to be slightly old-fashioned and dated even from the first day of its publication. This naturally leads on to the question of the reception of the King James Bible.

# 12

## TRIUMPH:
## THE FINAL ACCLAMATION
## OF THE KING JAMES BIBLE

By 1850, the King James translation had triumphed. What was once a curiosity had become a classic. The nineteenth century showered praise on the King James Bible, viewing it as one of the high points of English literary achievements and perhaps the greatest contribution to the spiritual ennobling of the human race. Such judgments are inevitably projected on to earlier generations, giving the impression that the genius and brilliance of the translation were universally recognized from the outset. It is thus tempting to believe that the new translation was rapturously received on publication, being acclaimed immediately as a lasting monument of English literature as much as hailed as a superb new translation of the word of God.

Yet history gives us no warrant for any such extravagant opinions. Indeed, the evidence at our disposal suggests that many saw the final appearance of the new translation as something of an anticlimax. There were those who would indeed speak of the King James Bible in the highest possible terms—but such a judgment lay over a century away. The irrefutable evidence is that, far from rushing out to buy or make use of this new translation, people preferred to use an English translation from fifty years earlier—the Geneva Bible.

The simple truth is that the "new Bible" was initially regarded with polite disinterest. Nobody at the time really liked the new translation very much. Even some of those who were prominently involved in the translation of the King James Bible seemed hesitant to use it, preferring to cite from the Geneva Bible instead—hardly a commendation for their work. The King James Bible might be the Bible of the English religious and political establishment; it had a long way to go before it became the Bible of the English people.

This chapter tells the story of how an ugly duckling became a swan; how a translation that at first singularly failed to excite the popular imagination went on to be acclaimed as "the noblest monument of English prose"—to use the phrase of Robert Lowth (1710–87), sometime Professor of Poetry at Oxford University. It is a long and fascinating story, which can here only be told in part.

## EARLY REACTIONS

THE PUBLICATION OF the King James Bible in 1611 occasioned no fanfares of welcome, or accolades of praise. The event caused scarcely a ripple to pass over the face of English society at the time. England had far more important things to worry about than its new Bible. Religious controversies over the question of predestination in the Low Countries were beginning to have an influence in England, and were causing increased religious polarization. Politically, there were concerns about Spanish ambitions in the Low Countries, which could easily involve England in a new military conflict.

The small degree of reaction that could be discerned was generally negative in tone. One response was particularly critical, and deserves mention. When the translators of the King James Bible were selected, some individuals who believed that they were highly suited to the task found that they had been passed over. One scholar who saw himself as belonging to this category of overlooked geniuses was Hugh

Broughton (1549–1612). Broughton had pressed the case for a new translation of the Bible during the reign of Queen Elizabeth, and had been frustrated by the lack of progress that was achieved. The news that James I was to commission a new translation initially seemed to him to be a most excellent matter.

Contemporary reports suggest that Broughton was a notoriously grumpy old man who disliked working with others, and had an exaggerated sense of his own importance. The world of letters has always been heavily populated with such types, and it is quite likely that Broughton's reputation as a *prima donna* had preceded him, persuading those close to the King that he could never work on a committee. Broughton was, in any case, heavily involved in a biblical translation project of his own choosing—the revision of the Geneva Bible. This was never completed.

Broughton professed himself "crossed" by the new translation, and declared that the only useful thing that could be done with it was to burn it. Broughton's death in 1612 prevented him from developing his criticisms of the new translation, as much as improving upon it through his own revision of the Geneva Bible. However, there were others who were displeased with the new translation, and sought to secure revisions at the earliest possible stage.

Yet such calls were not taken with any great seriousness until the 1640s, when the issue became polarized for political reasons. The King James Bible had been commissioned by a king. As Parliamentarians—who argued for the authority of the English Parliament over the English monarch—gained influence around this time, the question of who should authorize a new translation of the Bible became a serious political issue. For many, it was *Parliament* that should commission a new authorized version—and that authority would derive from the English people, not the English monarch. As Parliamentarians were generally Puritan in their religious outlook, it was not surprising that the Geneva Bible should be suggested as a candidate for such "authorization."

It is, therefore, no cause for surprise to learn that the opponents of

Puritanism during the reign of Charles I did all they could to eliminate the influence of this Bible, with its marginal notes.

## THE BATTLE OF THE BIBLES: CHARLES I AND THE WAR AGAINST THE GENEVA BIBLE

As a result of pressure from the authorities, after 1616 the printing of the Geneva Bible ceased in England. The work now had to be
imported from the Netherlands. This, however, did nothing to stem its
sales. James I seems to have been relatively unconcerned over this
matter, and did not consider the suppression of the importation of this
rival to his own translation to be a matter of pressing importance. He
cordially disliked the Geneva Bible, but believed that his own new
translation would eventually displace it without any need for special
action on his part.

However, the death of James I and the accession of his son,
Charles I, in 1625 saw a change in the religious climate within
England. Charles's marriage to the French princess Henrietta Maria
had caused considerable popular resentment, partly on account of her
being a foreigner, and partly because she was a Roman Catholic.
Radical Protestants were alarmed at the prospect of a monarch who
would be openly sympathetic to the Roman Catholic cause throughout Europe.

Charles appointed the high churchman William Laud as Archbishop of Canterbury in 1633. Archbishop Laud was clearly troubled
by the continuing popularity—and correspondingly high sales—of the
Geneva Bible. Under Charles I, religious tensions had worsened, with
overt opposition between Puritans and Anglicans emerging at point
after point. England was divided into the factions that would shortly
take opposing sides in the civil war, pitching Puritan against Anglican,
Parliamentarian against Royalist. The Geneva Bible, with its notes, was
seen as the Bible of the Puritans, and the King James Bible as the Bible
of the establishment. For Laud, the continuing circulation of the

PORTRAIT OF KING CHARLES I
ATTRIBUTED TO THE WORKSHOP OF
SIR ANTHONY VAN DYCK (1599–1641)

Geneva Bible was, therefore, a significant contributing cause to the religious tensions of his day, which threatened to tear England apart.

Yet it was not the Genevan translation as such that caused Laud and his supporters such headaches. The real problem lay with the extensive marginal notes, which offered guidance to the reader as to how the text was to be interpreted and applied. Although the Geneva Bible dated from two generations earlier, its critique of the abuse of monarchical powers might have been written with Charles I's reign in mind. As has been already noted, some of these comments (see page 141) caused such offence to James I, and therefore were partly responsible for his desire for a new English translation.

James's son, Charles I, felt similarly threatened by the Genevan challenge to the doctrine of the divine right of kings. Charles had absorbed much of his father's belief in this doctrine, and saw it as essential to the religious and political well-being of his kingdom. William Laud, Archbishop of Canterbury, had a strong personal vested interest in maintaining both the monarchy and the established Church of England, and rightly saw the doctrines of the Geneva Bible's marginal notes as a serious threat to the situation. It was thus natural for Laud to want to minimize the influence of the Geneva Bible at this point. But what could he do? One option might have been to mount a major theological critique of the Geneva Bible, by publishing immense numbers of learned treatises countering its criticisms of the doctrine of the divine right of kings. But this would take time, and would have little impact at the popular level. Laud was aware that there was a much simpler solution. All that was needed was an order banning the Geneva Bible from England. But what reason could be given? In the end, Laud hit on an ingenious solution. To support the Geneva Bible, he argued, was unpatriotic.

Laud suggested that the Geneva Bible posed a threat to the livelihood of patriotic English printers, whose livelihoods were being threatened by the importation of cheap and well-produced Geneva Bibles. The commercial success of the Geneva Bible seemed to Laud to offer an entirely reasonable excuse to suppress it. As the work was

J. COCHRAN'S 1830 ENGRAVING OF
VAN DYCK'S PORTRAIT OF WILLIAM LAUD,
ARCHIBISHOP OF CANTERBURY

printed abroad, Laud argued, would not permitting its continued import threaten the English printing industry as a whole? The Geneva Bibles printed in Amsterdam were better in every respect than the early printings of the King James Bible. If market forces alone were allowed to dictate the outcome of this economic battle of the Bibles, the Geneva Bible would dominate the English market. It may be added that the costliness of the King James Bible was the direct result of Robert Barker's monopoly on the text, which allowed him to profit extensively from the work. Laud, however, passed over this awkward point, and summed up his objections to the Genevan text as follows:

> By the numerous coming over to the [Geneva Bible] from Amsterdam, there was a great and a just fear conceived that by little

*and little printing would quite be carried out of the Kingdom. For the books which came thence were better print, better bound, better paper, and for all the charges of bringing, sold better cheap. And would any man buy a worse Bible dearer, that might have a better more cheap?*

Laud thus had a simple economic and patriotic reason for wishing to block the importation of Geneva Bibles. Although Laud was careful to present his reasons for wishing to limit, and even terminate, the circulation of these Bibles in England as fundamentally patriotic and economic in motivation, many realized that this was merely a convenient excuse for suppressing a work that he disliked for religious reasons. The Geneva Bible had its origins within Calvinist circles, and was seen as being overtly supportive of a Puritan agenda. A simple answer to Laud's concerns about the future of the English printing industry lay to hand: permit production of the Geneva Bible *in England*. But this option does not appear to have been given serious consideration.

Samuel Johnson once remarked that "patriotism is the last refuge of a scoundrel." Perhaps it is unfair to suggest that Laud was scurrilous in what he did. But whatever its morality, Laud's action proved highly effective. The flow of the subversive text into England was staunched. The final known edition of the Geneva Bible was published in 1644. As a result, the King James Bible enjoyed a new commercial success— the word "popularity" is not yet apposite. However, it was not long before a compromise was developed that allowed the Genevan notes a new lease on life in England. The popularity of the Geneva Bible rested not so much on the translation itself, as on the explanatory material appended to the translation. So why, some reasoned, should not the Geneva translation be replaced with the King James Bible, while retaining the Genevan notes? Between 1642 and 1715, at least nine editions—eight of which originated in Amsterdam—are known of the King James Bible with the Geneva notes.

But many Puritans regarded this as an unsatisfactory compromise, and pressed for the replacement of the King James Bible. With the outbreak of the English civil war in 1642, an opportunity arose to challenge the authority of the King James Bible.

## AMBIVALENCE: THE PURITAN COMMONWEALTH

IN THE CLOSING years of the reign of Charles I, the growing political influence of Puritanism began to become of importance to the reception of the King James Bible. The new emphasis upon the authority of Parliament—as opposed to that of the king—within Puritan circles led to demands for revision of the translation to be undertaken by the state. Parliament, it was argued, should commission a new translation, which would eliminate the errors and ecclesiastical bias of the King James Bible. William Laud had been one of the most formidable opponents of the Geneva Bible, and a staunch defender of the King James Bible. However, Laud found himself outmanoeuvred by an increasingly confident Puritan Parliament. In 1641, he was imprisoned in the Tower of London; in 1645, he was executed.

With Laud out of the way, serious opposition to the King James Bible gathered momentum. Calls for the revision of the translation became increasingly frequent and strident. In a sermon delivered before the House of Commons, assembled at the church of St. Margaret's, Westminster, on August 26, 1645, John Lightfoot (1602–75) argued the case for a revised translation, which would be both accurate and lively:

> *It was the course of Nehemiah when he was reforming that he caused not the law only to be read and the sense given, but also caused the people to "understand the reading." And certainly it would not be the least advantage that you might do to the three nations, if not the greatest, if they by your care and means might come to understand the proper and genuine reading of the Scripture by an exact, vigorous and lively translation.*

The Parliamentary Grand Committee for Religion eventually agreed to order a subcommittee to look into this matter. It was clear that the complaints against the King James Bible could be broadly divided into two categories: the many misprints in the printed versions of the text, which caused confusion to readers; and, perhaps more seriously, questions concerning the accuracy of the translation itself. A Parliamentary group that crystallized around Henry Jessey (1601–63), noted for his competence in sacred languages, concluded that the literary style of the King James Bible left something to be desired; "many places which are not falsely may be yet better rendered." Similar comments can be found in Robert Gell's *An Essay Towards the Amendment of the Last English Translation of the Bible* (1659).

Yet perhaps one may conjecture that a political issue coloured this discussion, in that hostility to the King James Bible reflected a perception that it was hostile to Puritanism—or at least that it lacked the Puritan emphasis that made the Geneva Bible so satisfying to its readers. One Parliamentary group, meeting in 1652–53, argued that the King James Bible used "prelatical language"—in other words, the traditional church terminology, such as "bishop." This practice, which was specifically laid down in Richard Bancroft's rules for the translators, was offensive to many Puritans. It reminded them of the religious establishment that they had worked hard to overthrow. There was also new and increased resistance from many Puritans to the inclusion of the Apocrypha in the King James Bible. The Westminster Confession of Faith would reject the inclusion of this group of works in Bibles; some Puritans wanted immediate action on this matter.

It might be thought that the period of the Puritan Commonwealth would have seen a new lease on life for the Geneva Bible. In fact, this was not the case. Perhaps there was a realization that the Geneva translation was not as good as might be hoped. In any case, the marginal notes could be had by other means. In the first year of the Commonwealth, an edition of the King James Bible with the

Genevan notes was published, with official backing, in London. The *Soldier's Pocket Bible*, issued in 1643, consisted of selections from the Geneva Bible. The following year saw the final reprint of the Geneva Bible, which henceforth virtually disappeared from the radar screens of English religious controversy.

This is a curious fact, and its explanation remains far from clear. The simplest explanation is economic, and relates to the continuation of earlier monopoly regulations under the Commonwealth. Oliver Cromwell conferred the monopoly on the King James Bible to John Field and Henry Hills in 1656, during which year Field also became printer to Cambridge University. Field was widely regarded as a monopolist on a grand scale, and it is possible that Field, wishing to gain as much as possible from his monopoly on the King James Bible, sought to discourage the publication of rival versions, or the development of revisions. Entirely plausible though this explanation may be, it must be stressed that we simply do not know with any certainty the true reasons for the waning in popularity of the Geneva Bible at a time when it might have been expected to enjoy a surge in popularity.

The Commonwealth thus came to an end without the anticipated surge in popularity and influence of the Geneva Bible. Oliver Cromwell, who was installed as "Lord Protector" of the English nation in December 1653, failed to ensure the Puritan succession. As a result, his death in September 1658 led to the Puritan government falling apart. The resulting political instability eventually led to the restoration of the monarchy in 1660. With Charles II restored to the English throne, and a growing public backlash developing against the excesses of the period of the Puritan Commonwealth, the earlier Puritan opposition to the King James Bible virtually guaranteed that it would be the established translation of the new administration.

PORTRAIT OF OLIVER CROMWELL
BY ROBERT WALKER (1607–60)

## RESTORATION:
## THE FINAL ACCEPTANCE OF THE
## KING JAMES BIBLE

THE RESTORATION OF Charles II in 1660 put an end to any talk about revising the King James translation, or replacing it with any rival. Charles's concern was to restore the Church of England to its proper place in English society, and regain the stability that had been so painfully lacking in recent years. The publication of the Book of Common Prayer in 1662 alongside the King James translation of the Bible was designed to ensure religious conformity and security, so that the problems of the past might be left behind. The King James Bible was now seen as a pillar of Restoration society, holding together church and state, the bishops and monarch, at a time when social cohesion was essential to England's future as a nation. The Act of Uniformity (1662), which brought into being a new Book of Common Prayer, firmly upheld the establishment of the Church of England. Nobody wanted to return to the chaos of the Puritan Commonwealth. England turned its back on Puritanism as quickly and totally as Germany disowned its Nazi past after the Second World War.

This was bad news for the Geneva Bible, which was now viewed as a seditious text, giving theological support to a politically and religiously discredited section of English society. To praise or to possess the Geneva Bible could spell instant social death. It had become a potent symbol of a period in English history that was both feared and despised by the leaders of the polite culture of the Restoration.

With the restoration of the monarchy, to popular acclaim, the "battle of the Bibles" had ended. The King James Bible had finally triumphed over its rival. The grounds of that triumph may partly rest in its eloquence, or in the excellence of its translation. Yet the most significant factor in its final triumph appears to have been the fact that it was associated with the authority of the monarch at a time when such authority was viewed positively. In marked contrast, the Genevan Bible was marginalized, not on account of the quality of its translation or English prose, but because it had been the preferred translation of the detested Puritan faction, who had now been comprehensively routed, militarily and politically.

The "new translation"—as the King James Bible was still termed even late in the seventeenth century—was still regarded with some misgivings at the opening of the eighteenth. Yet it was during this century that a decisive change in attitude toward the "new translation" developed. It is virtually impossible to point to any defining moment or event that crystallized the perception that this was indeed a great work of religious literature; but at some time during this century, perhaps around 1750, such a perception settled over the work, and would remain in place until the end of the First World War. If the first 150 years of its history were encumbered with hints of discontent, criticism, and suspicion, its next 150 years were characterized by something at times approaching uncritical adulation.

When, why, and how did this take place? It is impossible to say. Perhaps an increasing distance from the origins of the translation began to allow the work to be endowed with the characteristics of a classic. Perhaps a fading of memories allowed rival versions—such as the Geneva Bible or the Bishops' Bible—or hostile initial reactions to be forgotten. Perhaps familiarity dulled the senses to the weaknesses of the translation, or allowed well-known words to become embedded in the memory. Whatever the reasons—and these remain less than fully understood—there is no doubt that a decisive and irreversible change came about in the esteem in which the King James Bible was held in England and beyond.

Yet the triumph of the King James Bible was not limited to Great Britain (within which the translation continues to be known as the "Authorized Version"). The expansion of British economic and military influence in the later eighteenth and nineteenth centuries was preceded and accompanied by missionary work, based on the King James Bible. Wherever English-language versions of Christianity sprang up, these would usually be nourished by this definitive translation. The impact of the King James Bible on the language and worship of Christianity in Africa and Australasia has been immense.

The Christian church in America represents by far the most important English-language community of faith outside the British Isles. The story of how the King James Bible was received in North America thus merits especially close attention. How did a translation so closely linked with the British establishment fare in this former colony, which broke those links during the War of Independence?

## THE KING JAMES BIBLE IN AMERICA

THE ENGLISH LANGUAGE was brought to America by English colonists, who began to settle in the region in the late sixteenth century. The settlement of America thus took place around the time when the English language itself was undergoing a major period of transition, on which both the works of Shakespeare and the King James Bible were significant influences. English was, of course, by no means the only European language that became established in America around this time.

Several waves of European immigration led to Dutch, French, German, Italian, Spanish, and Swedish becoming established, often in very specific geographical regions. The emergence of English as the dominant, and finally the official, language of the United States is a fascinating and complex matter, and cannot be told in detail in this chapter, but is of significance in demonstrating the influence of the King James Bible on the shaping of written and spoken English in the region.

Three major periods can be distinguished in the European settlement of North America.

1. From the settlement of Jamestown in 1607 to 1788 when the new federal constitution was finally ratified. At this stage, some 90 per cent of the immigrant population, which was mostly to be found east of the Appalachian Mountains, was from the British Isles, and hence predominantly English-speaking.
2. From 1787 to about 1860, during which the immigrant population moved westward, eventually reaching the Pacific Ocean. This period can be thought of as ending with the Civil War. The failure of the Irish potato harvest in 1845 led to massive emigration from Ireland, and the establishment of large Irish immigrant communities in cities such as Boston.
3. The third phase saw increased emigration from southern Europe, including Italy, as well as from parts of Asia.

While all of these periods are of considerable interest to American historians, the first is of special importance to our story. This was the settlement of the original thirteen colonies on the Eastern seaboard, stretching from Maine to Georgia. The earliest New England settle-

THE LANDING OF THE PILGRIMS AT PLYMOUTH
ON DECEMBER 11, 1620, BY CURRIER & IVES

ments were in the Massachusetts Bay area. However, the tidewater district of Virginia was also of importance. Jamestown was founded in 1607, and the colony attracted many refugees from England, especially under the reign of Charles I. Although some were Anglicans, the evidence suggests that many were Puritans, fleeing what they regarded as an oppressive England to find religious toleration in the New World.

It was clear from the outset that many of those settling in the American colonies had strong religious reasons for wishing to leave England. America was to be the promised land, the Atlantic Ocean the Red Sea, and England under Charles I and Archbishop William Laud was the new Egypt. The resonances with the great biblical account of the exodus of the people of God from Egypt and the settlement in a new land, prepared for them by God, were too obvious to miss.

The émigrés brought their Bibles with them to the New World. These were not simply reminders of the lands they had left behind; they were also to serve as a spiritual and literary resource in their new lives. It would be many years before the American colonies could sustain a printing industry. Many of the families who settled in the colonies had one book only—and that was the Bible. The evidence strongly suggests that the first English Bible to be brought to the New World was the Geneva Bible. Not only had this been available longer, it was the translation of choice for the Puritans, who valued its extensive annotations. The Geneva Bible offered both text and commentary, which served as a framework to interpret the hand of providence that had delivered them from Egypt and brought them to this new Canaan.

Gaps soon opened between the forms of English spoken in America and Britain. American English preserved features of both the written and spoken English of the seventeenth century, which were soon eroded in England itself. Standard American English is in many ways reminiscent of the spoken English of the seventeenth and eighteenth centuries. Phrases such as "I guess," nouns such as "platter" and verbal forms such as "gotten"—all of which go back to Chaucer—dropped out of use in England, yet were retained in America.

Despite substantial immigration to America from other European nations, and the presence of a large number of Native American languages, English became *de facto* the language of the United States. The gradual dispersion of the English-speaking population throughout the entire continent of North America ensured its geographical universality. Other languages might predominate in certain localities; English was spoken throughout.

The literary text that shaped American Christianity in this formative phase proved to be the King James Bible. Its prominent place in the public life of the prerevolutionary American colonies ensured that

English continued to be written after the fashion of England. Cut off from their linguistic homeland, the colonists found that the text of the Bible was an important means of sustaining both their religious faith and their English prose. Both their faith and their language was nourished and governed by the King James translation.

There is no doubt that the King James Bible was a formative influence on the shaping of American English. As the great American man of letters Noah Webster (1758–1843) pointed out, "the language of the Bible has no inconsiderable influence in forming and preserving our national language." Its role in public discourse was guaranteed through its prominent role in the worship of the churches and in private devotion. As the complex history of American Christianity makes abundantly clear, often highly charged debates on practically every aspect of Christian life and thought broke out regularly. Yet the common factor that united the warring factions was often the King James Bible. The lowest common denominator of English-speaking American Protestant Christianity, especially in the nineteenth century, was the King James Version of the Bible.

## THE FIRST PRINTED AMERICAN BIBLES

PRECISELY ON ACCOUNT of their colonial status, the American colonies were subject to the restrictions of British law. The King James Bible could not be produced legally in America, but had to be imported from England. Production could be carried out only at authorized centres in London, Cambridge, and Oxford. Some American writers took the view that the "privilege" granted by the British crown for the production of the King James Bible applied only to editions without added comments, and, therefore, considered producing annotated and illustrated editions, thus bypassing the copyright difficulty. Yet such schemes foundered. The simple fact was that there was such a scarcity of high-quality paper and printing type in America that the production of a book as large as the Bible was beyond the means of American printers at this stage.

These economic restrictions did not apply to Bible translations in other languages, or to portions of the Bible in versions other than the King James Bible. The first book to be printed in British North America was the famous *Bay Psalm Book* of 1640, which was a translation of the Psalms undertaken by Richard Mather, John Eliot, and Thomas Weld. John Eliot is also of importance to our story for another reason—he was responsible for the translation of the Bible into a Native American language. The largest group of North American native languages is usually known as Algonquian, which includes the languages of the Blackfoot and Cheyenne. Eliot produced the first printed Bible in North America in one of the Algonquian languages. In view of his importance, it is worth considering Eliot in a little more detail.

John Eliot was born in Widford, Hertfordshire, England, on July 31, 1604. During his time as a student at Cambridge University, he came under the influence of the leading Puritan divine Thomas Hooker. His Puritan views fell foul of the repressive religious policies of William Laud and he chose to emigrate from England, eventually arriving at Boston in 1631. The following year, he became pastor of Roxbury, a few miles from the centre of Boston, where he would remain for the rest of his life.

Eliot was interested in the culture and language of the Native Americans who lived around Roxbury, and made a point of studying and learning Natic (as this regional variant of Algonquian is known). He began to preach in this language, and was able to attract support for his missionary work in the region, eventually managing to gain parliamentary approval in 1649 for the establishment of the Society for the Propagation of the Gospel in New England. His translation and production of the Bible into Natic took place over the period 1661–63, using a professional printer, Marmaduke Johnson, sent over from England in 1660 on a three-year contract. The Bible runs to 1,200 pages, and could not have been produced without the technical means and assistance provided from London.

The first complete Bible to be published in North America in a

European language appeared in 1743. This was not, as might be thought, in English, but German, reflecting the sizable German immigrant community. Its appearance brought new pressure for an English Bible to be produced locally, rather than having to import one from Europe. In July 1777, a petition was placed before the "Continental Congress of the United States of North America now sitting in Philadelphia" by three local clergymen, requesting the printing of an American Bible. As far as can be seen, no action resulted from this petition. It was concluded "that the proper types for printing the Bible are not to be had in this country, and that the paper can be procured, but with such difficulties and subject to such casualties as render any dependence on it altogether improper." Instead, it was recommended that twenty thousand English Bibles should be imported from Europe.

The restrictions placed on the production of the King James Bible in North America were, of course, the direct result of the colonial status of the region. It was axiomatic that British publishing privileges applied in the British colonies. However, the political status of the entire region was called into question through growing American hostility to British economic privileges in the region, particularly taxation. The American Revolution (1776–83) witnessed the overthrow of British power, and put an end to any means by which British economic privileges might be enforced.

The scene was now set for the production of an American edition of the King James Bible, free of the kind of restrictions that had proved such a difficulty earlier. In the event, the initiative for such a move came not from any official state or federal body, but from a private individual. Robert Aitken was born in Dalkeith, Scotland in 1734, where he had learned the craft of book production. He established himself in the book trade in the Scottish town of Paisley. Frustrated by his lack of success, however, he decided to make an exploratory visit to America to discover whether he could make a living there.

In May 1769, Aitken and his family moved to Philadelphia, where he established himself initially as a bookseller, and subsequently as a printer and publisher. He set up his printing house at the sign of the "Pope's Head," which was only a few doors away from the coffee-house that was the gathering point for revolutionary activists. Aitken began to publish the *Pennsylvania Magazine* in January 1775; a year later, he was entrusted with the publication of the journals of Congress. When Congress withdrew to the relative safety of Baltimore in December 1776, Aitken was urged to follow; Aitken, however, decided to remain in Philadelphia. The British finally with-drew from the city in June 1778. The following month, Aitken adver-tised an edition of the New Testament in the *Pennsylvania Evening Post*. This edition had evidently been set up and produced the previ-ous year, as Aitken's accounts make reference to some sales in August 1777.

It is, however, clear that Aitken's real ambition was to produce the first English Bible to be printed in America. Congress itself had been aware of the importance of this step. In 1780, the following resolu-tion, introduced by James McLene of Pennsylvania and John Hanson of Maryland, was passed:

> *That it be recommended to such of the States who may think it convenient for them that they take proper measures to procure one or more new and correct editions of the Old and New Testament to be printed and that such states regulate their printers by law so as to secure effectually the said books from being misprinted.*

Yet nothing seems to have come of this proposal. Perhaps aware of growing interest in this possibility, Aitken presented a "memorial"—a modern equivalent of which might be a "memorandum"—to Congress, proposing a new Bible. He was already known in congres-sional circles, of course, through his publishing work, and could have every expectation that his proposal would be taken seriously.

Aitken, however, did not wait for congressional approval before beginning his work. The text to be printed was, of course, the King

James Bible, with the Apocrypha omitted. The dominant forms of Christianity in the United States at this time were sympathetic to the exclusion of these works, and Aitken saw no difficulty in responding accordingly. In any case, the resulting work would be easier and less costly to produce on account of this omission.

It is perhaps a harsh judgment to suggest that Aitken may have hoped to secure a privilege on the printing of American Bibles comparable to that enjoyed by the King's Printer in England. Yet certain telling indicators point in this direction. Aitken sought congressional approval and endorsement for his text. In the event, this was forthcoming. After an examination of specimen copies by its two chaplains, Congress approved Aitken's Bible on September 10, 1782, allowing Aitken freedom to publish its specific recommendation in any manner he liked.

> *The United States in Congress assembled highly approve the pious and laudable undertaking of Mr. Aitken, as subservient to the interest of religion, as well as an instance of the progress of arts in this country, and being satisfied from the above report of his care and accuracy in the execution of the work, they recommend this edition of the Bible to the inhabitants of the United States, and hereby authorize him to publish this recommendation in the manner he shall think proper.*

Aitken promptly inserted the congressional endorsement in the front matter of his text, which he finally published on September 25, 1782. In effect, Aitken's was promoted as an "authorized" version of the Bible, the authorization no longer originating from the king of England, but from the Congress of the United States. Aitken produced ten thousand copies of his Bible, set in brevier type on American-made paper. The work was 1,452 pages in length.

Aitken's Bible did not have the impact he had hoped for. The ending of hostilities with England led to the reopening of trade routes, with the result that imported Bibles from Britain and Europe were once more available—at considerably lower cost. Aitken sought to protect his position and investment, petitioning Congress in 1789 to grant him an exclusive license to print Bibles in the United States for fourteen years. (The parallels with the British privilege system cannot be overlooked.) Congress declined this proposal, clearly believing that a free trade in Bibles was essential. By 1800, twenty-four editions of the English Bible were available. By then, Aitken was in serious financial trouble. In 1791, he revealed to John Nicholson, Receiver General of Taxes for the State of Pennsylvania, that he had sustained a loss of four thousand pounds on his Bible.

Yet Aitken's activities had ensured that the King James Bible—despite its British establishment pedigree—would be the translation of choice of the United States. Even in the closing decades of the twentieth century, American Christianity continued its love affair with this translation. As rival translations—such as the Revised Standard Version—began to gain the upper hand in the period immediately following the Second World War, a staunch defence of the integrity of the King James Bible was mounted by its supporters in the United States. It was argued that the King James Bible was more accurate as a translation, was based on a more reliable text than its rivals, and used sombre and sober language appropriate to such a dignified topic. A series of popular polemical works argued that the King James Bible alone represented the authentic "Word of God"; all other versions involved distortions, additions, or other changes detrimental to the reliability of the text. Although these views are typical of a decided minority of conservative American Protestants, they remain an important witness to the continuing respect and admiration in which the King James Bible is widely held.

The production of the "New King James Bible"—which appeared over the period 1979–82—can be seen as an attempt to build on the perceived strengths of the traditional translation, including its "quality of translation" and "majesty of style." Although perhaps allowing itself to be understood as a new *edition* of the King James Bible, the work is actually a revision of the text, aiming to retain the "elegant literary style" and "beauty" of the original, while making such minor translation changes as seemed necessary.

The production of the New King James Bible is perhaps one of the most telling signs of the continuing importance of the original translation of 1611. In popular Christian culture, the King James translation is seen to possess a dignity and authority that modern translations somehow fail to convey. Even four hundred years after the six companies of translators began their long and laborious task, their efforts continue to be a landmark for popular Christianity. Other translations will doubtless jostle for place in the nation's bookshops in the twenty-first century. Yet the King James Bible retains its place as a literary and religious classic, by which all others continue to be judged.

# AFTERWORD

"The English Bible—a book which, if everything else in our language should perish, would alone suffice to show the whole extent of its beauty and power." Thus wrote Lord Macaulay in 1828, foreshadowing the immense esteem in which the Victorian era would hold the King James Bible.

## THE TRANSPARENCY OF THE TEXT

PERHAPS THE GREATEST tribute to its success lies in the simple fact that, for nearly two centuries, most of its readers were unaware that they were actually reading a *translation*. George Bernard Shaw had Henry Pickering admonish Eliza Doolittle to remember that "you are a human being with a soul and the divine gift of articulate speech: that your native language is the language of Shakespeare and Milton and The Bible; and don't sit there crooning like a bilious pigeon." For Shaw, and his age, the King James translation of the Bible *was* the Bible. The translation achieved a transparency that allowed its readers to forget that they were reading what was originally written in a foreign language. Demands for revision of the translation were met with the highly significant retort: "If the King James Bible was good enough for St. Paul, it's good enough for me." The idea of inspiration, which was traditionally applied to the biblical texts in their original languages, now came to be applied to the English translation of the King James Bible itself.

Although hints of this can be seen in the late eighteenth century, the trend reached its climax in the middle of the nineteenth century. The prominent American writer Alexander Wilson McClure (1808–65) published a work entitled *The Translators Revised*, in which he lavished praise on their achievements, and set out his belief that:

> *The first half of the seventeenth century, when the translation was completed, was the Golden Age of biblical and oriental learning in England. Never before, nor since, have those studies been pursued by scholars whose vernacular tongue is English with such zeal and success. This remarkable fact is a token of God's providential care of his Word as deserves most devout acknowledgement.*

This gives an insight concerning the early seventeenth century that was apparently denied to those fortunate enough to live then— that it was a Golden Age of biblical learning and translation. An increasing historical distance, not to mention a certain lack of knowledge of the early history of the translation, allowed this heady nostalgia to settle over the reputation of the King James Bible.

Yet this definitive and authoritative work was actually a translation. This point was completely lost to most in the nineteenth century—even the clergy. Richard Whately (1787–1863), Archbishop of Dublin from 1831, caused consternation at his diocesan conference of clergy when he produced a copy of the King James Bible, and declared: "Never forget, gentlemen, that this is not the Bible." Gasps of astonishment were heard throughout the auditorium. After a moment's pause for effect, he continued, "This, gentlemen, is only a *translation* of the Bible." Perhaps it was "only" a translation—but it was the only translation that English-language culture knew and used for the best part of two hundred years. It was inevitable that it should have a deep impact on the shaping of that language. Jean Paul once remarked that "every language is a dictionary of faded metaphors." The English language can be thought of as a dictionary of such images and phrases, many of which can be traced back to the King James Bible. The phrases and images that it deployed have often survived, whereas the specific religious beliefs they conveyed have not.

## THE POWER OF RELIGIOUS PROSE

THE PROSE OF the King James Bible had the power to move and convert, and exercised a powerful hold over the mental world of generations of English-speaking people. In his journal entry for Sunday February 20, 1763, James Boswell (1740–95)—the celebrated biographer of Dr. Samuel Johnson—wrote of the impact of the Old Testament story of Joseph:

> *This forenoon I read the history of Joseph and his brethren, which melted my heart and drew tears from my eyes. It is simply and beautifully told in the sacred writings. It is a strange thing that the Bible is so little read. I am reading it regularly through at present. I dare say that there are many people of distinction in London who know nothing about it. Were the history of Joseph published by some genteel bookseller as an eastern fragment and circulated amongst the gay world, I am persuaded that those who have any genuine taste might be taken in to admire it exceedingly and so by degrees have a due value for the oracles of God.*

Boswell clearly took the view that a literary appreciation of the Bible would lead to a recognition of its religious merits.

Similar themes can be found in American writings of the same period. Timothy Dwight's 1772 work *A Dissertation on the History, Eloquence and Poetry of the Bible* can be seen as a strident affirmation of the literary value of the King James Bible, and an important anticipation of later attitudes toward the text. Samuel Jackson Pratt's *The Sublime and Beautiful of Scripture*, which dates from the same period, made some similar points:

> *I am thus particularly earnest to display in this work the literary excellence of the Holy Bible, because I have reason to apprehend it is too frequently laid by under a notion of its being a dull, dry and unentertaining system, whereas the fact is quite otherwise: it contains all that can be wished by the truest intellectual taste, it enters more sagaciously and more deeply into human nature, it develops character, delineates manner, charms the imagination and warms the heart more effectively than any other book extant; and if once a man would take it into his hand without that strange prejudicing idea of flatness, and be willing to be pleased, I am morally certain he would find all his favorite authors dwindle in the comparison, and conclude that he was not only reading the most religious book but the most entertaining book in the world.*

In part, the immense influence of the King James Bible lay in the fact that it was the only biblical translation known by a culture that was generally well disposed toward the public and private reading of the Bible. The inescapability of the language and imagery of the King James Bible led to them being incorporated into the language and literature of the English-speaking peoples. The great English art critic and cultural historian John Ruskin (1819–1900) made it clear that his own work had been immeasurably shaped by the prose of the Bible, which he had absorbed deeply:

> *From Walter Scott's novels I might easily, as I grew older, have fallen to other people's novels; and Pope might, perhaps, have led me to take Johnson's English, or Gibbon's, as types of language;*

*but, once knowing the 32nd of Deuteronomy, the 15th of First Corinthians, the Sermon on the Mount, and most of the Apocalypse, every syllable by heart, and having always a way of thinking with myself what words meant, it was not possible for me, even in the foolishest times of youth, to write entirely superficial or formal English.*

Ruskin saw the language of the King James Bible as a major influence on his own style. Other writers of this period could easily bear witness to the same point.

This Bible conveyed religious teachings using language that inspired its readers to meditation and worship, rather than dulling them by the wooden communication of doctrines and demands. Iris Murdoch made this point when she spoke of the King James Bible and the Book of Common Prayer (1662) as

*. . . great pieces of literary good fortune, when language and spirit conjoined to produce a high unique religious eloquence. These books have been loved because of their inspired linguistic perfection. Treasured words encourage, console, and save.*

For Murdoch, the religious themes of the Bible need not have been phrased in such an eloquent and enriching way. The glory of the King James Bible was that the English language was raised to new heights by being put to the service of this supreme goal—the rendering in English of the words and deeds of God.

## TAMING THE TEXT: NAUGHTY WORDS AND A PRUDISH CULTURE

YET SOMETIMES THE King James rendering of some biblical passages was just too explicit for some of its more tender readers. As English and American society became more polite and cultivated, it became increasingly unfashionable to speak directly and openly of certain parts of the human body, and their embarrassing anatomical functions. Both the King James Bible and the writings of William Shakespeare were singled out as being potentially seditious, in that they could lead sensitive young people—especially gentle young ladies—astray through their direct, coarse and offensive language. The solution to this dilemma was to sanitize both texts, and make them less scandalous to such sensitive persons.

The English word "bowdlerize" was originally coined around 1836 to mean "to edit heavily someone else's work, so that it conforms with your notions of propriety." The word derives from Dr. Thomas Bowdler (1754–1825), who published in 1818 an edited version of Shakespeare's works entitled *The Family Shakespeare*. Its chief selling point was indicated on its title page, which informed its readers that "those words and expressions are omitted which cannot with propriety be read aloud in a family." Although this edition met with an adverse critical reaction, the general public loved it.

Encouraged by the success of this venture, Bowdler next cleaned up Gibbon's *History of the Decline and Fall of the Roman Empire*. Again, Bowdler drew attention to his work's "careful omission of all passages of an irreligious or immoral tendency." Bowdler went on to say, in what seems to have been a singular lapse of modesty, that Gibbon himself would have approved of his deletions, and that his edition would henceforth be known as the definitive edition of this classic work.

What is not often appreciated is that polite Victorian society, both in England and the United States, had similar difficulties with the King James Bible, which was altogether too frank about certain matters for their comfort. The general issues were set out in Matthew Gregory Lewis's novel *The Monk* (1796), a work that was regarded itself with considerable distaste in the Victorian period. Lewis's novel tells of a worthy and responsible mother, sensitive to her social situation, who was quite convinced that allowing her daughter, Antonia, to read the Bible would lead to all kinds of sexual dysfunction:

*That prudent Mother, while She admired the beauties of the sacred writings, was convinced that, unrestricted, no reading more improper could be permitted a young Woman. Many of the narratives can only tend to excite ideas the worst calculated for a female breast: Every thing is called plainly and roundly by its name; and the annals of a Brothel would scarcely furnish a greater choice of indecent expressions. Yet this is the Book which young Women are recommended to study; which is put into the hands of Children, able to comprehend little more than those passages of which they had better remain ignorant; and which but too frequently inculcates the first rudiments of vice, and gives the first alarm to the still sleeping passions.*

Happily, this most worthy mother hit upon a brilliant way of allowing her daughter to benefit from what she regarded as the inspiring passages in the Bible, and avoid the somewhat explicit statements in others:

*She had in consequence made two resolutions respecting the Bible. The first was that Antonia should not read it till She was of an age to feel its beauties, and profit by its morality: The second, that it should be copied out with her own hand, and all improper passages either altered or omitted.*

What is being described is, of course, the "bowdlerization of the Bible," if we might be allowed this anachronism.

Similar concerns were expressed by that great American man of letters, Noah Webster, responsible for an influential dictionary that helped establish the distinctive aspects of American spelling. Webster was alarmed by a series of biblical passages that he regarded as "offensive," "unseemly," and "distasteful." Words to which he took particular exception include "piss," "privy member," "prostitute," "teat," "whore," and "womb."

This tendency to censor the language of both Shakespeare and the King James Bible can be seen as a monument to both their popularity and their acknowledged influence on the shaping of the English language. To change them would be to change the English language. The genteel censors doubtless meant well, and do not deserve quite the full torrent of critical abuse that was heaped upon them. It is, however, a reminder that we shall always be plagued with censorious bores who demand we all use language that they find acceptable and are "adapted to modern views of propriety" (to use an 1828 phrase of William Alexander, who was critical of the crudeness of the language of the King James Bible).

## THE DEMAND FOR REVISION

WITH THE PASSING of time, the demand for revision of the King James translation has gained momentum. The English language has changed considerably since 1611, causing difficulties in interpretation at points. Yet such is the status of the King James Bible that there has been intense resistance to any revisions to the text. Many feel that this text, like Shakespeare's works, is vested with the dignity and sanctity of a classic, and cannot, therefore, be revised. There is no doubt that the King James Bible is a model English text, which can be studied as a landmark in the history of the English language, and is to be seen as a major influence on English literature, especially in the eighteenth and nineteenth centuries.

But the awkward fact remains that those who produced the King James Bible did not see their labours in quite this way. They saw their work as a *translation*—that is, something that aims to convey to its readers the meaning of another text, written at a different time and place, and in another language. By definition, no translation can be perfect. The King James Bible may indeed be esteemed as an excellent translation of the word of God by the standards of 1611 and beyond. Yet translations eventually require revision, not necessarily because they are defective, but because the language into which they translated itself changes over time. Translation involves aiming at a moving target, which has accelerated over the centuries. English is developing more quickly today than at any time in its previous history. Some words have ceased to be used; others have changed their meanings. When a translation itself requires translation, it has ceased to serve its original purpose.

The King James translators themselves were alert to the need to ensure faithful and accurate translation of the Bible into living English. The English of 1611 is not the English of the twenty-first century. It can mislead us, simply because English words have changed their meaning. For example, consider the sentence:

> *For this we say unto you by the word of the Lord, that we which are alive* and *remain unto the coming of the Lord shall not prevent them which are asleep (1 Thessalonians 4:15).*

A modern reader would find this puzzling, in that the 1611 meaning of the word "prevent" does not correspond to its modern sense. For the King James translators, "prevent" meant what we now understand by "precede" or "go before"—not "hinder." As linguistic change now means that the King James Bible has the potential to mislead and confuse, there is a clear case for revision of the translation. The extent of that revision is a matter for discussion; its necessity is beyond doubt. Like any living language, English changes over the years. Linguistic development is simply a sign of life, in that a language is being used and adapted to new situations.

The King James translators were perfectly aware of their need to provide a faithful and accurate translation of the Bible for their day and age. That day and age are now many centuries behind us. The paradox is that those who insist that we retain the King James Bible as the only English translation of the Bible actually betray the intentions and goals of those who conceived and translated it—namely, to translate the Bible into living English.

King James's translators honoured and made use of the English translations that already lay to hand. These were the existing land-marks, to which the King James translators added their own—perhaps the greatest. But the journey continues. Its direction has been mapped and guided by Tyndale, Coverdale, and the six companies of transla-tors whose achievement has been celebrated and documented in this volume. It has yet to end; indeed, it will not end, until either history is brought to a close or English ceases to be a living language. The true heirs of the King James translators are those who continue their task today, not those who declare it to have been definitively concluded in 1611.

## CONCLUSION

LET THE LAST word go to the translators. Addressing their readers, they declare their "desire that the Scripture may speak like itself, as in the language of Canaan, that it may be understood even of the very vulgar." Ordinary people were to be given a pathway into the text, which its translators believed to be the doorway to salvation, and the only hope and consolation for the world of their day. Without actu-ally intending to, those translators produced a literary milestone. We can still celebrate both their achievements—the superb translation of the Bible that they intended to create, and the classic work of English literature that was an accidental, yet most welcome, outcome. Our culture has been enriched by both aspects of the King James Bible. Sadly, we shall never see its equal—or even its like—again.

# A COMPARISON OF HISTORIC
# ENGLISH TRANSLATIONS:

## PSALM 23

In what follows, the first four verses of this very familiar psalm are presented, allowing an appreciation of the distinctive styles and orthographies of the major English versions from the Wycliffite translations of part of the Bible of c.1384 to the King James Bible of 1611. One modern translation—the Revised Standard Version of 1952—is included as a reference point; note how the pattern set by the King James Bible has had a deep impact on this leading twentieth-century translation.

### WYCLIFFITE BIBLE, C. 1384

*The Lord gouerneth me, and no thing to me shal lacke; in the place of leswe where he me ful sette. Ouer watir of fulfilling he nurshide me; my soule he conuertide. He broghte doun me vpon the sties of rightwisnesse; for his name. For whi and if I shal go in the myddel of the shadewe of deth; I shal not dreden euelis, for thou art with me. Thi gherde and thy staf; tho han confortid me.*

## COVERDALE BIBLE, 1535

*The LORDE is my shepherde, I can wante nothinge. He fedeth me
in a grene pasture, and ledeth me to a fresh water. He quickeneth
my soule, & bringeth me forth in the waye of rightuousnes for his
names sake. Though I shulde walke now in the valley of the shadowe of death, yet I feare no euell, for thou art with me: thy staffe
& thy shepehoke comforte me.*

## MATTHEW'S BIBLE, 1537

*The Lord is my shepherde, I can want nothynge.
He fedeth me in a grene pasture, & ledeth me to a fresh water.
He quickeneth my soule, & bryngeth me forth in the waye of rygh-
tuousnes for hys names sake.
Though I shulde walke now in the valley of the shadow of death,
yet I feare no euell, for thou art wyth me: thy staffe & thy shepehoke comforte me.*

## GREAT BIBLE, 1539

*The Lorde is my shepherde, therefore can I lack nothing. He shall
fede me in a grene pasture, & leade me forth besyde the waters of
comforte. He shall conuerte my soule, & bryng me forth in the
pathes of ryghteousnes for hys names sake. Yee though I walke
thorow ye valley of the shadow of death, I will feare no euell, for
thou art wyth me: thy rodde & thy staffe comforte me.*

## GENEVA BIBLE, 1560

*The Lord is my shepherd, I shal not want.
He maketh me to rest in grene pasture, & leadeth me by the stil
waters.
He restoreth my soule, & leadeth me in the paths of righteousnes
for his Names sake.
Yea, though I shulde walke through the valley of the shadow of
death, I wil feare no euil: for thou art with me: thy rod and they
staffe, they comfort me.*

## BISHOPS' BIBLE, 1568

*God is my sheephearde, therfore I can lacke nothyng: he wyll cause me to repose my selfe in pasture full of grasse, and he wyll-leade me vnto calme waters.*

*He wyll conuert my soule: he wyll bring me foorth into the pathes of righteousnesse for his name sake.*

*Yea though I walke through the valley of the shadowe of death, I wyll feare no euyll: for thou art with me, thy rodde and thy staffe be the thynges that do comfort me.*

## DOUAI OLD TESTAMENT, 1609–10

*Our Lord ruleth me, and nothing shal be wanting to me: in place of pasture there he hath placed me.*

*Upon the water of refection he hath brought me up: he hath converted my soule.*

*He hath conducted me vpon the pathes of justice, for his name.*

*For, although I shal walke in the middes of the shadow of death, I wil not feare evils: because thou art with me.*

*Thy rod and thy staffe: they have comforted me.*

## KING JAMES BIBLE, 1611

*The LORD is my shepheard, I shall not want. He maketh me to lie downe in greene pastures: he leadeth mee beside the still waters.*

*He restoreth my soule: he leadeth me in the pathes of righteousnes, for his names sake. Yea though I walke through the valley of the shadowe of death, I will feare no euill: for thou art with me, thy rod and thy staffe, they comfort me.*

## REVISED STANDARD VERSION, 1952

*The LORD is my shepherd, I shall not want; he makes me lie down in green pastures. He leads me beside still waters; he restores my soul. He leads me in paths of righteousness for his name's sake. Even though I walk through the valley of the shadow of death, I fear no evil; for thou art with me; thy rod and thy staff, they comfort me.*

# A BIBLICAL TIMELINE

The following chart is intended to help identify the major landmarks leading to the production of the King James Bible. It is not intended to be exhaustive, but simply to help locate some of the major events that led to the production of this work, and which affected its early reception.

1456 Johannes Gutenberg produces the first printed Bible, in Latin
1509 Henry VIII becomes king of England
1516 Erasmus publishes first printed Greek New Testament
1517 Indulgence controversy; Martin Luther posts the Ninety-Five Theses
1520 Luther publishes *The Appeal to the German Nobility*, demanding that lay people be allowed to read the Bible for themselves
1521 Diet of Worms; Luther works on translating the New Testament
1522 Luther publishes German translation of the New Testament
1525 William Tyndale's first attempt to publish the New Testament in English is thwarted by Cochlaeus

1526 The first complete English edition of the New Testament is published by William Tyndale in Worms

1530 Tyndale publishes his translation of the Pentateuch (the first five books of the Old Testament)

1531 Tyndale publishes his translation of Jonah

1532 Thomas Cranmer appointed Archbishop of Canterbury

1534 Henry enacts Supremacy and Uniformity Acts

1535 Coverdale Bible published—first complete English Bible. Execution of Sir Thomas More (July). City of Geneva declares itself to be a Protestant republic

1536 Dissolution of the monasteries; John Calvin arrives in Geneva; William Tyndale executed (October)

1537 Matthew's Bible published

1539 Great Bible published

1540 Execution of Thomas Cromwell, advocate of Protestant ideas and champion of English translations of the Bible

1547 Death of Henry VIII; succeeded by Edward VI

1553 Death of Edward VI; succeeded by Mary Tudor. English Protestants begin to seek refuge in Europe, including Geneva

1556 Execution of Thomas Cranmer

1557 Publication of William Whittingham's Geneva New Testament

1558 Death of Mary Tudor; succeeded by Elizabeth I

1559 Elizabethan "Settlement of Religion." Religious refugees begin to return to England from their exile in Europe

1560 Geneva Bible published

1568 Bishops' Bible published

1569 Geneva Bible published in Scotland

1571 Every cathedral ordered to set up a Bishops' Bible for regular use

1582 Douai-Rheims New Testament published

1583 John Whitgift appointed Archbishop of Canterbury

1587 Execution of Mary, Queen of Scots

1588 English navy defeats Spanish Armada

1603 Elizabeth I dies; succeeded by James VI of Scotland

1604 Hampton Court Conference, which took decision to publish new English translation of the Bible; death of John Whitgift, Archbishop of Canterbury; succeeded by Richard Bancroft

1609 Publication begins of the Douai-Rheims Old Testament; completed 1610

1610 Final editing of new Bible translation; death of Richard Bancroft, Archbishop of Canterbury

**1611 Publication of the King James Bible**

1618 Thirty Years War breaks out

1625 Death of James I; succeeded by Charles I

1642 English civil war breaks out

1648 Charles I defeated

1649 Execution of Charles I

1653 Oliver Cromwell becomes Lord Protector of England

1658 Death of Cromwell

1660 Restoration of the monarchy; return of Charles II to England

1662 Act of Uniformity; Book of Common Prayer

1675 King James Bible published by Cambridge University Press

# LIST OF WORKS
# CONSULTED

*The first printed catalogue of the Bodleian Library 1605, a facsimile: Catalogus librorum bibliothecæ publicæ quam Thomas Bodleius eques auratus in academia Oxoniensi nuper instituit.* Oxford, England: Bodleian Library, 1986.

Allen, Ward, *Translating for King James: Notes Made by a Translator of King James' Bible.* Nashville, Tenn.: Vanderbilt University Press, 1969.

Anderson, Benedict R. O., *Imagined Communities: Reflections on the Origin and Spread of Nationalism.* New York: Verso, 1991.

Anderson, Christopher, and Samuel Irenæus Prime, *Annals of the English Bible.* New York: Robert Carter, 1856.

Ashley, Maurice, *Oliver Cromwell and the Puritan Revolution.* London: English Universities Press, 1958.

Avis, F. C., "Book Smuggling into England During the Sixteenth Century." *Gutenberg Jahrbuch* (1972), 180–97.

———, "England's Use of Antwerp Printers, 1500–1540." *Gutenberg Jahrbuch* (1973), 234–40.

Backus, Irena, "Laurence Tomson and Elizabethan Puritanism." *Journal of Ecclesiastical History* 28 (1977), 17–27.

————, *The Reformed Roots of the English New Testament*. Pittsburgh, Pa.: Pickwick Press, 1980.

Barker, Henry, *English Bible Versions: A Tercentenary Memorial of the King James Version*. New York: New York Bible and Common Prayer Book Society, 1911.

Barnstone, Willis, *The Poetics of Translation: History, Theory, Practice*. New Haven, Conn.: Yale University Press, 1993.

Baskerville, Edward J., *A Chronological Bibliography of Propaganda and Polemic Published in English Between 1553 and 1558 from the Death of Edward VI to the Death of Mary I*. Philadelphia: American Philosophical Society, 1979.

Baugh, Albert C., and Thomas Cable, *A History of the English Language*. 4th ed. London: Routledge, 1993.

Bennett, H. S., *English Books and Readers 1475 to 1557*. Cambridge, England: Cambridge University Press, 1969.

Benson, Arthur Christopher, *The Life of Edward White Benson, Sometime Archbishop of Canterbury*. 2 vols. London: Macmillan, 1899.

Berger, Samuel, *Histoire de la Vulgate pendant les premiers siècles du moyen âge*: New York: Olms, 1976.

Bergier, Jean-François, "Zur den Anfänge des Kapitalismus: Das Beispiel Genf." *Kölner Vorträge zur Sozial- und Wirtschaftsgeschichte* 20 (1972), 3–29.

Betteridge, Maurice S., "The Bitter Notes: The Geneva Bible and its Annotations." *Sixteenth Century Journal* 14 (1983), 41–62.

Blake, N. F., *A History of the English Language*. Basingstoke, England: Macmillan, 1996.

Bliss, Robert M., *Restoration England: Politics and Government, 1660–1688*. London; New York: Methuen, 1985.

Bloy, C. H., *A History of Printing Ink, Balls and Rollers, 1440–1850*. London: Wynken de Word Society, 1967.

Braidfoot, Larry, *The Bible and America*. Nashville, Tenn.: Broadman Press, 1983.

Bridges, Ronald F., and Luther Allan Weigle, *The King James Bible Word Book: A Contemporary Dictionary of Curious and Archaic Words Found in the King James Version of the Bible*. Nashville, Tenn.: Nelson, 1994.

Bruce, F. F., *The English Bible: A History of Translations*. London: Lutterworth, 1961.

————, *History of the Bible in English: From the Earliest Versions*. 3rd ed. New York: Oxford University Press, 1978.

Bühler, Curt F., *The Fifteenth-Century Book*. Philadelphia: University of Pennsylvania Press, 1960.

————, *The University and the Press in Fifteenth-Century Bologna*. Notre Dame, Ind.: University of Notre Dame Press, 1957.

Burnet, Gilbert, *A History of the Reformation of the Church of England*. 3 vols. Dublin: Gunne, Smith and Bruce, 1730–32.

Bush, Douglas, *English Literature in the Earlier Seventeenth Century, 1600–1660*. Oxford History of English Literature. 2nd ed. Oxford, England: Clarendon Press, 1962.

Butler, Pierce, *The Origin of Printing in Europe*. Chicago: University of Chicago Press, 1940.

Butterworth, Charles C., *The English Primers, 1529–1545; Their Publication and Connection with the English Bible and the Reformation in England*. Philadelphia: University of Pennsylvania Press, 1953.

————, *The Literary Lineage of the King James Bible, 1340–1611*, Philadelphia, Pa.: University of Pennsylvania Press, 1941.

Caird, George, *The Language and Imagery of the Bible*. London: Duckworth, 1980.

Campbell, A. P., *The Tiberius Psalter*. Ottawa: University of Ottawa Press, 1974.

Cardwell, Edward, *Documentary Annals of the Church of England*. Oxford, England: Clarendon Press, 1844.

————, *A History of Conferences and Other Proceedings Connected with the Revision of the Book of Common Prayer from the Year 1558 to the Year 1690*. Oxford, England: Clarendon Press, 1840.

Carleton, James George, *The Part of Rheims in the Making of the English Bible*. Oxford, England: Clarendon Press, 1902.

Carlin, Norah, *The Causes of the English Civil War*. Oxford, England: Blackwell Publishers, 1999.

Carson, Don A., *The King James Version Debate*. Grand Rapids, Mich.: Baker Book House, 1979.

Carter, Harry, *A View of Early Typography up to About 1600*. Oxford, England: Clarendon Press, 1989.

Chaix, Paul, *Les livres imprimés à Genève de 1550 à 1600*. 2nd ed. Geneva: Droz, 1966.

————, *Recherches sur l'imprimerie à Genève de 1550 à 1564; Étude bibliographique, économique et littéraire*. Geneva: Droz, 1954.

Collinson, Patrick, "England and International Calvinism," in Menna Prestwich (ed.), *International Calvinism*. Oxford, England: Oxford University Press, 1985, 197–223.

————, *The Religion of Protestants: The Church in English Society 1559–1625*. Oxford, England: Clarendon Press, 1982.

Cook, Albert S., *The Bible and English Prose Style: Selections and Comments*. Philadelphia: R. West, 1977.

————, *Biblical Quotations in Old English Prose Writers: Second Series*. Philadelphia: West, 1977.

Cook, Albert Stanburrough, *The Authorised Version and Its Influence*. Folcroft, Pa.: Folcroft Library Editions, 1976.

————, *Biblical Quotations in Old English Prose Writers*. Norwood, Pa.: Norwood Editions, 1976.

Cooper, Lane, *Certain Rhythms in the English Bible*. Ithaca, N.Y.: Cornell University Press, 1952.

Cottle, Basil, *The Triumph of English 1350–1400*. London: Blandford, 1969.

Cruttwell, Patrick, "Fresh Skins for Good Wine." *Hudson Review* 23 (1970), 546–56.

Daiches, David, *The King James Version of the English Bible. An Account of the Development and Sources of the English Bible of 1611 with Special Reference to the Hebrew Tradition*. Hamden, Conn.: Archon Books, 1968.

Daniell, David, *William Tyndale: A Biography*. New Haven, Conn.: Yale University Press, 1994.

Danner, Dan G., "The Contribution of the Geneva Bible of 1560 to English Protestantism." *Sixteenth Century Journal* 12 (1981), 5–18.

Davies, Hugh Sykes, "Sir John Cheke and the Translation of the Bible." *Essays and Studies* 5 (1952), 1–12.

Davies, Julian, *The Caroline Captivity of the Church: Charles I and the Remoulding of Anglicanism 1625–41*. Oxford, England: Clarendon Press, 1992.

Dees, Jerome Steele, *Sir Thomas Elyot and Roger Ascham*. Boston, Mass.: G. K. Hall, 1981.

Eadie, John, *The English Bible: An External and Critical History of the Various English Translations of Scripture*. London: Macmillan, 1876.

Eales, Jacqueline, *Puritans and Roundheads: The Harleys of Brampton Bryan and the Outbreak of the English Civil War*. Cambridge, England: Cambridge University Press, 1990.

Eisenstein, Elizabeth, *The Printing Press as an Agent of Change: Communications and Cultural Transformations in Early Modern Europe*. 2 vols. Cambridge, England: Cambridge University Press, 1979.

———, *The Printing Revolution in Early Modern Europe*. Cambridge, England: Cambridge University Press, 1983.

Febvre, Lucien, and Henri-Jean Martin, *The Coming of the Book*. London: Verso, 1984.

Ferrell, Lori Anne, *Government by Polemic: James I, the King's Preachers and the Rhetoric of Conformity, 1603–1625*. Stanford, Calif.: Stanford University Press, 1998.

Figgis, J. N., *The Theory of the Divine Right of Kings*. Cambridge, England: Cambridge University Press, 1896.

Fincham, K., and P. Lake, "The Ecclesiastical Polity of James I." *Journal of British Studies* 24 (1985), 173–192.

Fincham, Kenneth, *The Early Stuart Church, 1603–1642*. London: Macmillan, 1993.

———, *Prelate as Pastor: The Episcopate of James I*. Oxford, England: Clarendon Press, 1990.

Fletcher, H. George, *Gutenberg and the Genesis of Printing*. New York: Pierpoint Morgan Library, 1994.

Fox, John, *The Influence of the English Bible on English Literature*. New York: s.n., 1911.

Freeman, James M., *A Short History of the English Bible*. Normal Outline Series. New York: Phillips & Hunt, 1879.

Frerichs, Ernest S., *The Bible and Bibles in America*. Atlanta, Ga.: Scholars Press, 1988.

Fuller, Thomas, *The Church History of Britain from the Birth of Jesus Christ until the Year 1648*. Oxford, England: Oxford University Press, 1845.

Garcia de la Fuente, Olegario, *Antología del latín bíblico y cristiano*. Málaga, Spain: Edinford, 1990.

———, *El latín bíblico y el español medieval hasta el 1300*. Logroño: Diputación Provincial, 1981.

Gardiner, John Hays, *The Bible as English Literature*. Folcroft, Pa.: Folcroft Library Editions, 1978.

Gaunt, Peter, *Oliver Cromwell*. Historical Association Studies. Cambridge, Mass.: Blackwell Publishers, 1996.

Gordon, Ian A., *The Movement of English Prose*. London: Longman, 1966.

Graff, Harvey B., *The Legacies of Literacy*. Bloomington, Ind.: Indiana University Press, 1987.

Greenslade, S. L., "English Versions of the Bible, 1525–1611," in S. L. Greenslade (ed.), *The Cambridge History of the Bible: The West from the Reformation to the Present Day*. Cambridge, England: Cambridge University Press, 1963, 141–74.

Gregg, Pauline, *Oliver Cromwell*. London: J. M. Dent, 1988.

Gruber, Michael, *The English Revolution; A Concise History and Interpretation*. New York: Ardmore Press, 1967.

Guppy, Henry, and John Rylands Library, *Miles Coverdale and the English Bible, 1488–1568*. Manchester, England: The Manchester University Press, 1935.

Hall, Basil, *The Genevan Version of the English Bible*. Presbyterian Historical Society of England. Annual lecture, 1956. London: Presbyterian Historical Society of England, 1957.

Hall, David D., *Cultures of Print: Essays in the History of the Book*. Amherst, Mass.: University of Massachusetts Press, 1996.

Hall, Verna M., and Rosalie J. Slater, *The Bible and the Constitution of the United States of America*. 1st ed. San Francisco, Calif.: Foundation for American Christian Education, 1983.

Hammond, Gerald, "English Translations of the Bible," in Robert Alter and Frank Kermode (ed.), *The Literary Guide to the Bible*. London: Collins, 1987, 647–66.

———, *The Making of the English Bible*. Manchester, England: Carcarnet, 1982.

Hargreaves, Cecil, *A Translator's Freedom*. Sheffield, England: Sheffield Academic Press, 1993.

Hatch, Nathan O., and Mark A. Noll, *The Bible in America: Essays in Cultural History*. New York: Oxford University Press, 1982.

Haugaard, W.P., *Elizabeth and the English Reformation: The Struggle for a Stable Settlement of Religion*. Cambridge, England: Cambridge University Press, 1968.

Havelock, Eric A., *The Muse Learns to Write: Reflections on Orality and Literacy from Antiquity to the Present*. New Haven, Conn.: Yale University Press, 1988.

Healy, Thomas F., and Jonathan Sawday, *Literature and the English Civil War*. Cambridge, England: Cambridge University Press, 1990.

Heaton, William James, *The Puritan Bible and Other Contemporaneous Protestant Versions*. London: F. Griffiths, 1913.

Hibbert, Christopher, *Cavaliers & Roundheads: The English Civil War, 1642–1649*. New York: Scribners, 1993.

Hill, Christopher, *The English Bible and the Seventeenth-Century Revolution*. London: Penguin Books, 1993.

Hills, Margaret Thorndike, and American Bible Society, *The English Bible in America; A Bibliography of Editions of the Bible & the New Testament Published in America, 1777–1957*. New York: American Bible Society, 1961.

Hirsch, Rudolph, *Printing, Selling and Reading, 1450–1550*. Wiesbaden, Germany: Otto Harrassowitz, 1974.

Hoare, Henry William, *Our English Bible: The Story of Its Origin and Growth*. Rev. ed. New York: Dutton, 1925.

Hope, J., "Second Person Singular Pronouns in Records of Early Modern Spoken English." *Neuphilologische Mitteilungen* 94 (1993), 83–100.

Hudson, Anne, "Wyclif and the English Language," in Anthony Kenny (ed.), *Wyclif in His Times*. Oxford, England: Clarendon Press, 1986, 85–103.

Hunt, Geoffrey, *About the New English Bible*. London: Oxford University Press, 1970.

Jessop, T. E., *On Reading the English Bible*. Peake Memorial Lectures, no. 3. London: Epworth, 1958.

Johnson, A. F., *Type Designs: Their History and Development*. London: André Deutsch, 1966.

Kamesar, Adam, *Jerome, Greek Scholarship, and the Hebrew Bible: A Study of the Quaestiones Hebraicae in Genesim*. Oxford, England: Clarendon Press, 1993.

Kantorowicz, E. H., *The King's Two Bodies: A Study in Medieval Political Theology*. Princeton, N.J.: Princeton University Press, 1957.

Kilgour, Frederick G., *The Evolution of the Book*. New York: Oxford University Press, 1998.

Knowles, Gerry, *A Cultural History of the English Language*. New York: Oxford University Press, 1997.

Knox, Ronald, *On Englishing the Bible*. London: Burns & Oates, 1949.

Lake, Peter, *Anglicans and Puritans? Presbyterianism and English*

*Conformist Thought from Whitgift to Hooker*. Boston, Mass.: Unwin Hyman, 1988.

Lehmberg, Stanford E., *Sir Thomas Elyot, Tudor Humanist*. New York: Greenwood Press, 1969.

Lewis, C. S., "The Literary Impact of the Authorised Version," in *They Asked for a Paper: Papers and Addresses*. London: Geoffrey Bles, 1962, 26–50.

Littlejohn, David, *Dr. Johnson and Noah Webster: Two Men and Their Dictionaries*. San Francisco: Book Club of California, 1971.

Lloyd Jones, G., *The Discovery of Hebrew in Tudor England: A Third Language*. Manchester, England: Manchester University Press, 1983.

Lowes, John Livingston, "The Noblest Monument of English Prose," in *Of Reading Books*. London: Constable, 1930, 47–77.

MacCulloch, Diarmaid, *Thomas Cranmer: A Life*. New Haven, Conn.: Yale University Press, 1996.

Marsden, Richard, *The Text of the Old Testament in Anglo-Saxon England*. Cambridge Studies in Anglo-Saxon England. 15. Cambridge, England: Cambridge University Press, 1995.

Martin, Charles, *Les Protestants anglais réfugiés à Genève au temps de Calvin 1555–60*. Geneva: Jullien, 1915.

Martin, J. W., "The Marian Regime's Failure to Understand the Importance of Printing." *Huntington Library Quarterly* 44 (1981), 231–47.

McAfee, Cleland Boyd, *The Greatest English Classic: A Study of the King James Version of the Bible and Its Influence on Life and Literature*. Folcroft, Pa.: Folcroft Library Editions, 1977.

McGrath, Alister E., *The Intellectual Origins of the European Reformation*. Oxford, England: Blackwell, 1987.

———, *Luther's Theology of the Cross: Martin Luther's Theological Breakthrough*. Oxford, England: Blackwell, 1985.

McMurtrie, Douglas C., *The Corrector of the Press in the Early Days of Printing*. Greenwich, Conn.: Condé Nast, 1922.

———, *Proofreading in the Fifteenth Century: An Examination of Evidence Relating to Correctors of the Press at Work in Paris Prior to 1500*. Greenwich, Conn.: Condé Nast, 1921.

———, *The Gutenberg Documents*. New York: Oxford University Press, 1941.

Meredith, P., "The York Cycle and the Beginning of Vernacular Religious Drama in England," in *Le Laudi Drammatiche umbre delle Origini*. Viterbo, Italy: Centro di Studi sul Teatro Medioevale e Rinascimentale di Viterbo, 1981, 311–33.

Metzger, Bruce M., *The Early Versions of the New Testament: Their Origin, Transmission and Limitations*. Oxford, England: Oxford University Press, 1977.

Micklethwait, David, *Noah Webster and the American Dictionary*. Jefferson, N.C.: McFarland, 1999.

Miller, John, *Restoration England: The Reign of Charles II*. London; New York: Longman, 1985.

Milton, Anthony, *Catholic and Reformed: The Roman and Protestant Churches in English Protestant Thought, 1600–1640*. Cambridge, England: Cambridge University Press, 1995.

Monter, E.W., "Historical Demography and Religious History in Sixteenth-Century Geneva." *Journal of Inter-Disciplinary History* 9 (1979), 399–427.

Moris, Guerra, "Santi Pagnini traducteur de la Bible," in Irena Backus and Francis Higman (ed.), *Théorie et practique de l'exégèse*. Geneva: Droz, 1990, 191–98.

Morrill, J. S., *Oliver Cromwell and the English Revolution*. London; New York: Longman, 1990.

———, *The Revolt of the Provinces: Conservatives and Radicals in the English Civil War, 1630–1650*. New York: Barnes & Noble, 1976.

Moulton, W. F., *The History of the English Bible*. 2d ed. New York: Cassell Petter & Galpin, 1878.

Mozley, James F., *William Tyndale*. London: SPCK, 1937.

Mullan, John, *Sentiment and Sociability: The Language of Feeling in the Eighteenth Century*. Oxford, England: Clarendon Press, 1988.

Needham, Paul, "Johann Gutenberg and the Catholicon Press." *Papers of the Bibliographical Society of America* 76 (1982), 395–456.

Nida, Eugene A., and Charles R. Taber, *The Theory and Practice of Translation*. Leiden, The Netherlands: E. J. Brill, 1982.

Norton, David, *A History of the Bible as Literature*. 2 vols. Cambridge, England: Cambridge University Press, 1993.

Oberman, Heiko A., *Luther: Man Between God and the Devil*. New Haven, Conn.: Yale University Press, 1989.

O'Callaghan, E. B., *A List of Editions of the Holy Scriptures and Parts Thereof Printed in America Previous to 1860*. Detroit, Mich.: Gale Research Co., 1966.

Opfell, Olga S., *The King James Bible Translators*. Jefferson, N.C.: McFarland, 1982.

Orlinsky, Harry Meyer, and Robert G. Bratcher, *A History of Bible Translation and the North American Contribution*. Biblical Scholarship in North America. Atlanta, Ga.: Scholars Press, 1991.

Paine, Gustavus Swift, *The Learned Men*. New York: Crowell, 1959.

Pare, Philip Norris, *Eric Milner-White, 1884–1963*. London: SPCK, 1965.

Pattison, T. Harwood, *The History of the English Bible*. Philadelphia: American Baptist Publication Society, 1894.

Payne, J. D., *The English Bible: An Historical Survey*. London: Wells Gardner Darton, 1911.

Pollard, A. W., "The New Caxton Indulgence." *The Library* 9 (1928), 86–89.

Pollard, Arthur W., *Records of the English Bible: Documents relating to the Translation and Publication of the Bible in English, 1525–1611*. London: Oxford University Press, 1911.

Pope, Hugh, *English Versions of the Bible*. St. Louis, Mo.: Herder Book Co., 1952.

Price, Ira Maurice, *The Ancestry of Our English Bible: An Account of Manuscripts, Texts, and Versions of the Bible*. 4th ed. Philadelphia: The Sunday School Times Company, 1909.

Quiller-Couch, Arthur, *On the Art of Reading*. Cambridge, England: Cambridge University Press, 1920.

Reed, R., *Ancient Skins, Parchments and Leathers*. New York: Seminar Press, 1972.

Reed, Ronald, *The Nature and Making of Parchment*. Leeds, England: Elmete, 1975.

Ridley, Jasper Godwin, *John Knox*. New York: Oxford University Press, 1968.

Rodes, Robert E., *Lay Authority and Reformation in the English Church: Edward I to the Civil War*. Notre Dame, Ind.: University of Notre Dame Press, 1982.

Roots, Ivan Alan, *Commonwealth and Protectorate: The English Civil War and Its Aftermath*. New York: Schocken Books, 1966.

Rosenau, William, *Hebraisms in the Authorized Version of the Bible*. Philadelphia: R. West, 1978.

Rupp, E. Gordon, *Six Makers of English Religion, 1500–1700*. London: Hodder and Stoughton, 1957.

Ruppel, Aloys, *Johannes Gutenberg*. 3rd ed. Nieuwkoop: De Graaf, 1967.

Russell, Conrad, *The Causes of the English Civil War*. Oxford, England: Clarendon Press, 1990.

Ryan, Lawrence V., *Roger Ascham*. Stanford, Calif.: Stanford University Press, 1963.

Rydén, Mats, *Relative Constructions in Early Sixteenth-Century English, with Special Reference to Sir Thomas Elyot*. Uppsala, Sweden: Almqvist & Wiksell, 1966.

Sachse, William L., *Restoration England, 1660–1689*. Cambridge, England: Published for the Conference on British Studies at the University Press, 1971.

Sambrook, James, *The Eighteenth Century: The Intellectual and Cultural Context of English Literature 1700–1789*. London: Longman, 1986.

Schaff, Philip, et al., *The Revision of the English Version of the New Testament*. New York: Harper & Brothers, 1873.

Schwarz, M., "James I and the Historians: Towards a Reconsideration." *Journal of British Studies* 13 (1974), 114–34.

Scrivener, F. H. A., *The Authorized Edition of the English Bible (1611)*. Cambridge, England: Cambridge University Press, 1884.

Shriver, F., "Hampton Court Revisited: James I and the Puritans." *Journal of Ecclesiastical History* 33 (1982), 48–71.

Simms, Paris Marion, *The Bible in America; Versions That Have Played Their Part in the Making of the Republic*. New York: Wilson-Erickson, 1936.

Spence, Hersey Everett, and James Cannon, *A Guide to the Study of the English Bible*. 3d ed. Nashville, Tenn.: Cokesbury Press, 1927.

Spurr, John, *English Puritanism, 1603–1689*. Social History in Perspective. New York: St. Martin's Press, 1998.

Stoughton, John, *Our English Bible: Its Translations and Translators*. New York: Scribner and Welford, 1878.

Trevor-Roper, Hugh R., *Archbishop Laud, 1573–1645*. 3rd ed. Basingstoke, England: Macmillan Press, 1988.

Tyacke, N. R. N., *Anti-Calvinists: The Rise of English Arminianism c. 1590–1640*. Oxford, England: Oxford University Press, 1987.

Unger, Harlow G., *Noah Webster: The Life and Times of an American Patriot*. New York: John Wiley & Sons, 1998.

Weigle, Luther Allan, *The English New Testament from Tyndale to the Revised Standard Version*. New York: Greenwood Press, 1969.

Westcott, Brooke Foss, and William Aldis Wright, *A General View of the History of the English Bible*. 3d rev. ed. London; New York: Macmillan, 1905.

White, Paul, *Predestination, Policy and Polemic: Conflict and Consensus in the English Church from the Reformation to the Civil War*. Cambridge, England: Cambridge University Press, 1992.

Whitley, William Thomas, *The English Bible Under the Tudor Sovereigns*. London: Marshall Morgan & Scott, 1937.

Wild, Laura Hulda, *The Romance of the English Bible: A History of the Translation of the Bible into English from Wyclif to the Present Day*. Garden City, N.Y.: Doubleday Doran, 1929.

Wilkinson, Lancelot Patrick, *Eric Milner-White, 1884–1963: Fellow Chaplain and Dean, Dean of York; A Memoir Prepared by Direction of the Council of King's College, Cambridge*. Cambridge, England: King's College, 1963.

Willey, Basil, "On Translating the Bible into Modern English." *Essays and Studies* 23 (1970), 1–17.

Willoughby, Harold R., Thomas Cranmer, and Herndon Wagers, *The First Authorized English Bible, and the Cranmer Preface*. Chicago: University of Chicago Press, 1942.

Wilson, Derek A., *The People and the Book: The Revolutionary Impact of the English Bible, 1380–1611*. London: Barrie and Jenkins, 1976.

Wormald, J., "James VI and I: Two Kings or One?" *History* 68 (1983), 187–209.

Wosh, Peter J., *Spreading the Word: The Bible Business in Nineteenth-Century America*. Ithaca, N.Y.: Cornell University Press, 1994.

Wright, John, *Historic Bibles in America*. New York: T. Whittaker, 1905.

Zagorin, Perez, *The English Revolution: Politics, Events, Ideas*. Aldershot, England; Brookfield, Vt.: Ashgate, 1998.

# ILLUSTRATION CREDITS

Doubleday and the author would like to acknowledge the following for permission to reproduce the illustrations contained herein:

Silvio Fiore/SuperStock (p. 11); The Huntington Library, Art Collection and Botanical Gardens, San Marino, California/SuperStock (p. 16); Stationers' Hall, London/Bridgeman Art Library, New York (p. 17); Stock Montage/SuperStock (pp. 20, 103); Culver Pictures/SuperStock (p. 30); Palazzo Barberini, Rome, Italy/ET Archive, London/SuperStock (p. 40); Culver Pictures (pp. 42, 89, 153, 283); Belvoir Castle, Leicestershire/ Bridgeman Art Library, New York (p. 60); American Bible Society, New York City/SuperStock (pp. 74, 96, 122, 208, 213); National Portrait Gallery, London/Bridgeman Art Library, New York (pp. 92, 110); Private Collection/ Phillip Mould, Historical Portraits Ltd., London/Bridgeman Art Library, New York (p. 108); Private Collection/Bridgeman Art Library, New York (pp. 116, 137, 184); Guildhall Library, Corporation of London/Bridgeman Art Library, New York (p. 186); Phillip Mould, Historical Portraits Ltd., London/Bridgeman Art Library, New York (p. 281); Scottish National Portrait Gallery, Edinburgh, Scotland/Bridgeman Art Library (p. 288); Superstock, Inc., Collection, Jacksonville/SuperStock (p. 292).

# INDEX

*Page numbers of illustrations appear in italics.*

331

81–82; French as language of the elite, 24, 25, 26–28, 30; Geneva Bible, initial Elizabethan response to, 124–27; Geneva Bible and Protestant ideas, 99–129, 141–48, 161–62; "Great Bible," 95, *96*, 97–98, 99, 124, 198, 204, 269, 312; Gunpowder Plot, 170; Hundred Years War, 29; King Charles I, 168–69, 280, 282–85; King Charles II, 227, 257, 287, 288; King Edward VI, *108*, 109, 115; King Edward VII, 166; King Henry V, 29; King Henry VIII, 34, *60*, 61–66, 90, 91, 95, 112, 135–36; King James I, 69, 113,129, 135–36, *137*, 138–41, 143, 145, 147, 148, 149–50, 153–71, 199, 219–20, 226–27, 257; King Richard II, 21; Latin, use of, 28–29, 34–35, 68–69; Luther's writings in, 68; "Matthew's Bible," 91–93, 94, 198, 312; missionary societies, 227–28; nationalism and national identity, rise of, 2, 25–26, 28–31, 171; Parliament, 285–87; Peasants' Revolt, 1381, 21; persecutions of Protestants, 109, 112, 117; printing of Bibles, 198–99; Protestant identity of, 130–35; Puritan Commonwealth, 285–87; Puritans, 149–61, 226–27, 279–87, 289; Queen Elizabeth I, 6, 25, 28–31, 63, *116*, 117, 124–27, 130–36, 138, 157, 167, 199; Queen Elizabeth II, ix; Queen Mary I, 61, 107, 109, *110*, 112–13, 114, 117, 130; Reformation in, 61–66, 68; "Settlement of Religion" (1559), 117, 125, 126, 127, 132, 149, 154; smuggled books into, 84; Spanish Armada defeat, 129, 131; Tyndale Bible, 73–80, *74*; Tyndale Bible, attempt to suppress, 80–89; Wycliffite vernacular Bible, 19–23, 311–12. *See also* King James Bible ("Authorized Version")
*English Expositor, An* (Bullokar), 259
English language: acceptance of foreign terms and phrases, 258–62; American, 290–91; banned by English church, 33–35; Bible in, 19–23, 59, 65–66, 67–98, *see also specific Bibles*; bowdlerizing and prudishness, 305–8; church opposition to use, 32–35;

Elizabethan, 131–32; factors in shaping, 256–58; Hebraic phrases in, 258, 262–65; Henry V's use of, 29; "his" and "its," 274–76; "inkhorn" terms, 260; King James Bible, influence of, 1–2, 23, 24, 235, 252, 253, 254–56, 257–58, 259, 262–76; literature, early, using, 28; meditations printed in, 33–34; Middle English, 26–27; neologisms, 260; as peasant's language, 23, 24; in religion, 31–32, 68; rise as national language, 24–36; "sayeth" or "says," verbal endings, 271–74; Shakespeare's influence, 1, 253; standardization of spelling, lexical patterns etc, 258; "thou," "you," "ye," 266–67; Tyndale Bible, influence of, 79; vocabulary growth, 79, 90, 259–62
Ephesians *3:8–11*, 261–62
Erasmus of Rotterdam, 25, 35, 39, *40*, 51, 53, 55–58, 59, 69, 71, 241, 243–44
*Essay Towards the Amendment of the Last English Translation of the Bible, An* (Gell), 286
Estienne, Robert, 107, 116, 118, 120, 241
Exodus: *1*, marginal notes, Geneva Bible, 144–45; *1:19*, 145; *1:22*, 145; *6:3*, 235; *15:4*, 86; *20:14*, 216; *28:11*, 214–15; *30:2–3*, 275–76
Ezekiel, *2:3*, 232
Ezra, 230; *4:11–16*, 230; *4:17–22*, 230; *5:7–17*, 230; *10:2–3*, 169

Field, John, 287
Fisher, Jack, 2–3
Fisher, John, 63, 82
Foxe, John, 68, 109, 112
France: Calvin in, 104; cultural centre, 27; enmity with England, 29–30; language, development, 257; language as lingua franca of Europe, 27; language used by English elite, 24, 28–29; Latin Quarter, Paris, 35; Olivétan Bible, 91, 93; printers, 205–6; Reformation in, 106–7; vernacular Bibles, 26
Frederick the Wise, 49, 52
Fust, Johann, 13, 18, 205

# THE HOLY BIBLE,

Conteyning the Old Testament,

AND THE NEW.

Newly Translated out of the Originall
tongues: & with the former Translations
diligently compared and reuised, by his
Maiesties speciall Comandement.

Appointed to be read in Churches.

Imprinted at London by Robert
Barker, Printer to the Kings
most Excellent Maiestie.

ANNO DOM. 1611